The Complete Guide to Horse Careers

by Sue Reynolds

New Horizons Equine Education Center, Inc.
425 Red Mountain Road
Livermore, CO 80536

Published by New Horizons Equine Education Center, Inc., 425 Red Mountain Road, Livermore, Colorado 80536.

Page design and layout produced by Carol LoSapio @ BeyondWords.

Publisher's Cataloging-in-Publication Data
    (Provided by Quality Books, Inc.)
    First Printing, April 1998
    Second Printing, November, 1998
    Third Printing, November 2000

Reynolds, Sue (Susan L.), 1945-
    The complete guide to horse careers / by Sue Reynolds ;
  [edited by Bobette Host].
    p. cm.
    Includes bibliographical references.
    At head of cover title: New Horizons.

ISBN 0-9663559-0-3

    1. Horse industry—Vocational guidance. 2. Horse racing—
Employees—Vocational guidance. 3. Equine sports medicine—
Vocational guidance. I. Title.

SF285.25.R49 1998
636.1'0023   QBI98-306   98-65621

Table of Contents

Acknowledgments

For those of you entering the horse career world, and to those of you already working in the profession of your dreams, this acknowledgment is a combination of appreciation and encouragement. The year spent interviewing the nearly two hundred people who made this book possible was a year of new friendships and renewed admiration for the warmth, sincerity, honesty, and willingness of people to share and help others.

Most names that appear in the Resources section at the end of each chapter are the names of people who kindly took time to speak with me over the phone, to communicate over the Internet, and even to welcome me into their homes, offices, and most of all hearts. These are people who love what they do and generously shared that love, along with their expertise, insights, challenges, and rewards. Seldom have I encountered so many people so satisfied with their professions. My sincere thanks to all of you. You have enriched my life.

A special thanks to Colette May, founder of New Horizons Equine Education Center. Her love for horses and people inspired her to develop New Horizons' home education program and to ask me to research and write this book.

Thanks are also in order to Bobette Host. Bobette designed and performed the indexing and coordination of the book. An active horse person herself she invested herself personally in developing a quality book for people interested in pursuing a career in an industry she, too, loves.

Carol LoSapio, of Beyond Words, was not only a delight to work with, but she willingly altered her schedule and worked diligently and professionally to design and layout a professional and user friendly final product, Thanks, Carol.

A final and heartfelt thanks to my husband, Gaius, who accompanied me on interviews, encouraged me, fixed meals, and showed unlimited patience with my clutter and irregular work schedule.

Introduction

Grace, speed, endurance, beauty, companionship, pleasure, recreation, sport, competition — many things come to mind at the mere mention of the horse. Children are in awe of the horse to the point that one of the first words uttered by many infants is *horse*. Anthropologists claim to know more about the beginnings of the horse than they do about the history of man.

In North America, horses were first introduced when the Spanish adventurer Hernando Cortez landed on the east coast of what is now Mexico. He left more than a dozen horses with the indigenous people and allowed other horses to wander away. These roaming horses either formed wild herds or were captured by native people. From that point on, horses played a significant role in the development of the continent. They were an integral part of the life-style of many Native American groups. They led wagons filled with pioneers across the country, delivered the mail, plowed fields, and transported people to church, town, and social affairs.

When the automobile was invented, skeptics predicted that horses would be seen only in zoos. How wrong they were. Today, according to the *Horse Industry Directory* of the American Horse Council, there are 6,931,000 horses in the United States. The table shows the many roles horses play.

Horses in the United States

Horses used for recreational riding	2,970,000
Show horses	1,974,000
Racehorses and racehorse breeding stock	725,000
Farm, ranch, police, rodeo, and polo horses	1,262,000

The horse industry produces goods and services valued at $25.3 billion annually, and it is estimated to have a $112.1 billion impact on the economy, surpassed only by the metal industry and the radio and television broadcasting industry.

If you are wondering if there are employment opportunities in the horse industry, the response is an emphatic yes! According to the *Horse Industry Directory* of the American Horse Council, 619,400 people are directly employed by the horse industry on a part-time, seasonal, or full-time basis. Jobs indirectly related to horses, combined with employment involving direct contact, add up to more than 1.4 million full-time equivalent jobs.

As one part of the agricultural industry, the horse industry offers a variety of employment opportunities. Some careers require direct contact with horses, and others simply require knowledge of or background in horses. This book includes interviews of more than 150 people employed in a diversity of careers, ranging from trainers who spend most of their time on horseback, to attorneys who spend most of their time in research libraries, offices, and courtrooms. Horse businesses range from small backyard operations that supplement or even drain income, to large manufacturers of horse feed.

A love for horses and the desire to work with them, a preference for physical work, the enjoyment of working outdoors, and the avoidance of a nine to five routine are all reasons for seeking a career working directly with horses. Compared to many professions, horse-related work often involves an element of risk and extensive experience, and it frequently pays less than other employment. Most horse people achieve success after working their way up through the ranks as grooms, stable hands, interns, wranglers, assistants, or volunteers. Beginning pay is notoriously low, and weekly paychecks of $150 to $250 are common. While room and board and reimbursement for expenses may be included, the hours are usually long and irregular. Horses don't punch a time-clock and have no respect for holidays.

People peripherally involved in the horse industry — in the fields of equine product manufacturing, accounting, law, or sales — utilize their special talents and love for horses indirectly. Earnings in these fields are generally higher.

The twenty-first century promises to offer exciting opportunities for the horse enthusiast who has creativity and perseverance, and is willing to take a few risks and endure some financial sacrifices. As you read about the occupations of interest to you, you will discover that the trails leading to many horse careers are a bit rocky. However, according to those who have made the trip, the rewards are well worth the occasional hardship.

Chapter One

Experience, Education, and Writing a Résumé

Is experience alone enough to establish a career in the horse industry? Should you attend a vocational or a specialty school? Do you need a college education? Is an associate, bachelor's, master's, or graduate degree necessary? Do you need to work as an intern or apprentice?

The response to each of these questions depends on the career you choose to pursue. The upcoming chapters describe the experience and education required, or at least recommended, for each of the careers discussed. In this chapter, some general experience and educational considerations are presented along with suggestions for locating schools. As you explore your options, notice the variety of careers available. Here are some questions that will help you get started in your career exploration.

Considering a Horse Career
Start-Up Questions

1. Do you like to work inside or outside?_____
_____

2. Do you like physical or sedentary work?_____
_____

3. Are you dedicated to a particular breed or discipline?_____
_____

4. Do you like being around people or are you a loner?_____
_____

5. Do you prefer taking or giving directions?_____
_____

6. Are you willing to relocate?_____
_____

7. What are your salary needs or expectations?_____
_____

8. How much education and/or experience are you willing to pursue?
_____

EXPERIENCE AND BACKGROUND

Building a Foundation

Whether you are eight or eighty, you can begin now to gain one important qualification for landing a job in the horse industry: experience with horses. Although an education is the minimum criterium for certain professions, an education without experience may find you in the saddle without a horse to ride. While you gather experience and background in the horse industry, you will need to analyze the industry to identify areas that are sustaining themselves, fields that are growing, and changes that are taking place in the industry as a whole. Here are some ways to acquire background and experience.

Developing a Background in Horses

✓ Read! Subscribe to horse and breed publications. Read with the purpose of understanding the industry. Notice advertisements and want ads.

✓ Refer to the *Horse Industry Directory* of the American Horse Council for listings of organizations and publications and *The Blood Horse: The Source* for people in careers ranging from accounting to watering systems.

✓ Call or write to local people in your area of interest, or in related fields. Find out how they achieved their current position, the challenges they faced, and the recommendations they have. Start a career file of especially interesting occupations.

✓ Explore opportunities available through riding clubs, science clubs, 4-H, horse shows, rodeos, or polo events. Handle stock, order ribbons, run the concessions, or serve as a runner or secretary, and move into leadership positions.

✓ Join your local horse council.

✓ Visit local farms and training establishments.

✓ Visit local tack and feed stores. Scan the bulletin boards and talk with employees and owners for opportunities and contacts.

Using the Internet to Gather Information

The Internet is certain to play a role in the horse industry as we approach the twenty-first century. The horse industry is spread across the country, with employment opportunities frequently found in rural areas. Rarely are large numbers of positions or businesses located in any one area, with the exception of some parts of the ten largest horse states (Texas, California, Oklahoma, Colorado, New York, Ohio, Michigan, Pennsylvania, Washington, and Kentucky).

Horse Information on the Internet

You can access information several ways:

✓ Enter the site of a specific link, such as HorseWeb (*www.horseweb.com/ hw_hlink.htm*). This will give you access to a dozen pages of horse-related addresses on the net. Most of those pages also have links to other pages.

✓ Select a search engine. Common search engines include: Alta Vista (*http://www.altavista.digital.com*); Lycos (*http://www.lycos.com*); Yahoo (*http://www.yahoo.com*)

✓ After accessing a search engine, enter the topic of interest. For example, in Yahoo, when you enter the word *horse*, more than 30 categories with nearly 2,000 matches appear.

✓ For a more specific search, enter a more precise topic: horse training, horse sales, horse breed, horse rodeo, etc.

The Internet has hundreds of web pages loaded with topics that include horse sales, events, organizations, camps, positions, information networks, and betting opportunities. As you browse through the chapters of this book, you will see many references to web page addresses. To a neophyte, addresses look like a series of letters, numbers, slashes, and symbols, but they are easy to access, and they open pages filled with vast amounts of readily available information in the equine world.

If you want to access the Internet, you'll need a computer with 20 to 30 megabytes of hard disk space and 8 megabytes of Ram, a modem, a telephone line, and an Internet account. Check with friends who are on the Internet and with companies in your area for suggestions regarding each of the basics. Your area may have a local Internet server with which you can establish an account, or you might look into one of the large well-known servers such as America Online or CompuServe. Once you are online you can begin an exciting information journey.

Volunteer Work

Volunteers play an active and important role in the equine world. Volunteer work also demonstrates to a prospective employer an applicant's sincere intent to be a part of the horse industry. A volunteer position warrants the same respect and priority as a paid position. Being a volunteer gives you the opportunity to develop contacts with horse people, gain experience needed to obtain a paid job, and creatively serve others. In the horse world, many organizations would completely disappear if they had to operate without volunteers.

You can volunteer to work directly with horses and riders, feed and clean stalls, do office work, organize events, run concessions, lobby legislators, produce newsletters, or coordinate publicity. Virtually any job skill can be acquired or improved upon through volunteer work.

Volunteering for Fun and Work Experience

✓ The *Horse Industry Directory* of the American Horse Council is an excellent source for locating volunteer organizations. Here is just a sample of such volunteer groups.

✓ Horse welfare agencies and rescue groups (such as the American Horse Protection Association, California Equine Council, or Colorado Horse Rescue) help abused, endangered, abandoned, and unwanted horses through education and intervention.

✓ Breed organizations and registries.

✓ Equestrian sports, such as racing, horse shows, rodeos, fairs, and horse expositions.

✓ Local horse clubs, 4-H, Future Farmers of America, the United States Pony Club, horseman's associations, state fair offices.

✓ Therapeutic riding programs for physically, mentally, and emotionally disabled people. Contact: North American Riding for the Handicapped.

✓ Horseback riding events in the Special Olympics International for mentally retarded individuals, on a local, state, or international level.

✓ State horse councils to help promote the state's horse industry through trail maintenance, legislation, zoning, research, and education.

Exchange Programs

Would you like to develop career experience by working abroad? Communicating for Agriculture, a nonprofit organization founded in 1972 with the goal of promoting general health and welfare for people in agriculture and agribusiness, serves as the parent organization for Communicating for Agriculture Exchange Program (CAEP), the largest international agricultural exchange program in the nation. This program has placed trainees in equine related positions in foreign fields since its inception in 1986.

If you contact the office with a description of the location and type of work you would like, CAEP will search for the perfect fit. Support staff are available for anyone who runs into problems or needs counsel during a placement. Here are some other factors to consider if you would like to be placed in an agricultural (equine) position in a foreign country.

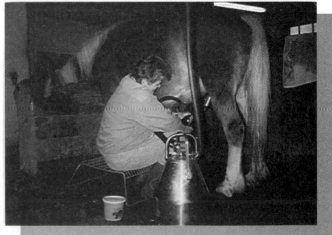

German mares' milk production, Communicating for Agriculture Exchange Program.

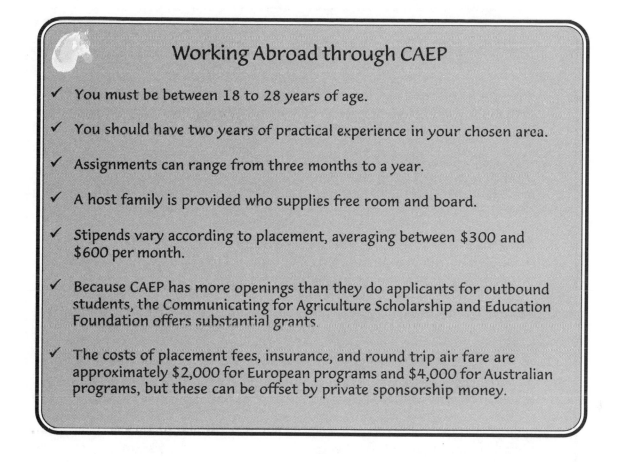

Working Abroad through CAEP

✓ You must be between 18 to 28 years of age.

✓ You should have two years of practical experience in your chosen area.

✓ Assignments can range from three months to a year.

✓ A host family is provided who supplies free room and board.

✓ Stipends vary according to placement, averaging between $300 and $600 per month.

✓ Because CAEP has more openings than they do applicants for outbound students, the Communicating for Agriculture Scholarship and Education Foundation offers substantial grants.

✓ The costs of placement fees, insurance, and round trip air fare are approximately $2,000 for European programs and $4,000 for Australian programs, but these can be offset by private sponsorship money.

Barbara Nelson, director of CAEP, has thirty years of experience with horses, ranging from showing, judging, training, and teaching to her present position. In 1997 she estimates that 130 inbound trainees from various foreign countries will find placements in the United States. Trainees can list their preference of working with hunter-jumper, dressage, eventing, riding schools, Western (reining, pleasure/halter, or cutting), breeding, or racing (track rider, jockey, and stable hand).

If you dream of travel — if you would like to learn how the horse industry operates in another country — if you are serious about making a career in the horse industry — this may be just the opportunity you are looking for.

Job-Hunting Considerations

Jobs that offer the opportunity to work directly with horses usually have the greatest appeal, and thus the competition for these jobs is often intense. If you are willing to take an entry-level position, such as stable hand, feed and clean-up crew, groom, counselor, or cook, with the idea of advancement, be sure the possibility of advancement exists before you accept the job. Be sure you are personally suited for the demands of an entry-level job. Be willing to settle for less to gain more in the future, but don't settle for just anything.

Set realistic expectations. Working with horses can be physically demanding. There is considerable turnover because many people enter the field with unrealistic ideas about the work and about themselves. As you read the following chapters, evaluate yourself while you look over the responsibilities and the work conditions shared by those in the professions that interest you. Then do some additional research to help you decide on the best profession for you.

If you have decided to start developing your experience with horses by seeking employment, here are some suggestions.

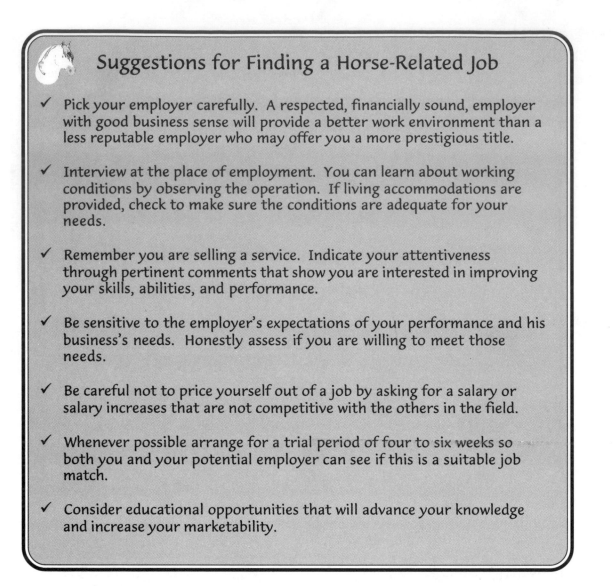

Suggestions for Finding a Horse-Related Job

✓ Pick your employer carefully. A respected, financially sound, employer with good business sense will provide a better work environment than a less reputable employer who may offer you a more prestigious title.

✓ Interview at the place of employment. You can learn about working conditions by observing the operation. If living accommodations are provided, check to make sure the conditions are adequate for your needs.

✓ Remember you are selling a service. Indicate your attentiveness through pertinent comments that show you are interested in improving your skills, abilities, and performance.

✓ Be sensitive to the employer's expectations of your performance and his business's needs. Honestly assess if you are willing to meet those needs.

✓ Be careful not to price yourself out of a job by asking for a salary or salary increases that are not competitive with the others in the field.

✓ Whenever possible arrange for a trial period of four to six weeks so both you and your potential employer can see if this is a suitable job match.

✓ Consider educational opportunities that will advance your knowledge and increase your marketability.

EDUCATION

Formal education is available in many forms. Distance education, or home education, is growing in popularity, as are on-campus classes. You need only pick the mode most appropriate for your needs.

Home Study Courses

If college is not an option for you at the present time, yet you desire to become more knowledgeable in horsemanship, you might consider home study or distance education courses. New Horizons Equine Education Center offers a series of step-by-step courses beginning with the basics of horsemanship through more advanced principles of equine management.

Working Student Programs

An increasingly popular alternative to college education is called the *working student program*. A person can gain practical knowledge and the skills required to become a trainer by going through a working student program. Originating in England, the concept differs from work study and internship programs. A designated number of lessons from a trainer, accommodations, and perhaps spending money, are traded for the student's labor in helping the trainer run the business. Feeding, mucking stalls, getting horses ready for riders, cooling them down, and grooming are common forms of labor. As skills are acquired, students often have the opportunity to assist in training.

Scheduling, communication, commitment, clear delineation of duties, and fairness to both parties are important elements in the success of this arrangement. Here are some suggestions for the person considering learning a trade as a working student.

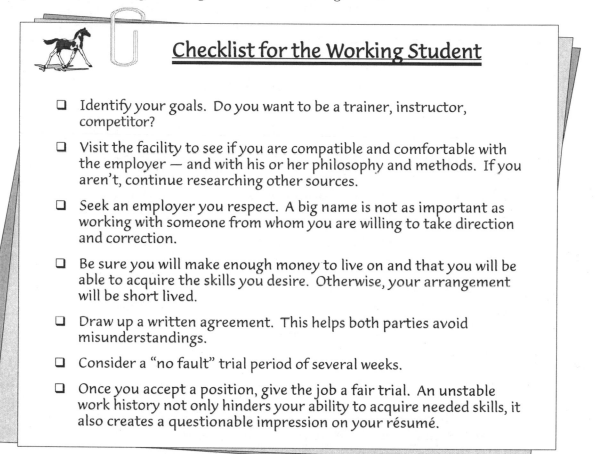

Checklist for the Working Student

❑ Identify your goals. Do you want to be a trainer, instructor, competitor?

❑ Visit the facility to see if you are compatible and comfortable with the employer — and with his or her philosophy and methods. If you aren't, continue researching other sources.

❑ Seek an employer you respect. A big name is not as important as working with someone from whom you are willing to take direction and correction.

❑ Be sure you will make enough money to live on and that you will be able to acquire the skills you desire. Otherwise, your arrangement will be short lived.

❑ Draw up a written agreement. This helps both parties avoid misunderstandings.

❑ Consider a "no fault" trial period of several weeks.

❑ Once you accept a position, give the job a fair trial. An unstable work history not only hinders your ability to acquire needed skills, it also creates a questionable impression on your résumé.

Clinics

Horse publications carry advertisements for clinicians who are recognized for their methods in a particular area of horse training or instruction. Many of these clinicians travel nationwide offering special training sessions and certifications. Once graduates of these clinics become certified, opportunities become available to conduct clinics under the well-known name of the sponsor.

For instance, Richard Shrake, the creator of Resistance Free™ Riding and Training Clinics offers a graduate course, master's course, and apprentice course. The apprentice course is mandatory for anyone who wants to become a Richard Shrake Resistance Free™ instructor or trainer. Each level of training lasts four days with a twelve-month hotline backup. The cost for each level is $1,250.

Linda Tellington-Jones offers training and certification based on developing a deeper understanding of animals. The three phases to her program are the Tellington-Touch, Learning Exercises from the Ground, and Joy of Riding.

There are many other reputable clinicians, some of whom are described in Chapter Six — Horse Training and Judging.

Trade Schools

If you desire to learn a specific trade — such as auctioneering, outfitting, stable or farm management, horseshoeing, training (racehorse or a specific discipline), instructing (for the handicapped or for a specific discipline), judging, massage therapy, or saddlemaking — then a trade school is a definite option. In the following chapters many of these specialties, along with resources for training, are presented.

Trade schools concentrate on training in one particular skill. The duration of the courses vary. Farrier (horseshoeing) schools, for instance, have courses of two weeks to an entire year in length.

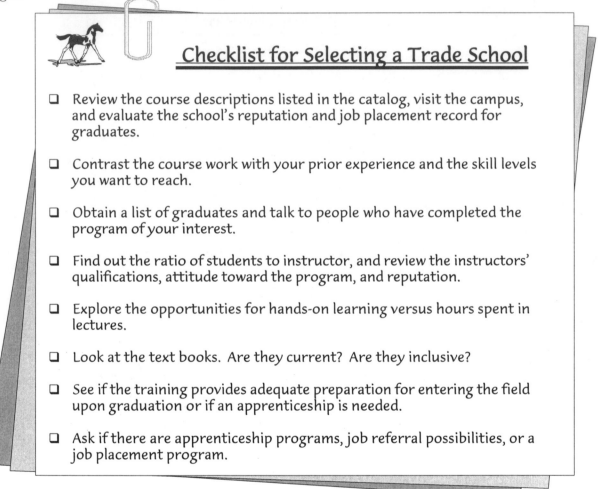

Checklist for Selecting a Trade School

❑ Review the course descriptions listed in the catalog, visit the campus, and evaluate the school's reputation and job placement record for graduates.

❑ Contrast the course work with your prior experience and the skill levels you want to reach.

❑ Obtain a list of graduates and talk to people who have completed the program of your interest.

❑ Find out the ratio of students to instructor, and review the instructors' qualifications, attitude toward the program, and reputation.

❑ Explore the opportunities for hands-on learning versus hours spent in lectures.

❑ Look at the text books. Are they current? Are they inclusive?

❑ See if the training provides adequate preparation for entering the field upon graduation or if an apprenticeship is needed.

❑ Ask if there are apprenticeship programs, job referral possibilities, or a job placement program.

Two-Year College Programs

Two-year college programs traditionally offer Associate of Arts or Associate of Applied Science degrees in equine studies, veterinary technology, or animal science. These focused studies are best suited for the student who is seeking a specific set of skills needed for a particular career. Careers as a judge, riding instructor, ranch or breeding farm manager, and veterinary technician fit into this category.

If you are considering eventually pursuing a four-year program, you should choose a broad-based curriculum in the two-year college, rather than a specialized one, and you should check out course requirements in the four-year college. The broader program offers more exposure to and greater understanding of the horse industry as a whole. If a two-year program is your primary focus, supplementing the course work with hands-on experience is highly recommended.

Use the checklist for trade schools in the previous section as a guide for finding a good two-year college program that suits your needs and interests.

Four-Year Degree Programs

Many four-year colleges and universities offer Bachelor of Arts or Bachelor of Science degrees in a wide variety of equine-related subjects. Although obtaining a four-year degree does not ensure job placement, it does open many doors that would otherwise be closed, especially if the degree is combined with practical experience. Employment opportunities in research, science, teaching, management, and sales are among the professions that usually require a minimum of a bachelor's degree. Many employers give preferential treatment to people with degrees.

Majors that can relate to the horse industry include: equine science, pre-veterinary medicine, animal science, agribusiness, agricultural engineering, agricultural economics, agricultural communications, recreation, environmental sciences, biochemistry, animal biology, and natural resource management.

Combining an equine science major with a secondary major, such as accounting, business, management, journalism, law, or computer science, expands your job marketability. If your horse career goal involves running a business of your own, it is helpful to take courses in bookkeeping, accounting, communications, marketing, and management.

Advanced Degrees

Graduate programs aimed at earning a Master of Arts, Master of Science, Doctorate of Law (J.D. or Juris Doctor), Doctor of Veterinary Medicine (D.V.M.), and other doctorate or Ph.D. degrees take an additional one to four years beyond the four-year degree. The most common advanced degree in the equine industry is that of D.V.M. When a horse career is mentioned, veterinary medicine is often one of the first that comes to mind. This career is discussed in detail in Chapter Four.

Advanced degrees in other related areas, such as animal science, physiology, horse nutrition, agriculture, agricultural engineering, agribusiness, accounting, and computer science, are beneficial in finding employment in the horse industry.

RÉSUMÉS

A résumé is an important marketing tool that presents a brief, concise, well-organized summary of your experience, education, and background. The purpose of a résumé is to convince the prospective employer that you merit an interview. During the interview the résumé serves as a visual reference and reminder of your qualifications. After the interview is over, the résumé provides the employer with a reminder of you and your qualifications.

Libraries, school guidance offices, professional companies, and some computer programs have forms for writing résumés. *Tips For Finding the Right Job*, a booklet by the United States Government Printing Office, provides additional information.

If you haven't already written a résumé, today is the best time to begin. Look for a form that appeals to you, modify it to your career goal objectives, and then make an effort to add new additions as they occur. Every time you earn an honor, perform a paid or volunteer task, or reach a new training or educational plateau, add it to your résumé. Addresses of schools, references, employers, or volunteer groups are usually readily available at the time the task is performed, but years later they may be hard to locate. And you might forget some important items if you don't record them while they are fresh on your mind.

SAMPLE RÉSUMÉ

NAME
Street Address · City, State Zip · Telephone Number · Fax Number

OBJECTIVE

Use the "Section Heading" button to create additional sections in your résumé (Objective, Education, etc). Use the "Small Caps" and "Italics" buttons to add visual interest as shown below.

PAID AND VOLUNTEER WORK EXPERIENCE

ORGANIZATION NAME
Title, Applicable Date(s)
Responsibilities and accomplishments.

ORGANIZATION NAME
Title, Applicable Date(s)
Responsibilities and accomplishments.

SKILLS AND EXPERIENCE WITH HORSES

- Bullets may be used here to create an attractive list of skills.

List all your skills, such as horse care, grooming, working with children or adults, nutrition, management of a specific horse business, and training abilities.

Include horse ownership, activities, lessons, trainers and their credentials, competitions, awards, and clubs (4-H, polo, pony, breed club, etc.).

EDUCATION

INSTITUTION NAME
Degree, Major and Year
Honors, related activities, accomplishments.

INSTITUTION NAME
Degree, Major and Year
Honors, related activities, accomplishments.

REFERENCES

A résumé is also important because it provides the first impression a school admissions board receives of an applicant. A professional, neat, error-free résumé that is concise, easy to scan, and a maximum of two-pages in length gives you a competitive edge. Having your résumé critiqued by a professional in the field may provide additional insights.

Keeping a journal of equine-related activities can also be helpful. For instance, thirteen-year-old Lacey Stevens, who has decided she will be a veterinarian, spent a summer riding with a local veterinarian, observing and assisting at times with surgeries, foaling, worming, and many other procedures. The journal in which she documents these activities will serve as an accurate reminder for the résumé she will need to write in five years.

Before listing people as references, ask if they are willing to be listed and be sure that they will give a good reference. When leaving a place of employment ask employers, supervisors, or fellow workers if they would write a short reference letter for you. (It's much better to do this before you leave. Contacting them at a later date is often difficult, and they may forget your specific job and the quality of your work.)

The Cover Letter

A well-written cover letter is an essential part of your résumé. This personalized letter introduces you and your special qualifications to the prospective employer.

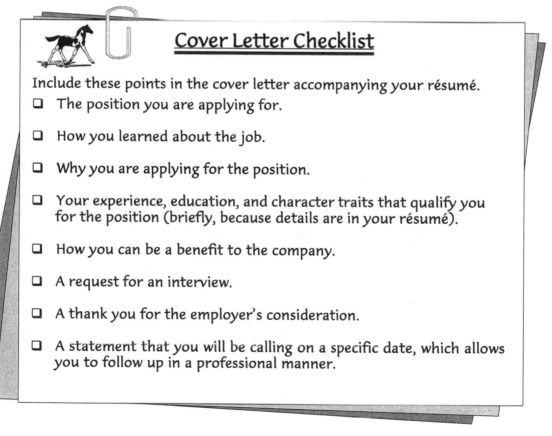

Cover Letter Checklist

Include these points in the cover letter accompanying your résumé.

- ❑ The position you are applying for.

- ❑ How you learned about the job.

- ❑ Why you are applying for the position.

- ❑ Your experience, education, and character traits that qualify you for the position (briefly, because details are in your résumé).

- ❑ How you can be a benefit to the company.

- ❑ A request for an interview.

- ❑ A thank you for the employer's consideration.

- ❑ A statement that you will be calling on a specific date, which allows you to follow up in a professional manner.

Interview Skills

Speaking skills. Once you acquire an interview, poise and ease in speaking are helpful. You might consider a speech class. If this is not feasible, tape record your conversation in a mock interview and play it back to gain insight on how well you express yourself. Avoid "uh," "yeah," and cliches.

Manners. Be courteous. Be prompt (it is polite to be on time or even a few minutes early), and demonstrate eye contact, respect, attentiveness, and, if you have a meal interview, proper eating etiquette.

Dress. Choose neat, clean clothing appropriate for the time and place of your interview. A suit and dress shoes may be appropriate for an office interview but are certainly out of place at a stable.

RESOURCES

Blood Horse: The Source, The. Special issue of the Thoroughbred Owners and Breeders Association publication. P.O. Box 4710, Lexington, Kentucky 40544-4710. (800)582-5604.

Communicating for Agriculture Exchange Program. Barbara Nelson, Box 677, Fergus Falls, Minnesota 56538. (800)432-3276. *http//www.cainc.org.*

Council of Better Business Bureaus. 4200 Wilson Blvd., Arlington, Virginia 22203. (703)276-0100. Can be contacted for information on accreditation of trade schools.

Equine Educational Programs Directory. Sue Struska, 403 N. Henderson Street, Williamston, North Carolina 27892-1830. Information on more than 300 schools and colleges with equine-related curricula.

Equine School and College Directory. Harness Horse Youth Foundation, 14950 Greyhound Court, Suite 210, Carmel, Indiana 46032-1091. (317)848-5132. *hhyfetaylor@iquest.net.* Includes farrier schools, equine degree programs, veterinary and veterinary technician programs.

Gateway's Career Guide for Horse Lovers. Gateway Publishing, Dept. 200-HR, P.O. Box 91294, Louisville, Kentucky 40291.

Horse Industry Directory. American Horse Council. 1700 K Street NW, Suite 200, Washington, D.C. 20006. (202)296-4031.

Internet College Web Sites:
    All Campus In-Sites: *http://www.allcampus.com*
    College Counsel College and Scholarship Superpage: *http://www.ccounsel.com*
    College NET: *http://www.collegenet.com*
    CollegeXpress: *http://www.collegexpress.com*
    Education and Career Center: *http://www.peterson.com*
    US News Colleges and Careers Center: *http://www.usnews.com/usnews/fair/home.htm*

Kreitler, Bonnie. *50 Careers With Horses.* Breakthrough Publications, 310 North Highland Avenue, Ossining, New York 10562. Lists trade schools and colleges.

New Horizons Equine Education Center. Colette May, 425 Red Mountain Road, Livermore, Colorado 80536. (970)484-9207. *http://www.frii.com/~nheec.*

North American Riding for the Handicapped Association. P.O. Box 33150, Denver, Colorado 80233. (800)369-7433. *http://www.narha.org.*

Peterson's Guide to Four-Year Colleges, Peterson's Guide to Two-Year Colleges, Peterson's Regional College Guides. (800)338-3282, extension 660. *custsvc@petersons.com.*

Shrake, Richard. *A Winning Way.* P.O. Box 4490, #2 Warbler West, Sunriver, Oregon 97707. (541)593-1868. *http://www.empnet.com/rshrake/.*

Special Olympics International. 1325 G. Street, Suite 500, Washington, D.C. 20005. (202)628-3630. Fax (202)824-0200.

Tellington-Jones, Linda. P.O. Box 3793, Santa Fe, New Mexico 87501-3793. (505)455-2945.

Tellington-Jones, Linda.   *TT.E.A.M. News International,* a newsletter. Fleet Street Publishing. 656 Quince Road, Gaithersburg, Maryland 20878. (301)977-3900.

Tips For Finding The Right Job. U.S. Government Printing Office. Superintendent of Documents, Public Documents District Center, Pueblo, Colorado 81009.

Chapter Two

Financing Your Education

Whether you are continuing your education after you graduate from high school or returning to school after you have been in the work world for awhile, financing is a major concern for most college-bound students and their families. Although many options are available, discovering the best avenue takes initiative, research, and time. It is time well spent because the rewards can be favorable. Among the funding options are internship programs, scholarships, private loan corporations, and federal financial aid.

INTERNSHIP PROGRAMS

Internships and apprenticeships are available in college communities during the school year. In addition, opportunities are usually available in surrounding and home neighborhoods during the summer, spring, and winter break. Some internships and apprenticeships are paid positions, but many are not. Often horse-related operations are willing to provide valuable training and experience in return for assistance. Check with the college placement office, professors, and advertisements in local publications.

SCHOLARSHIPS

Each year literally thousands of scholarships are available for students who take the time to research the opportunities and fill out applications. Many of these scholarships go unclaimed. There are legitimate sources for locating scholarships, but do be aware of fraudulent companies that charge a fee for giving you access to "unclaimed" scholarship and grant money. The list of scholarship sources is so extensive it could fill a book in itself.

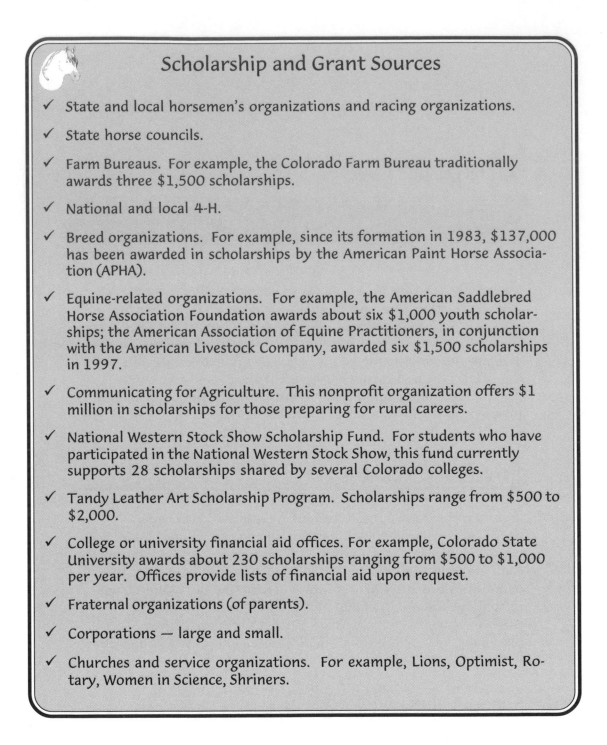

Scholarship and Grant Sources

✓ State and local horsemen's organizations and racing organizations.

✓ State horse councils.

✓ Farm Bureaus. For example, the Colorado Farm Bureau traditionally awards three $1,500 scholarships.

✓ National and local 4-H.

✓ Breed organizations. For example, since its formation in 1983, $137,000 has been awarded in scholarships by the American Paint Horse Association (APHA).

✓ Equine-related organizations. For example, the American Saddlebred Horse Association Foundation awards about six $1,000 youth scholarships; the American Association of Equine Practitioners, in conjunction with the American Livestock Company, awarded six $1,500 scholarships in 1997.

✓ Communicating for Agriculture. This nonprofit organization offers $1 million in scholarships for those preparing for rural careers.

✓ National Western Stock Show Scholarship Fund. For students who have participated in the National Western Stock Show, this fund currently supports 28 scholarships shared by several Colorado colleges.

✓ Tandy Leather Art Scholarship Program. Scholarships range from $500 to $2,000.

✓ College or university financial aid offices. For example, Colorado State University awards about 230 scholarships ranging from $500 to $1,000 per year. Offices provide lists of financial aid upon request.

✓ Fraternal organizations (of parents).

✓ Corporations — large and small.

✓ Churches and service organizations. For example, Lions, Optimist, Rotary, Women in Science, Shriners.

PRIVATE CORPORATIONS

Banks and private loan corporations are another avenue to research for college funding. For instance, the Wyoming Student Loan Corporation is a nonprofit company with 40 employees. It has $120 million dollars of assets, is government approved, and offers low-interest rates. This company provides a secondary market to lenders in Wyoming who make student loans under the Federal Family Education Loan program (FFEL). Check with banks and private corporations in your state for a similar company.

FEDERAL STUDENT FINANCIAL AID

The Federal Family Education Loan (FFEL) program is the largest single source of federal aid for students pursuing a college education. In 1994 they provided 6.7 million loans equaling $21.1 billion.

Applications for the Federal Student Financial Aid Program are available through most college or university financial aid offices. The loans are available to U.S. citizens or eligible noncitizens attending a participating college, making satisfactory academic progress, and working toward a degree. The programs include the following.

Federal Pell Grants

Available to undergraduate students, these loans do not have to be paid back. In 1996-1997, the largest Pell Grant was $2,470.

Federal Supplemental Education Opportunity Grants (FSEOG)

These undergraduate loans are administered directly through college or university financial aid offices. Amounts vary from $100 to $4,000, depending on financial need, when the application is filed, and the funding level of the school.

Federal Stafford and Direct Loans

Sometimes referred to as the *Direct Loan Program*, these funds come directly from the Department of Education of the federal government. If a school does not participate in this program, funds can be obtained from a bank, credit union, or other lender such as the Wyoming Student Loan Corporation. Federal Stafford Loans are available to U.S. citizens with a high school diploma or equivalent. Subsidized loans, where the government pays the interest while a student is in school and for the first six months after the student leaves school, also offer the possibility for deferred interest for those who qualify. Unsubsidized loans are available for those who do not have a financial need after obtaining a Pell Grant. Interest must be paid on these loans. Loan amounts range from $2,625 to $10,500, depending on eligibility and years enrolled in college.

Federal PLUS Loans

PLUS loans are available to undergraduate students who are dependent on a parent or legal guardian, are enrolled at least half time in school, and are citizens of the United States. Parents are legally responsible for repayment. PLUS loans are available through both the FFEL and Direct Loan programs. Parents must pass a credit check to qualify; however, those with no credit history will not be turned down. The yearly limit on a PLUS loan is equal to the cost of college attendance, minus any other financial aid received. The interest rate is variable, but will not exceed 9 percent.

Federal Perkins Loans

This low interest loan (5 percent in 1997) is available to both graduate and undergraduate students with exceptional financial need. Federal Perkins Loans are made with government funds and administered through the school. Up to $3,000 a year, or a maximum of $15,000, can be borrowed. Amounts depend on when the application is made, the funding level of the school, and the student's financial need.

Federal Work Study

Many colleges participate in work study programs that provide part-time employment for undergraduate and graduate students. Community service and work related to the recipient's course of study is encouraged to help students finance their education. Specific information can be obtained from the college placement office and from some department heads and instructors. Although most work study students have jobs in dorms, cafeterias, and other areas unrelated to the horse industry, some colleges and universities, such as Colorado State University, offer opportunities to gain experience in the breeding, training, or livestock programs. Work study programs pay by the hour and wages must be equal to or greater than the federal minimum wage.

The Internet

FastWeb offers a financial aid search through the web. The U.S. Department of Education's web page on Funding Your Education offers very specific information about types of funding, amounts of money available, and how to apply.

Bookstores and Libraries

Many scholarship resources can be purchased at a bookstore or reviewed at the local library.

INVESTMENT OPPORTUNITIES

For parents of young children who are planning ahead for college funding, there are many investment alternatives to consider. When making your selection, some issues to consider are the contribution amounts (gifts up to $10,000 each year per giver may be placed in a custodial account without triggering federal gift tax liability), convenience, ownership of funds, risk tax consideration, and the number of years until the child goes to college.

Banks, credit unions, and stock brokers can provide information on such investment alternatives as savings accounts, certificates of deposit, U.S. savings bonds, money markets, mutual funds, zero coupon bonds, and home equity loans.

RESOURCES

American Association of Equine Practitioners. Gina Preston. 4075 Iron Works Pike, Lexington, Kentucky 40511. (606)233-1968. *http://www.aaep.org.*

American Paint Horse Association (APHA). P.O. Box 961023, Fort Worth, Texas 76161. (817)439-3400, extension 320.

American Saddlebred Horse Association Foundation. 4093 Iron Works Pike, Lexington, Kentucky, 40511. (606)259-2742.

Colorado State University. Christy Lathan, Financial Aid Office. Lisa Martinez, Equine Science Department, Fort Collins, Colorado 80523. General Information: (970)491-1101. Equine Science: (970)491-8373.

Communicating for Agriculture. Barbara Nelson. Box 677, Fergus Falls, Minnesota 56538. (800)432-3276. *http//www.cainc.org.*

Equine School and College Directory. Harness Horse Youth Foundation. 14950 Greyhound Court, Suite 210, Carmel, Indiana 46032-1091. (317)848-5132. *hhyfetaylor@iquest.net.* Includes more than 40 scholarship sources, contact information, the number and amount of the scholarships awarded, and the requirements.

FastWeb. *http://www.fastweb.com.*

Financing a College Education: Investment Alternatives (booklet). University of Wyoming. Cooperative Extension Service, P.O. Box 3354, Laramie, Wyoming 82071-3354.

Horse Industry Directory. American Horse Council. 1700 K Street NW, Suite 200, Washington, D.C. 20006. (202)-296-4031. Lists breed organizations that may have scholarship funds available.

Kreitler, Bonnie. *50 Careers With Horses.* Breakthrough Publications, 310 North Highland Avenue, Ossining, New York 10562. Lists fourteen scholarship-sponsoring organizations.

National Western Stock Show Scholarship Fund. National Western Complex, 4655 Humbolt Street, Denver, Colorado. (303)353-5379.

Professional Rodeo Cowboy Association. 101 Pro Rodeo Drive, Colorado Springs, Colorado 80919. (719)593-8840. Request scholarship information.

Tandy Leather Art Scholarship Program. Box 791, Forth Worth, Texas, 76101. (800)433-5546.

U.S. Department of Education. *http://www.ed.gov/prog_info/SFA/FYE/index.html.*

Wyoming Student Loan Corporation. Phil Van Horn. 1920 Thomes, Suite 200, P.O. Box 3209, Cheyenne, Wyoming 82003-0209. (800)999-6541.

Chapter Three

The diversity of the horse industry offers a fertile field for private enterprise. Horse-related businesses range from large breeding facilities to small horse accessory shops. Career mobility and opportunities for change are plentiful, whether you want to start a new business, use your experience and background to change careers, or return to school to learn a new skill.

STARTING YOUR OWN BUSINESS

Many horse industry professions lead to the formation of privately owned businesses. People interviewed for this book often commented on the need for substantial business background. A veterinarian may start out working for a hospital or clinic, but may eventually purchase or start a private practice. Many trainers, instructors, boarding facility operators, clinicians, judges, farriers, sales agents, dude ranch owners — the list goes on — are self-employed.

If having your own business is one of your objectives, consider the start-up questions on the next page.

Small businesses with fewer than 50 employees have about a 10 percent success rate ten years after opening their doors. This 90 percent failure rate is frequently due to poor or nonexistent accounting and budgeting skills. *Income statement, balance sheet,* and *cash flow versus profit,* are basic terms you need to understand. You should seriously consider taking business classes through your local college or continuing education program.

You can explore your options further. Contact the Small Business Administration, establish a relationship with a bank that offers small business loans, review property issues that may create hazards or legal problems, and select a knowledgeable, helpful certified public accountant (CPA) to help you with tax issues and develop an efficient bookkeeping system.

Types of Businesses

Small businesses can be sole proprietorships, partnerships, and corporations.

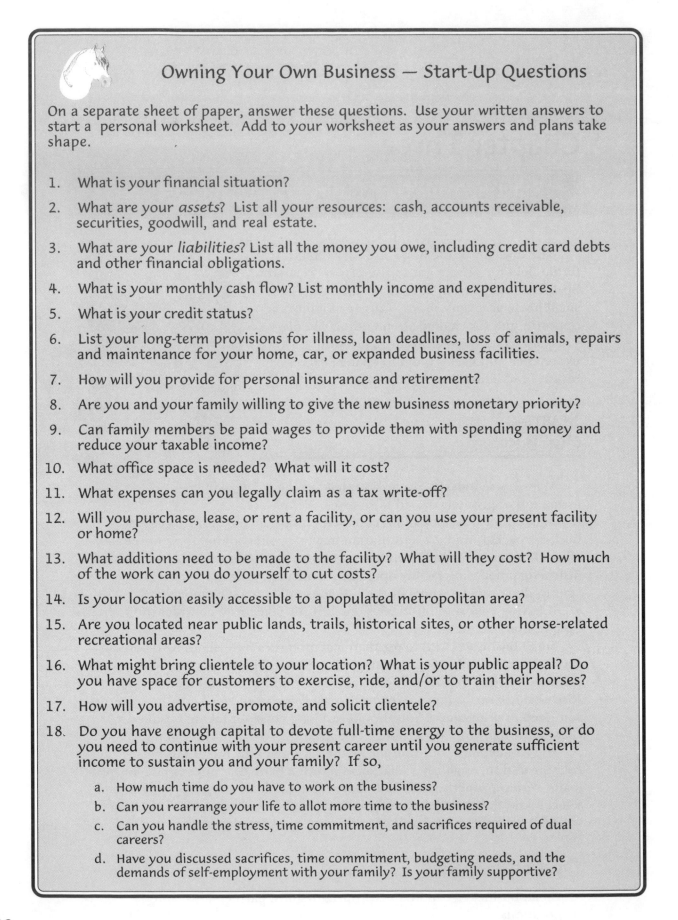

Owning Your Own Business — Start-Up Questions

On a separate sheet of paper, answer these questions. Use your written answers to start a personal worksheet. Add to your worksheet as your answers and plans take shape.

1. What is your financial situation?

2. What are your *assets*? List all your resources: cash, accounts receivable, securities, goodwill, and real estate.

3. What are your *liabilities*? List all the money you owe, including credit card debts and other financial obligations.

4. What is your monthly cash flow? List monthly income and expenditures.

5. What is your credit status?

6. List your long-term provisions for illness, loan deadlines, loss of animals, repairs and maintenance for your home, car, or expanded business facilities.

7. How will you provide for personal insurance and retirement?

8. Are you and your family willing to give the new business monetary priority?

9. Can family members be paid wages to provide them with spending money and reduce your taxable income?

10. What office space is needed? What will it cost?

11. What expenses can you legally claim as a tax write-off?

12. Will you purchase, lease, or rent a facility, or can you use your present facility or home?

13. What additions need to be made to the facility? What will they cost? How much of the work can you do yourself to cut costs?

14. Is your location easily accessible to a populated metropolitan area?

15. Are you located near public lands, trails, historical sites, or other horse-related recreational areas?

16. What might bring clientele to your location? What is your public appeal? Do you have space for customers to exercise, ride, and/or to train their horses?

17. How will you advertise, promote, and solicit clientele?

18. Do you have enough capital to devote full-time energy to the business, or do you need to continue with your present career until you generate sufficient income to sustain you and your family? If so,

    a. How much time do you have to work on the business?

    b. Can you rearrange your life to allot more time to the business?

    c. Can you handle the stress, time commitment, and sacrifices required of dual careers?

    d. Have you discussed sacrifices, time commitment, budgeting needs, and the demands of self-employment with your family? Is your family supportive?

Sole proprietorship. This is the least complicated, easiest to start type of business — business profits simply transfer to your individual tax return and you are taxed at that level. However, the liability risk is high for a sole proprietorship because if you are sued, not only are your business assets in jeopardy, so are your personal holdings.

Partnership. Two or more people join together to form a business partnership, which expands the expertise and capital base. It also increases the risk that a partner will incur unexpected, or unauthorized, expenses. With a partnership, the tax aspect is similar to that of the sole proprietorship, but the liability issue and assignment of responsibilities and rights can become quite complicated. Be sure to consult with an experienced CPA and attorney before entering into a partnership arrangement.

Corporation. As a legal entity owned by one or more stockholders, a corporation offers the most liability protection. It functions as a separate entity, can be sued in its own name, and is taxed separately. A lawyer can assist in filing the charter through your state, researching particular state requirements, and completing the paper work of describing the business's purpose, naming the shareholders, and meeting filing fee stipulations.

The disadvantage of forming a corporation is the possibility of double taxation on your profits when they are distributed to the shareholders. This money is first taxed at the corporate level and then at the individual level. If you want to arrange for the tax advantages of the sole proprietorship or partnership while receiving the liability protection of the corporation, you can file a small business election for an *S Corporation*. However, you should first research with your CPA the limitations and stipulations of this filing regarding the number of shareholders, types of shares, and limits on losses.

The Diversity of Horse Businesses

This book discusses many careers that involve owning and running a private business. In horse-related fields, the establishment of a private business is limited only by your imagination and creativity, as can be seen by surveying the great scope of products and services offered in the classified ads of any horse magazine on the newsstand. The success of such a business, however, will be determined by the demand and marketability of your product or service, your initiative and work ethic, your experience and marketing skills, and your willingness or ability to take a chance.

Speciality Businesses — Two Examples

A particularly innovative example of a small business that combines custom photo work, chocolate candy, and business cards is Creative Landmark Designs. Not only do they have edible business products, they also offer other custom chocolate novelty items that customers can display or eat. To promote their products, they attend trade and horse shows.

When Western riders think of a horse specialty business, saddlemaking comes to mind. Doug Krause of Eaton, Colorado, combined his love for horses, artistic eye, and skills to develop a leather, saddle, and mecate (pronounced *mə kä´ tā*) business. Doug's interest in braiding bull ropes began in high school when a bull-riding buddy introduced him to the skill. After graduating from college Doug found a gentleman he respected in the business and persistently pursued an apprenticeship. The man was weary of apprentices who would learn just enough saddlemaking to then leave and start a competing business. Doug's sincere interest, reflected by his individual study of the trade and his willingness to start as a clean-up volunteer apprentice, convinced the man to take Doug on. For four years, Doug apprenticed without pay while holding down a second job to pay the bills.

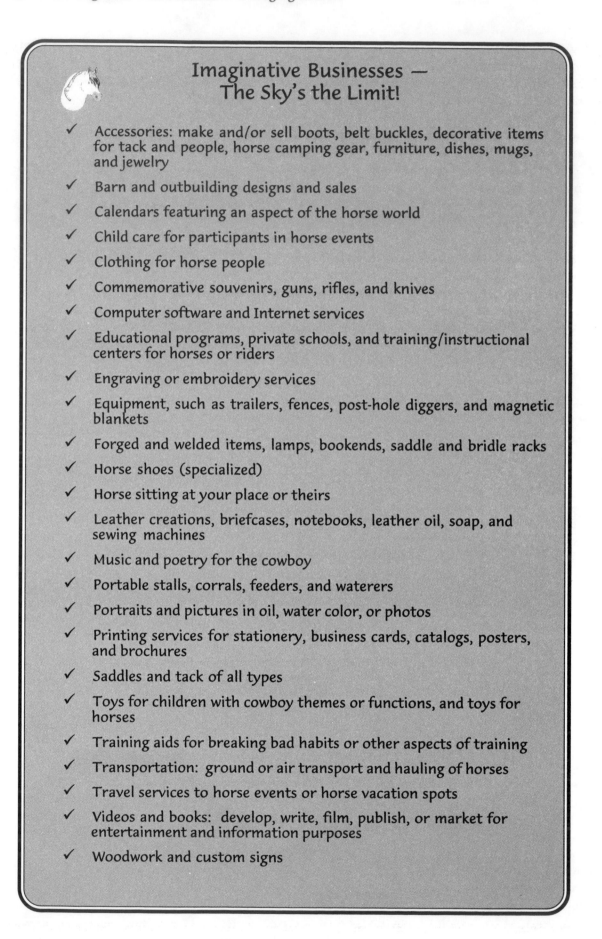

Imaginative Businesses — The Sky's the Limit!

✓ Accessories: make and/or sell boots, belt buckles, decorative items for tack and people, horse camping gear, furniture, dishes, mugs, and jewelry

✓ Barn and outbuilding designs and sales

✓ Calendars featuring an aspect of the horse world

✓ Child care for participants in horse events

✓ Clothing for horse people

✓ Commemorative souvenirs, guns, rifles, and knives

✓ Computer software and Internet services

✓ Educational programs, private schools, and training/instructional centers for horses or riders

✓ Engraving or embroidery services

✓ Equipment, such as trailers, fences, post-hole diggers, and magnetic blankets

✓ Forged and welded items, lamps, bookends, saddle and bridle racks

✓ Horse shoes (specialized)

✓ Horse sitting at your place or theirs

✓ Leather creations, briefcases, notebooks, leather oil, soap, and sewing machines

✓ Music and poetry for the cowboy

✓ Portable stalls, corrals, feeders, and waterers

✓ Portraits and pictures in oil, water color, or photos

✓ Printing services for stationery, business cards, catalogs, posters, and brochures

✓ Saddles and tack of all types

✓ Toys for children with cowboy themes or functions, and toys for horses

✓ Training aids for breaking bad habits or other aspects of training

✓ Transportation: ground or air transport and hauling of horses

✓ Travel services to horse events or horse vacation spots

✓ Videos and books: develop, write, film, publish, or market for entertainment and information purposes

✓ Woodwork and custom signs

During the last year of Doug's apprenticeship, the owner died. Doug managed the shop for a year and a half and then purchased it. Since then he has purchased four other shops, primarily to acquire the equipment. Today his shop, located at his home, contains usable and priceless tools and equipment dating back to the 1800s. If you aspire to work in leather, you need to realize that good equipment is expensive and hard to find. Doug has become proficient at reconditioning his machinery because much of it is no longer manufactured.

Doug's business is three businesses in one. His hand-crafted accessories, tack, and saddles provide an outlet for his artistic talents as he designs and carves each leather piece. A production line of motorcycle saddle bags for Harley Davidson provides a manufacturing business that turns a profit. And his custom horsehair work combines his artistic and business skills as he makes mecates and occasionally hitches and braids other items.

Doug's custom mecates begin with mane hair purchased from slaughter houses. The hair is then washed by hand, sorted, picked, spun into threads, and, with the assistance of a machine, twisted into ropes. Horse hair hitching is an artistic endeavor totally dependent on inspiration. Hitching a quirt takes about two hours per inch.

Whatever your specialty, Doug says you must be sure to research the market and the competition. One company found a way to mass produce hitched and braided products and now they sell for much lower prices than hand-hitched products.

Learning the saddle business from an established artisan was a privilege. Doug feels apprenticing to learn a trade is something a person should be willing to do for free or even to pay for if necessary.

Doug Krause places final touches on a handmade mecate.

Tips from the Experts — Doug Krause, Saddlemaker

- Saddle-making schools only prepare a person for an apprenticeship.
- Seek an established person to prepare you for the trade, but realize many are hesitant to take apprentices.
- Be willing to learn the trade in exchange for training, even if that means being a clean-up volunteer initially.
- It takes time to teach someone a trade, and *time is money* for the small businessperson.
- Develop your own unique style that makes your work distinctive.
- Research overhead carefully. Leather costs increase continually. Good thick saddle leather is at a premium because cattle are being bred smaller with thinner hides and brands often ruin leather.
- Consider adding a service or product that will financially support your more artistic, but less profitable, endeavors, as Doug's line of motorcycle saddle bags does.
- Understand that becoming proficient is a long journey.

CHANGING CAREERS

The days of selecting a life-long career in your twenties and continuing with it until retirement are a thing of the past. Today college classrooms are filled with non-traditional students who are following a dream or seeking a new challenge. Many employers are willing to hire people who are changing careers or are approaching "retirement age." For a person considering such a change, practical knowledge with hands-on experience is a winning combination.

Finances may demand that you continue your current profession while making the change, but that can work to your advantage by demonstrating to prospective employers your initiative and work ethic. Moonlighting in the horse industry can give you a valuable network of veterinarians, farriers, trainers, breeders, instructors, and writers. Don't hesitate to let these people know your goals and to seek their counsel.

Many individuals who were interviewed for this book moved into horse careers from other professions. Rich Reuter (see Chapter Nine — Working as a Farrier) had operated his own auto parts store for 30 years before he apprenticed for and began to practice his new trade as a farrier. Joe Rosenberg (see Chapter Four — Animal Health Professions) gave up his CPA practice, performed the most menial tasks for hourly wages in a veterinary clinic, and then entered

Changing Careers — A Worksheet

On a separate sheet of paper, complete these exercises. Use your written answers to start a personal worksheet. Add to your worksheet as your answers and plans take shape.

1. Develop a self-analysis chart with column headings: Work Experience, Education, Horse Experience, and Skills and Qualities

2. What are your preferences? What skills and subjects will you be the most motivated to learn and perform well?

3. What tasks do you strongly dislike?

4. What are your salary requirements?

5. What specific educational programs will help you achieve your goals? (To find out, re-read Chapter One in this guide and the chapters on careers that interest you.)

6. What additional experience do you need? Talk with people in the field of your interest. Research apprenticeships, on-the-job training, and experience through volunteer work.

7. How much financial risk can you handle? The minimum reserve recommended for someone who is changing careers is four to six months of cash on hand.

8. Will you need a loan? Check with local financial institutions or write to the Small Business Administration for information.

veterinary school. Annette Turno (see Chapter Seven — Stables and Riding Instruction) kept her full-time job as a veterinary technician while establishing a boarding facility. Laurie Krause (see Chapter Six — Horse Training and Judging) left her college teaching position to open a training business, while continuing to judge for horse shows part time. Each of these professionals has in common: a desire for change; motivation; and the willingness to work hard to pursue the skills, experience, and education needed for success.

Changing Careers to Meet a Need

Some people change careers because they identify a need that is not being met. Although Colette May grew up riding and working with horses on a ranch in Nebraska, she spent her early adult years as a public and private school teacher, while being involved in her daughters' horse activities. During those years she realized that very few equine education courses were available to the general public, so she began to gather information about equine training and management. In the 1970s she redirected her energies from teaching to developing equine education courses, and in 1986 she founded New Horizons Equine Education Center, Inc.

Colette May combined her educational and horse backgrounds to found New Horizons Equine Education Center.

The resulting home education programs naturally blend Colette's love of horses and her experience in education.

Today four major breed associations utilize New Horizons programs. Special courses have also been developed that target the educational needs of the professional and nonprofessional horse owner. A varied choice of classes, books, and learning aids have been developed to assist students of the horse throughout the world.

If you are creative, ready for a change, and/or willing to ride a challenging trail, then starting a new business or changing careers may be the route for you.

Tips from the Experts — Colette May, Equine Education

- Begin with what you love to do, and then combine that with your education and experience.

- Research your options: periodicals, targeted market, and professionals in the field.

- Acquire any additional skills or education the business requires.

- Learn how to market yourself and your product.

- Be aware of accounting and bookkeeping needs, or hire and consult a CPA.

- Don't over-extend. Start simple.

- Understand your first years are apt to be lean financially.

- Realize any new career takes many long hours to learn.

RESOURCES

Creative Landmark Designs. C. Michael Cotsworth. 2815 South York, Denver, Colorado 80210.

Johnson, George, Attorney At Law. Johnson Law Firm. 1775 Sherman Street, Suite 1825, Denver, Colorado 80203.

Krause, Doug. Saddlery. 19037 Weld County Road 74, Eaton, Colorado 80615.

New Horizons Equine Education Center. Colette May. 425 Red Mountain Road, Livermore, Colorado 80536. (970)484-9207. *http://www.frii.com/~nheec.*

Small Business Administration. 1441 L. Street NW, Washington, D.C. 20416.

Chapter Four

Animal Health Professions

In the United States alone there are 6.9 million horses. It's not surprising that the competitive animal health care sector requires thousands of well-trained, hard-working veterinarians, veterinary technicians, equine dentists, and a variety of alternative medicine practitioners to serve the horse industry.

Animal health care workers may work in: private practices (including home-based practices and mobile units); group-owned practices; clinics and hospitals; and combinations of all of these. Some veterinarians prefer specialization, which can range from practices dealing exclusively with horses, pets, dairy animals, food animals, surgery, ophthalmology, and exotics.

Animal health care industry jobs include research, development, evaluation, and marketing of new products and drugs. Although only a small proportion of jobs with federal, state, and local governments are related to horses, there are employment opportunities with agencies aimed at protecting public health and insuring safe food supplies and elimination of animal diseases. Likewise, military opportunities include biomedical research, disease prevention, and care for government-owned animals. College and universities provide teaching positions for graduate and undergraduate students, extension specialist positions, and laboratory and clinical research positions. Other horse-related health care possibilities include racetracks, circuses, environmental teams (studying wild horse and burro impact), animal shelters, wildlife management, and epidemiology.

VETERINARIANS

In addition to providing a valuable service to horses and people, veterinary medicine can provide a good income, with salaries averaging $32,000 for new veterinarians to close to $65,000 for established veterinarians. About 11 percent of the 57,000 veterinarians in the United States work mainly with horses, cattle, pigs, sheep, goats, and poultry. Of that 11 percent, about 6,000 are members of American Association of Equine Practitioners (AAEP). Approximately 3,500 of the AAEP members live in the United States, while the others live throughout the rest of the world. Of all the AAEP members, 47 percent practice exclusively with horses.

AAEP Members — Horse-Related Health Care

AAEP Members Who Practice Exclusively with Horses

45%	Work on pleasure and performance horses
23%	Do reproduction work
17%	Are racetrack practitioners
10%	Perform referral/surgical services
5%	Are employed in education, regulation, or industry-related jobs

The largest single employer of veterinarians is the United States government: more than 1,000 veterinarians work for the Animal and Plant Health Inspection Service (APHIS) of the Department of Agriculture. This aspect of veterinary medicine is described in more detail in Chapter Seventeen — Government and Law Enforcement Opportunities.

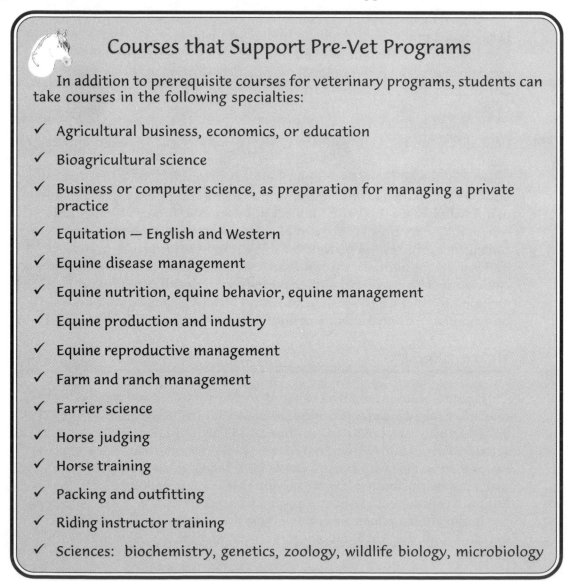

Courses that Support Pre-Vet Programs

In addition to prerequisite courses for veterinary programs, students can take courses in the following specialties:

✓ Agricultural business, economics, or education

✓ Bioagricultural science

✓ Business or computer science, as preparation for managing a private practice

✓ Equitation — English and Western

✓ Equine disease management

✓ Equine nutrition, equine behavior, equine management

✓ Equine production and industry

✓ Equine reproductive management

✓ Farm and ranch management

✓ Farrier science

✓ Horse judging

✓ Horse training

✓ Packing and outfitting

✓ Riding instructor training

✓ Sciences: biochemistry, genetics, zoology, wildlife biology, microbiology

How to Become a Veterinarian

Veterinarians must complete a rigorous educational program. In high school, students take all of the standard college preparatory classes, with two to three years of laboratory science (chemistry, physics, and biology) and three to four years of mathematics. However, high school graduates who lack these prerequisites can acquire them in college prior to applying to a veterinary school.

Six to eight years of college education beyond high school are required to obtain a Doctor of Veterinary Medicine (D.V.M.). A set four-year program is required for the veterinary program itself. Some schools offer two- to three-year pre-veterinary programs that do not require an undergraduate major. However, some colleges either require or strongly recommend that students declare an undergraduate major, because the numbers of applicants for veterinary programs far exceed the openings. In 1996, there were more than 6,400 applicants for approximately 2,300 first-year positions in veterinary schools in the United States. A four-year Bachelor of Science degree offers a solid career option while providing the applicant with a strong background for admission to the professional veterinary program.

If you haven't thought beyond the pre-veterinary goal, you might want to consider some related majors and relevant course work by utilizing college counselors/advisors and testing services, college catalogs, and such library resources as, *The Occupational Outlook Handbook.* An animal science major is excellent preparation for a veterinary practice focusing on livestock. A major in equine science, such as the one offered at Colorado State University, balances a rigorous biological program with practical experience.

Preliminary Considerations for the Prospective Veterinarian

If you are seriously considering the pursuit of veterinary medicine here is a list of insights to consider.

Be realistic. Veterinary work often looks glamorous from the outside but remember the hours are long and irregular, travel in rural areas where horses are kept is often required, the conditions can be challenging, and the science courses and other prerequisites are demanding.

Working with animals is only part of the job. Private practice veterinarians must deal with owners and clients, paper work, payroll, taxes, insurance, overhead, and retirement.

Develop a liking for science. Pre-veterinary and veterinary programs have heavy science and mathematics requirements.

Get as much experience as possible. College admission boards pay attention to volunteer and work experience, as well as extracurricular activities. Volunteer work helps you decide if veterinary medicine is right for you. Chapter One describes the many benefits of volunteering and internships, and lists volunteer groups to pursue. Some schools offer summer programs, such as Colorado State University's four-day Summer Vet Program, which includes presentations, demonstrations, laboratories, visits, and hands-on activities to help young people discover the many aspects of modern veterinary medicine.

Develop your résumé now. Write a projected résumé of experiences you would like to gain before and during your college years. Work to make that proposed résumé a reality. Meanwhile, keep a journal of all your experiences, educational achievements, and extracurricular activities (see Chapter One).

Apply yourself academically. Science courses accompanied by a grade point average of a B or better, combined with experience, will give you a competitive edge.

Carefully select an undergraduate college. A D.V.M. takes six to eight years of education beyond high school and can be very costly. Consider attending a less expensive undergraduate school near your home, which will allow you to save on room and board expenses. Seek a school with a good science program. If you have a veterinary school in mind, obtain a course checklist and use it as a guide, to avoid loss of credits when you transfer. For instance, Colorado State University's College of Veterinary Medicine allows 64 credits to be transferred from a two-year college and 96 credits from a four-year college. Three to four years of advanced science classes are normally required to meet admission requirements.

Most states have a veterinary school or an agreement with a school that saves on out-of-state tuition. Alaska, Arizona, Hawaii, Idaho, Montana, Nevada, New Mexico, North Dakota, Oregon, Utah, Washington, and Wyoming belong to the Western Interstate Commission for Higher Education (WICHE). Students from these states are eligible for in-state tuition at cooperating veterinary colleges. If you live in one of the above mentioned states, ask if the college of your choice has WICHE openings.

Check residency requirements. The number of openings for non-residents varies with each college. The College of Veterinary Medicine of Colorado State University offers approximately 25 non-resident positions out of approximately 130 yearly positions. The out-of-state (non-resident) tuition is nearly $28,000 for each year as opposed to the $8,300 per year for a resident or qualifying WICHE student. The in-state tuition for North Carolina State is $2,430, compared to $18,938 for non-residents. If you select an out-of-state school that isn't part of an agreement, you may want to consider living in the state and working for a year or two. If you are not attending a school in your parent's home state, you will probably need proof that you are financially independent (self-supporting and paying your own taxes).

Visit several colleges. Call for open house dates at the schools of interest. While visiting these informative events evaluate the campus, academic staff, placement program, living arrangements, curriculum, and veterinary emphasis. Talk with students and faculty members about the program's strengths and weaknesses.

Plan ahead. The application process takes nearly a year, and the competition is great. In 1996, 746 students applied for the 130 openings in Colorado State University's College of Veterinary Medicine. Students were evaluated on the following criteria:

Grade Point Average (GPA) on a minimum of 45 of the most recent semester credits. Few applicants were admitted with a GPA below 3.2. The average GPA was 3.64. If your grades are below the standard you might consider attending a community college and accumulating an excellent grade point average before applying to a D.V.M. program.

Graduate Record Examination Scores (GRE). The average verbal GRE score was 524. The average quantitative GRE was 616, and the average analytical GRE was 639. Booklets are available to help you prepare for this examination.

Quality of academic background. Ability to carry a full schedule, variety, and balance of courses.

Employment.

Involvement in extracurricular activities.

Evidence of leadership and achievement.

Experience working with animals.

Written communications skills as evidenced in a neat carefully prepared application.

Economic, cultural, social, or educational disadvantages.

Traveling the Road to Veterinary Medicine — Two Examples

Joe Rosenberg, a third-year graduate student in 1997 at Colorado State University, is an example of a non-typical candidate for veterinary school with an equine concentration. Born and raised in Hawaii, a state not renown for its animal or horse population, he had little exposure to horses. After completing graduate work in accounting, he became a certified public accountant (CPA) in Hawaii. Several years later Joe felt compelled to get out from behind his desk and books. He quit his job, started working as an hourly errand boy for a local vet, and found the profession to his liking. He was actually excited when he was promoted to the job of pooper scooper.

Determined to become a veterinarian even though he had never enjoyed science courses, Joe returned to college with a renewed perspective and attitude toward science. He enrolled in the University of Hawaii and obtained the required veterinary school science prerequisites in physics, chemistry, biology, genetics, and biochemistry. He also continued working for the local veterinarian, volunteered for other veterinarians, and devoted many hours as a volunteer in nonprofit organizations, including the Humane Society.

Hawaii is a member of the Western Interstate Commission of Higher Education (WICHE), which exempts out-of-state tuitions for some students from participating states. Joe looked over the participating veterinary schools and selected Colorado State University. He believes that financing his veterinary education will be worthwhile in the long run, and has acquired a loan for $18,000 a year ($5,000 of which is applied to tuition) at an interest rate of 8 percent. Even though the university does not require veterinary students to be mentored under an established veterinarian, the degree provides students with the minimal qualifications to be a veterinarian, and Joe feels book knowledge needs to be solidified with practice under supervision and assistance. Also, he is well aware of the practical benefits of being a CPA and recommends that students who expect to go into private practice acquire business, accounting, and marketing background.

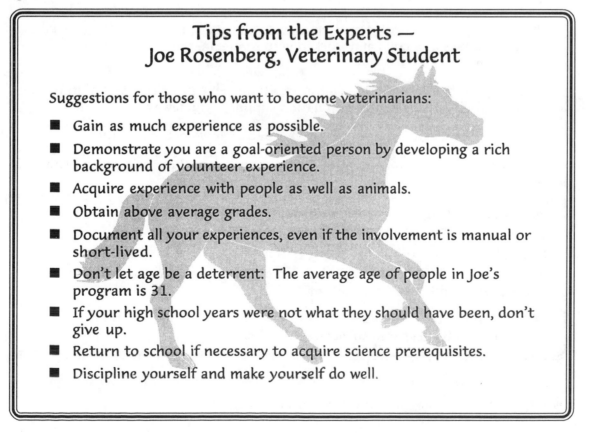

Tips from the Experts —
Joe Rosenberg, Veterinary Student

Suggestions for those who want to become veterinarians:

- Gain as much experience as possible.
- Demonstrate you are a goal-oriented person by developing a rich background of volunteer experience.
- Acquire experience with people as well as animals.
- Obtain above average grades.
- Document all your experiences, even if the involvement is manual or short-lived.
- Don't let age be a deterrent: The average age of people in Joe's program is 31.
- If your high school years were not what they should have been, don't give up.
- Return to school if necessary to acquire science prerequisites.
- Discipline yourself and make yourself do well.

An example of a veterinarian who became established and then shifted the emphasis of her practice is Melba Ketchum. In 1978, after graduating from Texas A & M University with her D.V.M., Dr. Melba Ketchum moved to her parent's home town of Carthage, Texas. Melba researched the potential clientele in this small ranch town and, convinced she could make a living, she acquired a bank loan and purchased a small animal hospital. As finances permitted, she invested several thousand additional dollars to buy other essential equipment. Within a year, Melba was earning a satisfactory living clearing between $40,000 to $60,000 a year. However, it was not without a lot of hard work and exceptionally long hours — as many as twenty hours a day. One Christmas Eve Melba did a C-section on a cow by a truck's headlights with snowflakes blowing in her face. As her practice expanded, she hired another veterinarian.

In 1985 Melba built a diagnostic laboratory next to her animal hospital. She still owns the hospital, but she now spends the majority of her time working in her laboratory, DNA Diagnostics, Inc./Shelterwood Laboratories. Melba has contracts with four breed registries to perform blood typing to analyze red blood cell factors, biochemical pole morphisms, DNA fragment sizes, and perform micro-satellite testing. DNA Diagnostics, Inc./Shelterwood Laboratories is one of four laboratories in the nation that perform blood typing. While contract blood typing is the primary business, DNA testing, research, diagnostic testing, and genetic mapping are also performed (60 horses were purchased for the laboratory to use for producing reagents). Today the laboratory employs ten people, including several office staff. The rest, all with backgrounds and degrees in science, include a veterinarian, a head technician, and medical technicians. Salaries range from $15,000 to $45,000.

Tips from the Experts — Melba Ketchum, D.V.M.

Suggestions for people who are pursuing careers in veterinary medicine:

- Work as much as you can along side a veterinarian. Melba was involved with horses as a child and worked with a veterinarian from the age of fifteen.

- Research the area where you want to establish a practice. Ascertain the probability of the animal population supporting a new veterinarian.

- Be cautious of salespeople with special low-cost medicine and equipment packages offered to newly opened practices. The high finance charges of these "deals" make it easy to get into insurmountable debt.

- Avoid setting up long-term accounts. Clients who are unacceptable to established veterinarians because of bad debts will seek out a new practitioner.

- Acquire a good background in accounting practices or hire an experienced trained accountant.

- Remember that animals are unaware of the time of day, weather, or holidays. Be prepared to work unusual hours.

RESEARCH

Certain colleges offer advanced or combined degrees that include an M.A., M.S., or Ph.D. to meet national standards for professionals trained to conduct research in industry, collegiate, or government agencies. Government research opportunities exist with agencies such as National Institutes of Health or Centers for Disease Control. Public health agencies are involved in policy and regulation development as well as disease prevention, animal health, and food safety.

Private industries and educational institutions have a variety of research needs. For instance, Colorado State University researchers specialize in genetic engineering, cell and molecular biology, biotechnology, environmental toxicology, and genetic disorders. It is important to note that without a D.V.M., research opportunities may be limited.

Dr. Dirk Vanderwall, Assistant Professor of Physiology at Colorado State University (CSU), practiced in New York State as a resident veterinarian at a Standardbred farm, acquired a Ph.D. in Equine Reproduction, and completed a post-doctoral appointment prior to coming on staff at CSU in 1994. At CSU he runs the clinical program in the Equine Reproductive Laboratory. The laboratory offers a full range of clinical services to owners, breeders, and veterinarians. Services include embryo recipient mares, client mares (bred to carry or produce embryos for transplanting), problem mares needing special attention, and research mares (bred for research projects). About 150 to 200 embryo transplants are performed, and approximately 100 mares are bred with cooled or frozen semen at the peak of the season. A program this size offers students a tremendous scope of hands-on experiences.

Each year, 5 to 6 graduate students (about 35 percent of the applicants) are accepted into the program. These students may be working towards the advanced degree in equine reproductive physiology either prior to or after gaining a D.V.M. The two-year graduate training program encompasses course work, research projects, and practical training. Of the 60 students in the program since its inception, an estimated 20 have gone into veterinary medicine and 20 into breeding farm management, and 20 students selected divergent, careers such as human reproduction and research.

It is interesting to note that junior and senior veterinary students specializing in equine medicine are only required to spend one week per year at the reproduction laboratory to gain exposure to this aspect of their career. However, students who desire more experience may choose to volunteer for additional hours.

Dr. Vanderwall conducts ongoing research projects involving new methods of preserving frozen and cooled stallion semen with a higher rate of fertility (the 65 percent to 75 percent fertility rate for fresh semen drops 10 percent for cooled semen and an additional 10 percent for frozen semen). The program is in the process of developing a freezing extender, new methods of evaluating potential fertility of semen, and new methods of assisted reproduction in mares. In situations where embryo transplants are not beneficial, several alternatives are being researched, including Gamete Inter-Fallopian Transfer.

Another program at the forefront of equine research is the Tennessee Equine Veterinary Research Organization (TEVRO) of the College of Veterinary

Dr. Dirk Vanderwall, Assistant Professor of Physiology at Colorado State University, with an embryo donor mare.

Medicine at the University of Tennessee. TEVRO is a nonprofit fund established to finance equine research in such areas as exercise physiology in the three-day event horse, blood viscosity in horses, uterine biopsy evaluation, laminitis, gastric ulcers, oncology, and the use of lasers in equine medicine and surgery.

The Equine Research Center at the University of Guelph publishes *Inside Equine* with current updates on research in various areas. Their approach to research integrates science and horse care/health. The library and reference database receives 40 trade publications with scientific and lay articles filed into the database. Several thousand articles are on that database with answers to questions regarding health care, farm management, reproduction, nutrition, and exercise physiology. In addition to information on research, the Equine Research Center offers an extensive horse industry networking service.

Research opportunities exist with many major manufacturing companies in the private sector, such as Purina Mills, Inc., and Farnam Industries (see Chapter Sixteen), which have laboratories to design research studies, perform the research, and develop products and programs based on the outcome. Organizations such as the American Farriers Association also have or support equine research programs.

If research is of particular interest to you, contact schools to discover their specialty areas. Dr. Vanderwall believes there will always be jobs for the dedicated and qualified individual with the right training, hands-on experience, and exposure to the many facets of research.

COOPERATIVE EXTENSION PROGRAMS — RESEARCH AND OUTREACH

Cooperative extension programs offer many horse-related employment opportunities. Originally developed to disseminate new ideas and research findings into communities through youth, horse programs are still considered the carrot that attracts young people to the programs. Every land grant college employs a State Extension Specialist, and each of that state's counties has a State Extension Director. Most directors have one or more agents who work with them on projects, one of which is the horse project. According to Dr. Ann Swinker, who serves as the Colorado State Extension Specialist, county agents serve as Agricultural Specialists, 4-H Youth Specialists, and Family Living Specialists.

Many positions throughout the United States offer educators opportunities to take part in on-going field research projects. In Colorado alone the cooperative extension delivers resources to 58 out of 63 counties. In the larger counties, or in counties with a high concentration of horses, such as Jefferson County, one or two people serve as Agriculture Specialists. With more than 260,000 horse projects for children, there is a need for qualified agents. Dr. Swinker suggests that anyone interested in becoming an extension agent attend a land grand college and obtain a minimum of a bachelor's degree in agriculture or animal science. Some states also require a master's degree in a related field. Good communication skills, leadership abilities, and a desire to teach and work with young people are essential.

Depending on academic degrees, experience, and location, salaries range from $28,000 to $70,000. As employees of Land Grant Colleges, extension agents, directors, and specialists are afforded the privileges of professors, including retirement, insurance, extended leave to further education, and vacation benefits. In addition, reduced tuition is available for faculty members and their families. Dr. Swinker used this benefit to obtain her Ph.D., a prerequisite for her position as State Extension Specialist. She administers the state program, teaches undergraduate classes, conduct workshops, co-chairs the State Horse Exposition in conjunction with the Colorado Horse Council, and assists in research projects.

The equine faculty at North Carolina State University College of Veterinary Medicine developed the Carolina Performance Horse Program (CPHP) in cooperation with the extension specialists in the College of Agriculture and Life Sciences. This program conducts research, clinical service activities, and client education, and addresses all aspects of performance horses, from riding ponies to leisure and pleasure, showing, dressage, and combined training. CPHP provides continuing education programs for horse owners at multiple locations around the state. A quarterly newsletter also assists in the dissemination of results of applied research in such areas as infectious diseases, surgery, colic, reproduction, drug pharmacokinetics in adult horses and foals, and pain management. The increasing population of horses over 20 years of age still performing, and then being kept for many years in retirement, has focused attention on geriatric disorders. Research has been directed to the status of immune function and endocrine changes in thyroid function. Equine clinicians, other professors at the college, six house officers, and several graduate students are engaged in research endeavors.

There are diverse opportunities with cooperative extensions. Call a college near you for information, and review the listing of veterinary schools at the end of this chapter.

ALTERNATIVE CARE

Alternative medicine is emerging as a viable approach to equine health care. Alternative medicine includes chiropractic, acupuncture, acupressure, massage, and the use of such high-tech tools as lasers and electro-magnets.

Chiropractic Medicine

The chiropractic approach is a holistic method of dealing with the health and performance conditions of a horse. As an adjunct or alternative treatment to veterinary medicine, chiropractic focuses on maintaining homeostasis of the nervous system by maintaining the proper functioning of the spinal column and joints. A horse may be a candidate for chiropractic if the horse: exhibits abnormal posture, head carriage, stiffness, plaiting, or shortened strides in one or more limbs; shows discomfort when being saddled or ridden; resents or refuses to perform certain gaits, lateral movements, or jumps; or has unusual gait abnormalities. Such conditions, referred to as subluxation/fixation, can be caused by traumas in trailering, poor fitting equipment, confinement, birth, or shoeing, and can be diagnosed and treated by a chiropractor. Chiropractors examine the entire horse, take a complete history, and evaluate gait, performance, range of spinal and extremital joints motion, muscle and bone palpation, conformation, and shoeing.

The American Veterinary Chiropractic Association (AVCA) maintains a school, Options for Animals, which offers intense lecture and laboratory courses. Full certification is achieved upon completion of written and oral practical exams and three case studies. AVCA originated in 1989 and has a staff of three employees plus six practitioners who instruct the courses. The association only accepts licensed human chiropractors and veterinarians. Nearly a dozen certified colleges have programs that combine this study with course work in anatomy.

Check with the state you wish to practice in for specifics. In some states, such as California, only a licensed veterinarian can do chiropractic on a horse. Other states allow licensed human chiropractors (Doctors of Chiropractic) to extend their practices to horses.

Acupuncture

Acupuncture dates back to China's Shang dynasty (circa 1766 – 1122 BC). Noted as a technique for treating certain types of painful conditions, an increasing number of today's veterinarians incorporate acupuncture into their treatment methods. Acupuncture involves inserting very fine needles into special sites on the surface of the body. This alters various biochemical and physiological conditions and the procedure can bring about numerous beneficial results, such as stimulation of the nerves and the body's defense system, increased circulation, and relieved muscle spasms. Treatment is administered to specific predetermined points called acupuncture points that correspond to four known neural structures.

The relatively painless treatments usually last from five to thirty minutes and are administered one to two times a week until the desired effect is achieved. Since diagnosis is an important part of the treatment, and only a veterinarian is licensed to diagnosis, it is recommended that an acupuncturist be a licensed veterinarian certified by the International Veterinary Acupuncture Society (IVAS). Some veterinarians will give patient referrals to trusted equine acupuncturists who are not veterinarians, depending upon the state regulations governing such referrals.

International Veterinary Acupuncture Society (IVAS) began in 1974 and has 1,300 members located throughout the world. There are 393 certified and 392 non-certified members in the United States. Certification is achieved after attending 120 hours of course work, completing a practical exam on a horse and a dog, satisfactory completion of a written exam of 150 questions, approval of a submitted case report, and 40 hours of internship with a certified veterinary acupuncturist.

Both the American Association of Equine Practitioners and the American Veterinary Medical Association consider acupuncture a viable treatment technique. It is a natural, safe treatment in which no drugs or chemical substances invade the body and complications are rarely seen.

Electroacupuncture, aquapuncture, moxibustion (use of heat and combustion), laser stimulation, gold implants, and acupressure are alternatives to acupuncture.

Magnetic Field, Low-Level Light, and Laser Therapies

Magnetic field therapy and low-level light therapy utilize external energy sources to reduce pain by inhibiting nerve conduction that affects cellular activity and to aid the body's healing mechanisms. These alternative health care treatments electrically stimulate deep muscles that are hard to reach through manual massage techniques.

Laser therapy treats a broad range of ligament, soft tissue and tendon injuries, navicular or founder conditions, inflammation, wounds, scar tissue formation, and arthritis. Various types of treatments and equipment are offered by a number of companies that have emerged over the years.

Homeopathy

Homeopathy (pronounced *hō mē op´ ä thē*, with the emphasis on the middle *o*) is based on the philosophy that all animals have a powerful ability to heal themselves, given the right stimulus and environment. Homeopathic medicines, referred to as *remedies*, use the extracts of plants, minerals, animals, bacteria, viruses, etc., and are administered in minute doses. They are intended to strengthen and balance the horse's own body functions in an attempt to cure, not just treat, a health problem. A Drop in the Bucket is one company that offers a catalogue of all-natural herbal remedies for horse health care, along with descriptions, uses, and lists of reference books for those interested in more detailed information.

VETERINARY TECHNICIAN

If you love working with horses, enjoy science, and like the prospect of treating horses medically, yet you don't want to invest the time and money involved in acquiring a Doctor of Veterinary Medicine, then you might be perfectly suited for the position of veterinary technician.

More than 70 accredited colleges, including junior and community colleges, have two- and four-year courses offering Associate in Applied Science degrees and bachelor's degrees. These programs are accredited by the American Veterinary Medical Association. To receive a degree, veterinary technicians enrolled in one of the accredited colleges or universities go through a process developed by the State Board of Veterinary Examiners. To prepare for the veterinary technician college program, high school students should take biology, chemistry, and other science courses.

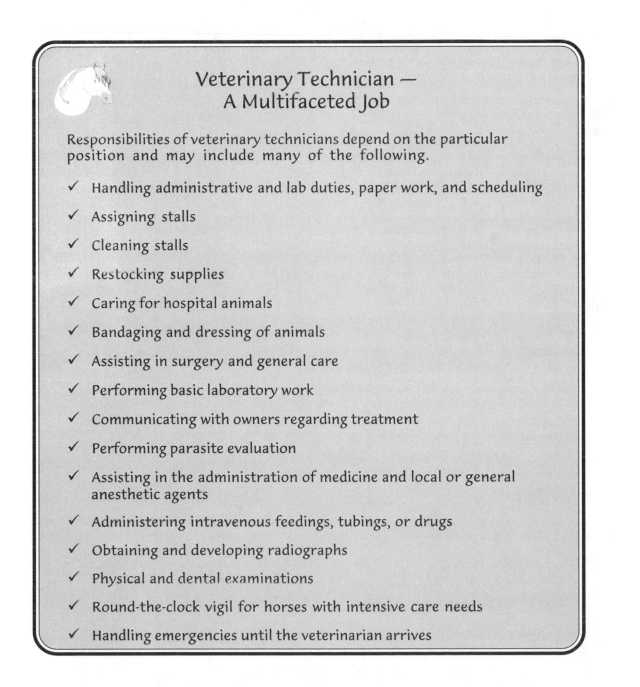

Veterinary Technician — A Multifaceted Job

Responsibilities of veterinary technicians depend on the particular position and may include many of the following.

- ✓ Handling administrative and lab duties, paper work, and scheduling
- ✓ Assigning stalls
- ✓ Cleaning stalls
- ✓ Restocking supplies
- ✓ Caring for hospital animals
- ✓ Bandaging and dressing of animals
- ✓ Assisting in surgery and general care
- ✓ Performing basic laboratory work
- ✓ Communicating with owners regarding treatment
- ✓ Performing parasite evaluation
- ✓ Assisting in the administration of medicine and local or general anesthetic agents
- ✓ Administering intravenous feedings, tubings, or drugs
- ✓ Obtaining and developing radiographs
- ✓ Physical and dental examinations
- ✓ Round-the-clock vigil for horses with intensive care needs
- ✓ Handling emergencies until the veterinarian arrives

Veterinary technicians work alongside a veterinarian and assist in a wide range of tasks. Flexibility is important because the job varies from day to day, and the hours can be irregular — if a horse needs night vigil, a technician is usually the first one called upon. In some universities and veterinary hospitals, such as the University of Pennsylvania Veterinary Center for Large Animals, veterinary technicians perform tasks similar to those of a nurse, only their patients are horses.

The field has many applicants. Therefore, it may be necessary to take a job in a related area and watch closely for openings. Experience in a related field can provide the added qualification that makes one applicant stand out over another.

Career Choices for the Veterinary Technician

In addition to working directly with a veterinarian, there are many alternatives open to veterinary technicians, although a few may require additional training or education. Among the alternatives are the following.

✓ Anesthesiology

✓ Bloodstock companies: pedigree evaluator, researcher, and analyst

✓ Breeding farm assistant

✓ Breed registry employee

✓ Business owner/manager (training, boarding, riding instruction, or breeding facility)

✓ Electrical stimulation or magnetic field therapy

✓ Dental technician

✓ Farm manager

✓ Forest service personnel

✓ Laboratory technician/assistant

✓ Massage therapy

✓ Physical therapy

✓ Pro-Rodeo Cowboy Association staff

✓ Radiology

✓ Research Assistant

✓ Sales representative for animal health products, feed companies, or supply companies

✓ Sports medicine

✓ Ultrasound

PHYSICAL THERAPY

Physical therapy offers another approach to dealing with horse injuries, especially those related to joints, muscles, ligaments, and tendons. Following the example of human physical therapists, equine physical therapists use a number of noninvasive techniques, excluding chiropractic, for rehabilitation of injuries. In cases of veterinary surgery, postoperative physical therapy is also becoming increasingly popular. For optimal results with therapy, feedback is needed. In equine therapy this feedback is dependent on the subjective evaluation of the owner, rider, trainer, veterinarian, and/or therapist, making team cooperation essential.

The American Veterinary Medical Association states that physical therapy performed by non-veterinarians should be under the supervision of or through the referral by a veterinarian, and should be limited to the use of stretching, rehabilitative exercises, hydrotherapy, applications of heat and cold, massage therapy, and stimulation by the use of low-level lasers, electrical sources, magnetic fields, and ultra sound.

State practice acts should be researched for policies concerning veterinary physical therapy. Most states require veterinary therapists to be licensed, certified, or to be an animal health technician educated in veterinary physical therapy or a licensed physical therapist educated in non-human anatomy and physiology.

Equine Physical Therapists — Two Practitioners

Don Doran, a third-generation horseman, has made his living working with horses for 25 years. Early in his career his central interest focused on injury recovery and rehabilitation. To further his knowledge, he attended and graduated from the Florida School of Massage, passed his state board tests, became licensed in Florida to practice massage, and went to work for the University of Florida's sports massage program. His personal interest at that time was the correlation of human and equine athletic injuries. Today Don Doran offers equine sports massage (ESM) programs and presents workshops and seminars around the country. The 12-day, 100-hour ESM professional program (Level 1) costs $1,295 and is available for people from all educational backgrounds, but enrollees must have knowledge of horsemanship and feel comfortable working around horses. A license from an accredited human massage therapy school is not a requirement but is strongly recommended either before or after attending an ESM program. An additional course offered by Don Doran is a six-day acupressure course that costs $695 and covers basic and in-depth techniques of non-intrusive stimulation of specific energy points in the horse's body.

Working as a local equine physical therapist is Harline Larkey. She graduated from Kansas State University with bachelor's and master's degrees, worked as a clinical social worker, and then decided to shift her focus to her passion: horses. After working as a veterinary assistant, she decided to become a certified equine sports massage (ESM) therapist. She attended Equi Touch in Loveland, Colorado. Course work included: equine anatomy and physiology; equine kinesiology; and

Harline Larkey, Charley Horse Equine Massage.

theories of massage, lameness, and shoeing; and hands-on application of ESM.   Upon graduation she opened her own business, Charley Horse Equine Massage.

As of 1997, there were no uniform state regulations concerning Equine Sports Massage and no certification is recognized by any state agency. However, certification demonstrates to clientele that a person does have training and knowledge in the techniques employed. Depending on the market, a $20 to $25 fee is standard for a 20 minute-session and $40 to $75 is standard for a 45-minute session.

DENTAL TECHNICIAN

One essential aspect of the health care of a horse is the maintenance of good dental health and functions. Gail Emerson, past president of the International Association for Equine Dental Technicians, views dental technicians as important members of the equine health care team. The head of the team is the veterinarian, and owners and trainers are other key members of that team.

Gail's full-time career as a dental technician involves lots of evening work. She works closely with local veterinarians, who can legally diagnosis and administer medications and drugs. Even though she restricts her work mainly to horses in her vicinity, she still averages about ten horses a day. Responsibilities include floating teeth, removing wolf teeth, and making occlusal adjustments. Her main outside travel is to the Belmont Race Track twice a year to examine young racehorses. Much of her work is preventative — caring for small abnormalities before a malocclusion develops.

Gail received an Associate Degree in Applied Science at the University of New York where her interest in dentistry began. She taught in Equine Animal Husbandry programs in the United States and in Australia. Upon returning to the States, she started her own business and became involved in the International Association for Equine Dental Technicians. The organization's goal is to assure that dental technicians are qualified and competent. To become certified, members must first pass a written test followed by an oral test, then a practical test. Certification in the organization provides members with verification of their competence, they receive a newsletter, and can take advantage of the association's referral system.

The equine dental technician is most frequently called upon to float teeth, and charges for this service range from $35 to $95. Corrective and occlusal work can demand as much as $150. A technician who has enough clientele to keep busy full time can gross annually as little as $25,000 and as much as $125,000. Initial expenses for appropriate equipment run in the vicinity of $10,000. As a small businessperson, the dental technician is responsible for his or her own insurance, taxes, vehicle expenses, phone bills, and retirement.

If you want to pursue a career as a equine dental technician, be sure to check your state's requirements. Some states restrict the performance of equine dental work, and some require that dental work be performed only under the supervision of a veterinarian. In 1996 an in-depth seminar was held during the American Association of Equine Practitioner's (AAEP) convention, after which a statement was released that said AAEP held that equine dentistry be performed only by licensed veterinarians or certified technicians under the employ of a licensed veterinarian. Much discussion and concern has been voiced about this statement by practicing dental technicians and horse owners.

Gail estimates that there are more than 1,000 full-time dental technicians. While no certification is required legally, Gail highly recommends certification, both for the horse's welfare and for the technician's personal assurance. In addition, Gail recommends that a technician have animal health background, an equine science-related degree, knowledge of bits and their usage, familiarity of horses, and good people skills. Dentistry, she maintains, is a demanding job — one that requires a love for horses over financial gain.

Resources

American Association of Equine Practitioners (AAEP). 4075 Iron Works Pike, Lexington, Kentucky 40511. (606)233-1968. *http://www.aaep.org*. Supports the health and welfare of horses and continuing education for veterinarians. Publishes: *AAEP Membership Directory, AAEP Report: News and Notes from the American Association of Equine Practitioners*, and *Shaping the Future of Equine Health*.

American Veterinary Chiropractic Association. Leslie Collins. 623 Main, Hillsdale, Illinois 61257. (309)658-2920. Options for Animals school provides instruction and certification for people who have a D.V.M. or a Doctor of Chiropractic.

American Veterinary Medical Association (AVMA). 1931 Meacham Road, Suite 100, Schaumburg, Illinois 60173. (800)248-2862. Each state has its own organization and set of practice acts. Publishes: *AVMA Directory, Journal of the AVMA*, and *Washington Veterinary News*.

Association of American Veterinary Medical Colleges (AAVMC). 1101 Vermont Avenue NW, Suite 710, Washington DC 20005-3521. (202)842-0773. *http://www.nmaa.org/aavmc* and *http://vet.futurescan.com/aavmc.html*. Publishes: *Journal of Veterinary Medical Education* and *Veterinary Medical School Admission Requirements in the United States and Canada*, which gives admissions requirements for the 27 veterinary schools in the United States and the four schools in Canada. Price: $14.95. To order: (800)638-0672.

Charley Horse Equine Massage. P.O. Box 304, Red Feather Lakes, Colorado 80545. (907)221-8588.

DNA Diagnostics, Inc./Shelterwood Laboratories. Dr. Melba Ketchum. P.O. Box 215, Highway 79 E, Carthage, Texas 75633. (903)693-6424. (800)693-6424.

Don Doran's Equine Sports Massage Programs. 14735 SW 71 Avenue Road, Achillea, Florida 34473-5102. (352)347-3747.

Drop in the Bucket, A. 586 Round Hill Road, Greenwich, Connecticut 06831. (203)863-1900.

Emerson, Gail, Dental Technician. P.O. Box 6103. Wilmington, Delaware 19804.

Equine Connection, The. (800)438-2838. Provides lists of equine veterinarians in specific geographic areas and educational resources on horse care.

Equi Touch. P.O. Box 7701, Loveland, Colorado. (970)635-0479. (800)483-0577.

Horse Report, The. A newsletter of the Equine Research Laboratory, School of Veterinary Medicine, University of California, Davis, California 95616-8589.

Inside Equine. Equine Research Centre, University of Guelph, Guelph, Ontario, N1G3W1. (519)837-0061.

International Association of Equine Dental Technicians (IAEDT). John Brochu, Secretary and Membership Chairman. 2207 Concord Pike #501, Wilmington, Delaware 19805. Voice Mail: (500)776-6095. Fax: (500)776-6096. *http://www.iaedt.com*. Offers certification program, sponsors an annual conference, and publishes a newsletter.

International Veterinary Acupuncture Society (IVAS). P.O. Box 1478, Longmont, Colorado 80502. (303)682-1167. Offers 120 hours of course work for certification for veterinarians in acupuncture.

Roberts, Dr. M. C. Chairman, Department of Food, Animal, and Equine Medicine. North Carolina State University. College of Veterinary Medicine. 4700 Hillsborough Street, North Carolina, 27606. (919)829-4200.

Rosenberg, Joe. 111.E Drake #7009, Fort Collins, Colorado 80525.

Swinker, Dr. Ann. Animal Science Department, Animal Science Building #108, Colorado State University, Fort Collins, Colorado 80523.

Vanderwall, Dr. Dirk, Assistant Professor of Physiology. Colorado State University, Fort Collins, Colorado 80523.

Veterinary, Health Care, and Other Publications. *http://aavmc.org/schools.htm.* Lists newsletters, directories, and annual publications, and provides links to veterinary school pages.

Western Interstate Commission for Higher Education (WICHE). P.O. Drawer P, Boulder, Colorado 80301-9752. (303)541-0214. *http://www.wiche.edu.*

Veterinary Schools in the U.S. and Canada

Auburn University. Animal Science Building, Room 212, Auburn, Alabama 36849-5517. (334)844-4546. *http://www.vetmed.auburn.edu.*

California, Davis, University of. Animal Science Department, Mark Hall 175, Davis, California 95616. (916)752-1360. *http://www.vetnet.ucdavis.edu.*

Colorado State University. Equine Science Program, Fort Collins, Colorado 80523. (303)491-7051. *http://www.vetmed.colostate.edu/index.html.*

Cornell University. Animal Science Department, 346 Morrison, Ithaca, New York 14853. (607)253-3771. *http://www zoo.vet.cornell.edu.*

Findlay, University of. 1000 North Main Street, Findlay, Ohio 45840-3695. Offers a pre-veterinary program and an equestrian program with opportunities to work with 350 privately owned horses each year.

Florida, University of. Animal Science Department, 106 Animal Science Building, Gainesville, Florida 32610-0125. (904)392-2381. *http://www.vetmed.ufl.edu.*

Georgia, University of. Livestock-Poultry Building, Athens, Georgia 30602. (706)542-3461.

Guelph, University of. Ontario Veterinary College, Guelph, Ontario N1G 2W1 Canada. (519)-824-4120. *www.uoguelph.ca/liaison/request/infocard.html.*

Illinois, University of. College of Veterinary Medicine, 2001 S. Lincoln, Urbana, Illinois 61801. (217)333-2760. *http://www.cvm.uiuc.edu.*

Iowa State University. College of Veterinary Medicine, Ames, Iowa 50011. (515)294-1250. *http://www.vetmed.iastate.edu.*

Kansas State University. College of Veterinary Medicine, Associate Dean's Office, Manhattan, Kansas 66506. (913)532-5660. *http://www.vet.ksu.edu.*

Louisiana State University. Animal Science Department, 105 J.B. Francioni Building, Baton Rogue, Louisiana 70803. (504)346-3200. *http://www.vtsas.vetmed.lsu.edu.*

Michigan State University. Department of Animal Science, 124 Anthony Hall, East Lansing, Michigan 48824-1225. (517)355-6509. *http://www.cvm.msu.edu.*

Minnesota, University of. College of Veterinary Medicine, Saint Paul, Minnesota 55108. (612)624-6244.

Mississippi State University. Animal and Dairy Science. Box 9815, Mississippi 39762. (601)325-1131. *http://www.pegasus.cvm.msstate.edu.*

Missouri-Columbia, University of. Department of Animal Science, Columbia, Missouri 65211. (314)882-7011. *http://www.hsc.missouri.edu/vetmed/docs/umc-cvm.html.*

Montreal, University of. Saint Hyacinthe, Quebec J2S 7C6. (514)773-8521.

North Carolina State University. Department of Animal Science, Box 7621, Raleigh, North Carolina 27695-7621. (919)829-4210. *www2.ncsu.edu/ncsu/cvm/cvmhome.html.*

Ohio State University. Department of Animal Science, 1800 Cannon Drive, Columbus, Ohio 43210. (614)292-1171. *http://www .et.ohio-state.edu.*

Oklahoma State University. Department of Animal Science, Stillwater, Oklahoma 74078-0102. (405)744-6648. *http://www.cvm.okstate.edu.*

Oregon State University. College of Veterinary Medicine, Corvallis, Oregon 97331-4801. (503)737-2098.

Pennsylvania, University of. College of Veterinary Medicine, 3800 Spruce Street Philadelphia, Pennsylvania 19104. (215)898-8841. *http://www.vet.upenn.edu.*

Prince Edward Island, University of. Atlantic Veterinary School, 550 University Avenue, Charlottetown, PEI C1A 4P3. (902)566-0958.

Purdue University. Department of Animal Science, 1026 Poultry Building, West Lafayette, Indiana 47907-7677. (317)494-7608. *http://www.vet.purdue.edu.*

Saskatchewan, University of. Western College of Veterinary Medicine, 52 Campus Drive, Saskatoon, Saskatchewan S7N 5B4 Canada. 306)966-7448.

Tennessee, University of. Department of Animal Science, 305 Student Services Building, Knoxville, Tennessee 37996. (615)974-7262. *http://www.funnelweb.utcc.utk.edu/vet.*

Texas A&M University. Department of Animal Science, College Station, Texas 77843. (409)845-5038. *http://www.cvm.tamu.edu.*

Tufts University. College of Veterinary Medicine, 200 Westboro Road, North Grafton, Massachusetts 01536. (508)839-5302 ext. 4700.

Tuskegee University. College of Veterinary Medicine, Tuskegee, Alabama 36088. (334)727-8174.

Virginia-Maryland Regional College of Veterinary Medicine. Blacksburg, Virginia 24061-0442. (540)231-5821. *http://www.vetmed.vt.edu.*

Washington State University. Department of Animal Science, Pullman, Washington 99164. (509)335-9515.

Wisconsin-Madison, University of. College of Veterinary Medicine, Madison, Wisconsin 53706. (608)263-6748.

Chapter Five

Horse Breeding

Diversity is a word used throughout this book because it so aptly describes the horse industry. Professionals within the field are often heard to say, "You sometimes have to undertake other business options to achieve your original goal," or " To make it in the horse world you have to work in two or more careers." These statements hold especially true in the breeding, training, instructing, boarding, and judging fields. Few people in these careers limit their work to one specific occupation. In this chapter we will view horse breeding through the eyes of people who have selected breeding as their primary focus, but not the only aspect, of their horse-related careers.

There are several trails that can lead to the career of horse breeding. Many horse

Colette May's Quarter Horse mare Seclusion and foal Diamond Rush at New Horizons Equine Education Center.

enthusiasts with years of experience in ranching, racing, rodeo, showing, auctioneering, training, and instructing have used their backgrounds to breed horses. Some people have taken an interest in the field, applied for an entry-level job or unpaid internship with a breeder, and thus learned the industry. Others with veterinary or veterinary technician aspirations, seek an education, followed by an apprenticeship, and then work at a college or private breeding facility. Still others take the career a step further and begin their own operation.

Breeding operations range in size from part-time hobbies, to businesses that combine breeding as a supplemental income with other occupations, up to large scale college and private full-time breeding operations that employ a wide range of paid and volunteer staff.

BREEDING AS A PART-TIME BUSINESS

Carol Kuiper of Silver Birch Ranch in Calhan, Colorado, uses her experience and knowledge of horses to perform appraisals, consultation services, horse training, and breeding of Paso Finos. Carol earns enough to travel to horse shows, clinics, workshops, and breed organizational meetings, and even occasionally turns a profit. She is the president of the Paso Fino Great Western Region of five states and serves as their delegate to National Paso Fino Association, Inc.

Carol owns thirteen Paso Fino mares and stands several stallions. With her Perlino Paso Fino (an almost totally white stallion), she can guarantee the color of a foal in utero bred to any color mare but black. If the Perlino or the Pinto throw color, the foal can command $6,000 to $18,000, while other foals command around $1,500 to $2,000.

Carol's expenses include feed, facility maintenance, insurance, and veterinary fees. Her husband, Hank, is a farrier and shoes their horses. Hank loves horses as much as Carol and enjoys showing their horses at fairs and shows. Carol has taken classes and clinics and is well-versed in artificial insemination procedures and abstracting blood for registration verification of parentage or pedigree analysis. Currently the National Paso Fino Association is considering verification of parentage by DNA testing using hair versus blood typing.

BREEDING AS A SUPPLEMENTAL INCOME

Born and raised on a horse and cattle ranch in Cheyenne, Wyoming, Chip Merritt learned how to ride a horse at about the same time he learned to walk. His grandfather, King Merritt, was the world champion single steer roper in 1945 and helped organize the Rocky Mountain Quarter Horse Association. He raised horses that were known for their ranch, rodeo, and match racing abilities. Chip's father, Hyde Merritt, carried on the family tradition and was instrumental in the advancement of the Hancock line of Quarter Horses. Chip planned to do the same — he respected and admired the Hancock line, their blue and roan color, and their sturdy, sensible, sound make-up. He attended the University of Wyoming on a rodeo scholarship and envisioned the time he would return to the family ranch where he would spend his days doing what he loved most.

The 1960s were a time of success and expansion for the Merritts, as they acquired a new ranch and added to their stock. But the 1970s brought soaring interest loan rates along with dropping cattle and horse prices. Untold tragedy followed when Chip's father was killed in a train crash. Bankers foreclosed on loans, forcing the Merritts to sell their ranches and liquidate about 140 head of horses. Chip's mother, Dee Dee Merritt, held on to three mares, and Chip kept six mares and two stallions.

Chip returned to college, earned a bachelor's degree in finance, entered the animal health industry as a sales representative for Lextron Inc., and began once again to build his herd of Hancock mares. Today he maintains twenty mares at a ranch in Laramie, Wyoming. The land and conditions lead to pasture breeding and little artificial insemination is used. His Hancock mares are known for their athletic ability and their ability to produce foals with a roan color. Many throw a foal a year, others every other year. Chip holds on to enough breeding stock to maintain his herd, and the rest he sells. His foals bring anything from $1,000 to $5,000.

At his home in Windsor, Colorado, Chip has corrals and foaling stalls, his own riding stock, and horses that are receiving medical attention or that he is training. He looks upon his involvement with horses as a way to supplement his income while staying involved in a life style he loves. Yet, with the right conditions he has had as many as fourteen colts for sale in one year. Because of his arrangement with his rancher friend and partner in Laramie, good pasture lands are available to his herd and little supplemental feeding is required. Chip reaps about 50 percent profit from his sale price.

Chip says if he were younger and had more capital and ranch land of his own, he would breed and train more horses and run cattle once again. Although feeding in the winter can be arduous, the discomfort is more than compensated for when he once again rides through the trees checking on his herd.

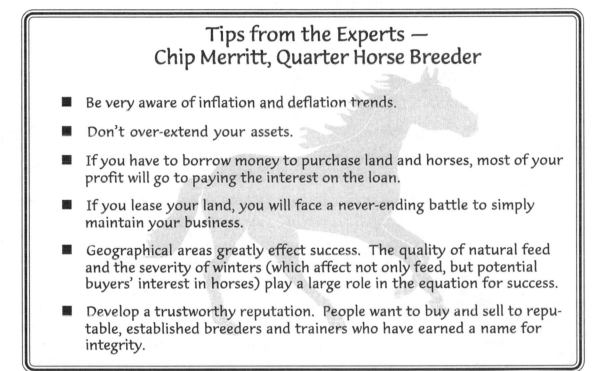

Tips from the Experts — Chip Merritt, Quarter Horse Breeder

- Be very aware of inflation and deflation trends.

- Don't over-extend your assets.

- If you have to borrow money to purchase land and horses, most of your profit will go to paying the interest on the loan.

- If you lease your land, you will face a never-ending battle to simply maintain your business.

- Geographical areas greatly effect success. The quality of natural feed and the severity of winters (which affect not only feed, but potential buyers' interest in horses) play a large role in the equation for success.

- Develop a trustworthy reputation. People want to buy and sell to reputable, established breeders and trainers who have earned a name for integrity.

BREEDING AS PART OF A LARGER HORSE BUSINESS

Charles and Cheryl Weatherell of CK Ranch in Buena Vista, Colorado, combined breeding, training, showing, and sales to develop a profitable business that grosses more than $100,000 a year. Specializing in the American Saddlebred, they stand their own stallion and breed several of their own mares, but focus on breeding outside mares. Educated in artificial insemination (AI) at Colorado State University, they breed using a balance of AI and live coverage. Operating their own collection station, they ship semen from Alaska to Florida. Shipping costs run $100 to $250, and stud fees for the American Saddlebred run $500 to $5,000, with the average fee running $2,500. The Weatherells run a full-service breeding operation.

In addition to breeding, training, and instructing, they board horses for $200 a month and run a full-scale sales operation, in which they act as brokers and charge a commission on sale prices. They advertise using videos, photos, publication advertisements, and booths at horse expositions, and they are considering the Internet for future advertising.

Tips from the Experts — Cheryl Weatherell, Breeder

- First, enjoy what you do. If it is drudgery, consider another occupation.

- Profit depends on: how hard you work, your location, and how you build your foundation. For most people, it will take five years to turn a profit.

- Be willing to start small and expand as finances permit. You might have to do low priority work until your goal is attained.

- Be willing to diversify: board, instruct, assist other trainers, clean stalls, do farrier work, AI, groom, etc.

- Analyze your expenditures.

- Discipline yourself not to overspend, and be careful of credit cards. If personal funds are not available, wait. Don't spend impulsively.

- Know your product.

- Deal with reputable people.

- We live in a suit-crazy world, so be sure to have adequate insurance, but don't become insurance poor.

BREEDING RACEHORSES

Breeding racehorses is the specialty of Ray Wardell. Ray grew up on a ranch near Pinedale, Wyoming. From his early youth he loved riding and rodeo. He passed this love on to his son Kelly, who was ranked as the number nine bareback bronc rider in 1997 at the ProRodeo National Finals in Las Vegas, Nevada. Racing and Quarter Horses, however, have a special allure for Ray. The faster the horse, the happier he is. Consequently, Ray focuses on raising racing Quarter Horses on his thousand acre ranch in Moorcroft, Wyoming. He has a couple of studs of his own, and a dozen or so mares, two-thirds of which have new foals. He breeds with both live coverage and artificial insemination. To enlarge his gene pool, Ray occasionally takes his mares to outside breeding facilities. Because he feels breeding is a finite science, Ray has become an avid student of pedigree. An average horse can't be effectively competitive anymore, according to Ray. Races are won by 1/100th of a second, so breeding of the best has become an intricate art. The best, Ray feels, means a combination of brains, control, speed, and conformation.

Ray believes in diversification and, although racing is his passion, he also breeds, buys, transports, and sells horses. One of his specialties is buying retired Quarter Horse racehorses, or racing his own horses until they no longer make money, and then conditioning and reselling them for rodeo. Racehorses with certain bloodlines adapt well to rodeo if the horses have the mental attitude to make such a transition. Conformation is also important. The key is to know what pedigree will make a good rodeo horse. Once the appropriate pedigree is ascertained, only minimal training is needed to transform these fast and trainable horses into barrel racing, bulldogging, and roping horses.

Ray sells his horses through advertisements in sale publications, by attending private and public sales, and by entering horses in claiming races. In 1979 he and nineteen other investors started a two-year-old stallion progeny futurity called the Diamond Classic Futurity Race, the largest total purse race in Wyoming. In conjunction with the race, he held a sale. He is no longer involved with the Diamond Classic, but this popular Wyoming race still has 20 berths. Each year $50,000 or more is added to the purse, and a three-year-old derby and a maturity race have been added.

The Diamond Classic is still a big racing event in Wyoming, but racing in Wyoming has changed drastically. There are only two major meets left — the Casper Meet (with the Diamond Classic) and the Evanston Meet. Due in part to these changes, 40 percent of Wyoming's racehorse breeders have left the business since 1991. This makes the sale of racehorses difficult and Ray has to travel as far as Canada to sell his horses. (For more about horse racing, see Chapter 10.)

Owning an Equine Reproduction Business

Jill Thayer, D.V.M., and her husband Vaughn Cook are co-owners of Royal Vista Equine, Inc. Although this full-scale reproduction facility specializes in the breeding of racehorses, it is not limited to breeding. In addition to breeding about 400 mares annually, they perform about 250 embryo transfers a year, breed about twelve of their own mares each year, travel to sales in the off-months of September through January to sell yearlings, perform haul-in reproductive veterinary work, stallion sperm collection, castration, and work with problem mares and stallions.

After receiving an undergraduate degree in equine science from Colorado State University, Jill spent several years managing the Colorado State University Equine Riding Center, worked for the Colorado State University Reproduction Center, and was employed as a veterinary assistant on a breeding farm. The breeding industry held a genuine lure for Jill. She knew she needed her Doctor of Veterinary Medicine degree to take her interest to the level she desired. You can only go so far as a technician, Jill said, and she had higher aspirations — a breeding farm of her own.

Upon Jill's graduation from graduate school, she and Vaughn leased a facility to begin their own operation. From 1990 to 1992 Vaughn continued to work at Colorado State University as the manager of the Equine Reproduction Unit. When the business began to thrive he retired from Colorado State University, and the couple purchased 80 acres west of Windsor, Colorado, to build their own new facility. Success resulted from: their combined passion for horses; working 15-hour days seven days a week; learning about equine reproduction through education, experience, and research; running an aggressive marketing campaign; and having an intelligent approach to the financial aspects of the business.

They calculated that in order to make their breeding facility a viable endeavor they would need to do 50 embryo transplants and breed 150-200 mares a year. They wanted a facility that could accommodate growth beyond that goal. They knew they would have to make some trade-offs to stay within their

Vaughn Cook and Jill Thayer, D.V.M, of Royal Vista Equine, perform an ultrasound.

projected budget. For instance, they could either install heated waterers or additional stalls. They opted to break ice in the winter and put in more stalls. They planned the facility in detail taking into consideration all their present and future needs.

Once the Royal Vista facilities were built, staff hired, and equipment purchased, the work began. Recordkeeping, reporting, and completing the forms for all the government regulations are a constant demand. Top that off with quarterly tax reports, year-end statements and taxes, payroll, purchasing, and billing. Jill feels that the several basic accounting classes she took in college were insufficient for someone who plans to do their own bookkeeping.

Royal Vista is primarily a reproduction unit, and horse owners are encouraged to pick up their mares as soon as possible after conception, which makes room for more mares. Jill figures that at $8 to $9 a day, they just break even on board and feed. Breeding fees vary from $1,000 up to a rare figure of $25,000. Stallions at Royal Vista are leased on a percentage basis.

The original breeding management system established by Vaughn and Jill is still closely adhered to. Because horses are long-day breeders, artificial lights are used to extend the daylight hours and thus extend the mares' breeding cycles, which allows breeding to begin as early as February. Once on site, mares are monitored closely.

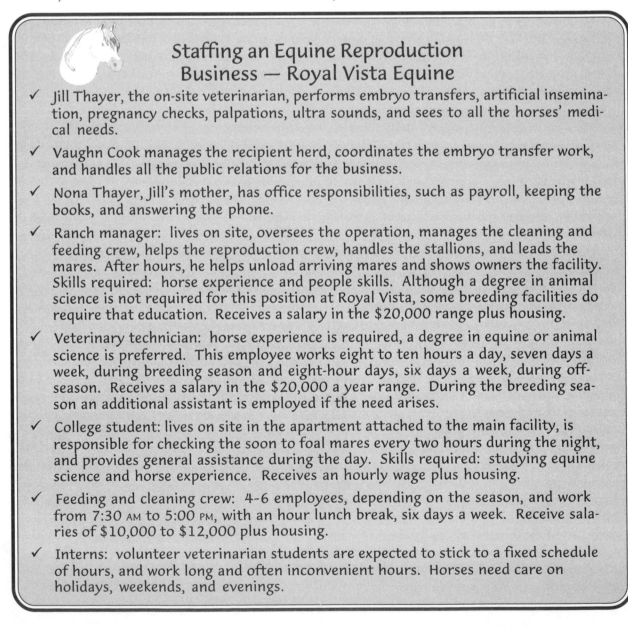

Staffing an Equine Reproduction Business — Royal Vista Equine

✓ Jill Thayer, the on-site veterinarian, performs embryo transfers, artificial insemination, pregnancy checks, palpations, ultra sounds, and sees to all the horses' medical needs.

✓ Vaughn Cook manages the recipient herd, coordinates the embryo transfer work, and handles all the public relations for the business.

✓ Nona Thayer, Jill's mother, has office responsibilities, such as payroll, keeping the books, and answering the phone.

✓ Ranch manager: lives on site, oversees the operation, manages the cleaning and feeding crew, helps the reproduction crew, handles the stallions, and leads the mares. After hours, he helps unload arriving mares and shows owners the facility. Skills required: horse experience and people skills. Although a degree in animal science is not required for this position at Royal Vista, some breeding facilities do require that education. Receives a salary in the $20,000 range plus housing.

✓ Veterinary technician: horse experience is required, a degree in equine or animal science is preferred. This employee works eight to ten hours a day, seven days a week, during breeding season and eight-hour days, six days a week, during off-season. Receives a salary in the $20,000 a year range. During the breeding season an additional assistant is employed if the need arises.

✓ College student: lives on site in the apartment attached to the main facility, is responsible for checking the soon to foal mares every two hours during the night, and provides general assistance during the day. Skills required: studying equine science and horse experience. Receives an hourly wage plus housing.

✓ Feeding and cleaning crew: 4-6 employees, depending on the season, and work from 7:30 AM to 5:00 PM, with an hour lunch break, six days a week. Receive salaries of $10,000 to $12,000 plus housing.

✓ Interns: volunteer veterinarian students are expected to stick to a fixed schedule of hours, and work long and often inconvenient hours. Horses need care on holidays, weekends, and evenings.

Tips from the Experts — Jill Thayer, D.V.M., Breeder

- Spend time, lots of it, in the industry you desire to enter.

- Take a long hard look at what you are getting into and make sure you are willing to make sacrifices.

- Realize that working in this industry is not a career, it is a way of life, and you'd better love it or you'll never last.

- Enter with your eyes open. Not only are there initial start-up costs, as listed above, but maintenance costs are continuous.

Every other day mares in estrus are bred by means of artificial insemination. Most are bred several times per cycle until they ovulate. Mares are not only teased (brought in the presence of a stallion to see if they are receptive) but also examined with the ultra sound machine to see if they are showing estrus. With the aide of the ultra sound, a 90 percent seasonal conception rate is averaged. On the off-days semen is collected from the on-site stallions and examinations of the mares are conducted. About 250 embryo transfers are conducted on these off-days as well as in the evenings of other days.

The demands of running Royal Vista are great, but Jill wouldn't trade it at this point in her life. At times she feels like she is going in ten directions at the same time and she does get frustrated, but she is doing what she has always wanted to do. She is only sad that she has no time to ride the animals she loves to be around.

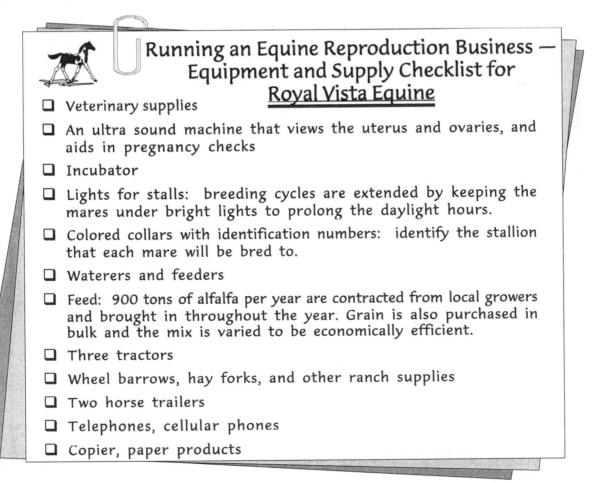

Running an Equine Reproduction Business — Equipment and Supply Checklist for <u>Royal Vista Equine</u>

- ☐ Veterinary supplies
- ☐ An ultra sound machine that views the uterus and ovaries, and aids in pregnancy checks
- ☐ Incubator
- ☐ Lights for stalls: breeding cycles are extended by keeping the mares under bright lights to prolong the daylight hours.
- ☐ Colored collars with identification numbers: identify the stallion that each mare will be bred to.
- ☐ Waterers and feeders
- ☐ Feed: 900 tons of alfalfa per year are contracted from local growers and brought in throughout the year. Grain is also purchased in bulk and the mix is varied to be economically efficient.
- ☐ Three tractors
- ☐ Wheel barrows, hay forks, and other ranch supplies
- ☐ Two horse trailers
- ☐ Telephones, cellular phones
- ☐ Copier, paper products

RESOURCES

CK Ranch. Cheryl and Charles Weatherell. 33525 Wapati Circle, Buena Vista, Colorado 81211. (719)395-8423.

Five Stars Ranch and Equestrian Center. Brad Ray, General Manager. 18850 Midway Ranch Road, Pueblo, Colorado 81001. (719)382-5601. Fax: (719)382-7561.

Half Fast Ranch. Ray Wardell. P.O. Box 250, Moorcroft, Wyoming 82721. (303)756-3668.

Merritt, Chip. 5330 East County Road 32E, Fort Collins, Colorado 80525. (970) 226-2086.

Royal Vista Equine. Jill Thayer and Vaughn Cook. 5412 East County Road 32 E, Fort Collins, Colorado 80525.

Silver Birch Ranch. Carol Kuiper. 14151 McClelland Road, Calhan, Colorado 80808. (719)347-2121.

Chapter Six

Training and Judging

With nearly seven million commercial and recreational horses in the United States, the need for qualified trainers and judges is striking. As you've probably deduced by now, disciplines in the horse industry frequently overlap. For instance, it is not unusual for students to refer to their trainers as instructors, and vice versa, even though they are distinct occupations.

Trainers teach horses good habits, skills, and behavior when they are being haltered, saddled, ridden, loaded in a trailer, or trained for a specific skill, such as working cattle, reining, dressage, jumping, and show disciplines. Good trainers are alert to signs of bad habits and immediately take corrective measures. In a sense, trainers explain their expectations to a horse and then train the horse to respond.

Although instructors may be peripherally involved in training horses, they concentrate chiefly on teaching students to ride with greater proficiency, in all the same skill areas — basic riding, reining, dressage, etc. Chapter Seven provides a more in-depth discussion of riding instruction and running a stable.

Many trainers and instructors use their expertise to judge horse events throughout the country. Likewise, due to the nature of the training and instructing business, many instructors and trainers have facilities where owners can board their horses. If you are considering starting a business in any of these areas, review Chapter Three and analyze your prospective capital outlay, accessible location, facility, and advertising costs. In addition, assess the competition in your area and be sure that you have something special to offer.

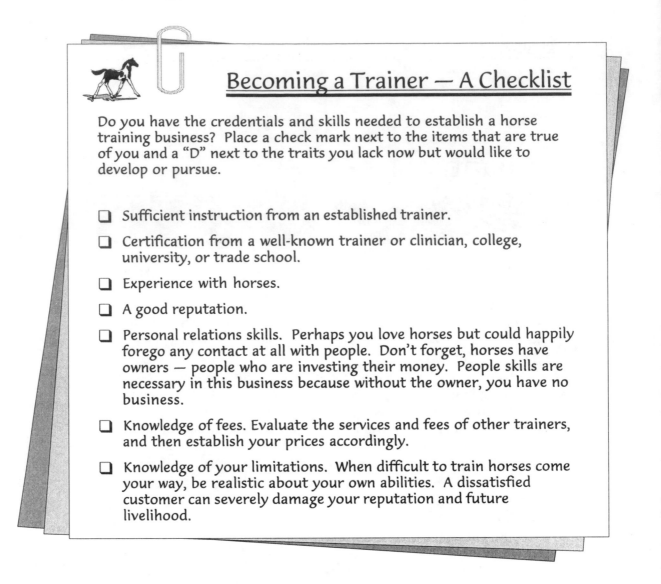

Becoming a Trainer — A Checklist

Do you have the credentials and skills needed to establish a horse training business? Place a check mark next to the items that are true of you and a "D" next to the traits you lack now but would like to develop or pursue.

☐ Sufficient instruction from an established trainer.

☐ Certification from a well-known trainer or clinician, college, university, or trade school.

☐ Experience with horses.

☐ A good reputation.

☐ Personal relations skills. Perhaps you love horses but could happily forego any contact at all with people. Don't forget, horses have owners — people who are investing their money. People skills are necessary in this business because without the owner, you have no business.

☐ Knowledge of fees. Evaluate the services and fees of other trainers, and then establish your prices accordingly.

☐ Knowledge of your limitations. When difficult to train horses come your way, be realistic about your own abilities. A dissatisfied customer can severely damage your reputation and future livelihood.

TIME MANAGEMENT

The amount of time required to adequately train a horse varies. Some horses will require only fifteen minutes a day of quality training. Others will demand much more time. But the time you actually work the horse is only a small part of being a trainer. Every aspect of the horse's care is your responsibility during the training period — the feeding program, appropriate tack, shoeing, length of time and frequency of pasture time, veterinary care, deworming, and/or vaccination needs. Proper care effects the horse's disposition and overall attitude, which in turn effect the horse's responsiveness to training. In judging, travel time to shows and time to study the current rule book are important factors to consider.

Seasonal weather conditions can also determine how you manage your time: scheduling and income can be directly effected by the time of year. Trainers and instructors on the West Coast, or in Arizona, Nevada, Florida, and other temperate climates may be able to work horses and riders year round. People in the Midwest, where weather makes it prohibitive to train without access to an indoor arena, may need to have a supplemental form of income.

HORSE TRAINING

Building Your Skills

Clinics offering in-depth information on a particular facet of training, instructing, and judging are a great way to develop skills and to share your own expertise. Trainers such as Richard Shrake, John Lyons, and Linda Tellington-Jones have developed successful and popular programs that have met with such a great demand they have taken their methods on the road in the form of clinics (see the section on Clinics in Chapter One). Other popular trainers include Buck Brannaman, Pat Parelli, and Marty Marten.

Trainers' incomes vary vastly and depend on such factors as location, climate, availability of an indoor arena, clientele, and number of horses the facility can maintain. Trainers usually charge fees for board and feed, in addition to training fees, which can range upward from $150 a month per horse, depending on the extent and type of training, the competition in the area, and the expertise of the trainer. Formal education is not always a prerequisite for a trainer. Vocational training, apprenticeship, and an associate or bachelor's degree in an equine-related program can be assets. Licenses and certification are not required except for racehorse trainers (see Chapter Ten).

Skill-Building through Clinics

Clinics can be found on a wide variety of topics, including the following.

✓ Business management skills

✓ Conditioning skills and methods

✓ Equine health care for owners and riders

✓ Exercise and conditioning techniques

✓ Judging skills and procedures

✓ Relaxation and massage

✓ Saddle skills emphasizing balance and form

✓ Selection of appropriate tack and equipment

✓ Specific skill or discipline techniques

✓ Trailering horses

An Example of Diversification

Many trainers are involved in other aspects of the horse industry while they train. Doug Kafka is such a person. If you happen to be in the wide open spaces between Laramie and Cheyenne, Wyoming, and you follow one dirt road and then another, less traveled, dirt road, you'll eventually cross a creek and come upon stables filled with horses, a huge rock adorned with a bull skull, as well as a rustic bunk house complete with authentic relics of days and events of long ago. You will have the distinct feeling of having arrived in the world of the cowboy. This is the home of Doug Kafka, trainer and owner of Triangle Bar Quarter Horses of Granite Cañon, Wyoming.

Doug Kafka of Triangle Bar Quarter Horses begins distance training.

Training is Doug's chief occupation along with raising Quarter Horses, but minutes after meeting Doug one soon ascertains that the title of trainer is only one of many that adequately describe this versatile cowboy. His heritage dates back beyond the tales he relates of his great-grandfather, Charles Lafayette Moore. Back when the West was really the West, Moore was coming up trail from Texas with a herd of longhorn cattle when he had an altercation with a man named Wiley. These two fellows only had one gun, and the fight needed to be settled. They threw the gun as far as they could, and then raced to retrieve it. Moore was the faster, and raw frontier justice took its course.

Doug's grandfather adds even more color to this cowboy's heritage. He was the Justice of the Peace for Dakota territory and married a spirited frontier gal, Mary Banner Garrett, who was not only the first elected woman Justice of the Peace but also the first United States Postmistress.

Doug has recorded much of his family history in short stories and cowboy poetry, which he both writes and recites. His home is a virtual museum of heirlooms and antiques. An artisan in his own right, he creates sculptures from black iron depicting the Old West. Doug has run a back hoe, put up grain elevators, cooked for large groups (including 122 traveling food editors for the National Beef Council in Cheyenne), been a wagon master, worked as a cowhand, and been on the payroll for several rodeo outfits. But training is the central theme of Doug's life.

From as young an age as he can remember, Doug has ridden and trained horses. He has participated in nearly every rodeo event, mostly on horses he trained. He has trained horses for individuals, small and large ranchers, and race tracks. He has worked for rodeo stock contractors, and trained horses to pull wagons. Most of his education is from experience, by working with some other great trainers, and by attending training seminars.

Every year, Doug works at the Cheyenne Frontier Days Rodeo, the Daddy of 'Em All. For many years he was a contestant, placing in the money in the Wild Horse Race 38 times. Now he trains, rides, and rounds up horses for this rodeo. A bonus to this hard work is the great opportunity to show off his excellently bred and trained horses to more than 300,000 people. He has sold horses in this great market from anywhere between $4,000 and $15,000.

Doug says that it's important not to limit yourself when you embark on a training career. Even though he has earned a commendable reputation and can draw top dollar for his horses, he still finds he must supplement his income in other ways.

Tips from the Experts — Doug Kafka, Trainer

- Gain as much experience as possible.
- Develop a reputation of honesty and integrity.
- Do quality work and stand behind that work, even if it means an initial loss of income.
- Be aware of the geographical and climatic benefits and disadvantages of your area.
- Understand the dangers presented by predators. In the mountainous area of Granite Cañon, which is over-populated with mountain lions, twelve colts and one mare were killed in six years.
- Be a sound business person.
- Make sure checks clear the bank before a horse leaves your premises.
- Keep excellent records, including all receipts of expenditures and income for tax and insurance purposes. Because of insufficient documentation, Doug received only a small percentage reimbursement when his colts were attacked by mountain lions.

Training Racehorses

Bob Johnson grew up around horses and followed in his father's footsteps by becoming a racehorse trainer. He acquired his trainer's license in 1977 by taking the racehorse trainer's test in Colorado. Reciprocity for licensing exists among most states, but some states require trainers to take the specific state's test. As long as trainers keep current in their own states, their licenses do not lapse.

Bob trains about 60 horses. In addition to his wife, Sheila, who is also actively involved in the business, he employs an assistant trainer, two jockeys, and about six grooms — one for every ten horses.

Training racehorses is Bob's major profession, but he is also involved in the family's 4,000-acre ranch in South Dakota, which is run by Bob's brother and dad. This ranch, homesteaded by his grandfather in the 1880s, houses an indoor arena and 44 box stalls. They have about 24 breeding mares, stand four studs, perform artificial insemination, and use the breeding expertise of Royal Vista Equine, Inc., when breeding a problem mare. In addition to horses, they also run about 350 head of cattle.

It is not unusual for Bob to race horses in several places. In June of 1997, he had seventeen horses turned out waiting for the Evanston Meet in Wyoming while he traveled to Arapahoe Park in Colorado with 21 horses. At the same time his wife was at Canterberry, Minnesota, with another 22 horses.

Bob primarily runs two- and three-year-old horses in stakes races. When horses pass the three-year eligibility, they are sold. Some join the rodeo circuit, others go to arena people, and still others are used for breeding.

Bob grew up with horses, racing, and ranching. In fact, his grandfather owned a Kentucky Derby winner in the early 1900s. Consequently he believes that experience is the best way to learn the business. If you weren't fortunate enough to grow up around horses, Bob says, work your way through the ranks. Schooling can help, but nothing takes the place of hands-on experience. Bob feels that instinct is as important as training. When you know intuitively what to do with a problem horse, then you have that special instinct a trainer needs. Training is not just an adventure, but a demanding job that requires a great deal of travel and time away from family. It also requires versatility — not only is Bob a trainer, he's an employer, horse transporter, breeder, salesman, bookkeeper, and horseman.

JUDGING

According to the American Horse Council, horse shows produce approximately 25 percent of the money generated by the horse industry. Throughout the year specific breed shows, children's shows, 4-H shows, national and internationally renown shows, and shows of every imaginable size and duration are held around the country. Shows feature Western classes, such as reining, Western pleasure, and trail, and English classes, such as dressage and hunt seat equitation. The increase in the number of indoor

arenas has made it possible for many parts of the country to expand their show season. For each of these shows, judges are needed.

The American Horse Show Association (AHSA) was founded in 1917, when showing horses was not complicated. But today society is more mobile and horse shows have grown in scope and frequency; consequently, competition has heightened. AHSA, a major sponsor of horse shows, has a comprehensive rule book that is used nationwide. Many other breed organizations have rule books that follow AHSA rules closely but add specific rules pertinent to their breed.

Three times a year, the licensing committee of AHSA meets to review all applications. If they deem an applicant qualified (usually sixteen references from experienced judges are required), they issue a *small r status* with stipulations of which class of shows can be officiated. After two years and judging at least two rated shows, the applicant can apply for *large R status*. If you would like to pursue becoming a judge, you may contact AHSA for the specifics of the breed and disciplines of your interest.

Judging — Dave Johnson's Perspective

Dave Johnson, of North American Equine Services[SM], combines judging with training, volunteer work, and his appraisal and expert witness business. Dave has served as an AHSA licensed judge for 27 years. He is a member of the board of directors and vice president and chairman of Zone 8 (Arizona, Colorado, New Mexico, and Utah); chairman of the Show Standards and Ad-Hoc Safety Committee; and member of the Marketing and Development and Exhibitors' Committees. As a *large R status* judge with AHSA, Dave travels frequently.

Learner judges often ask Dave if they can assist at shows and Dave is very selective about agreeing. Judging is a delicate and precise business. He only accepts learner judges who demonstrate sincerity, genuineness toward horses and people, and a responsive attitude toward constructive criticism and learning.

Judging — Anna Jane White-Mullin's Perspective

Anna Jane White-Mullin combines her judging with writing, clinic presentations, volunteer work, Internet marketing, and training. Anna uses the Internet to advance her business, and has found this to be both profitable and time consuming, but she knows the web is the advertising medium of the future, so she sticks with it. It is not unusual for Anna to spend three hours a day answering e-mail questions that are later posted on her site as reference material. She began her web page in August of 1996. After it was listed in *Horse Show Magazine*, the publication of AHSA, she had a significant increase in her readership and received several requests for clinics and judging.

Anna is a recorded judge with the AHSA. She received her judging license after submitting written recommendations from many current judges and meeting the stringent enrollment criteria set forth by the AHSA. Her fees for judging are $300 a day plus expenses (food, lodging, and car travel at $ .25 a mile). Anna enjoys judging, traveling, and staying involved in the discipline she loves.

Anna also travels and puts on hunt seat equitation clinics. These clinics include three two-hour lessons a day. The first half-hour of each lesson is a lecture. Her fee for producing a clinic is $500 a day plus expenses.

In 1984, Anna wrote her first book, *Judging Hunters and Hunter Seat Equitation*. This book quickly became a best-selling equestrian work and was followed by a second work, *Winning: A Training and Showing Guide for Hunter Seat Riders*. As a result of her books, lecturing opportunities have opened up for her.

Tips from the Experts — Anna Jane White-Mullin, Judge, Trainer, Author

Anna has a button on her web page that includes tips. Some of the tips she offers to aspiring judges are listed here.

- Capitalize on your background in horses.
- Seek creative ways to use your learned skills, talents, and interests to earn a living.
- Take advantage of cyberspace to advertise your skills and products.
- By necessity be a self-starter.
- As a self-employed person, plan for your own retirement and insurance benefits.
- Obtain high-quality training with top trainers. (Anna was fortunate to train under such coaches as Gordon Wright, George Morris, Ronnie Mutch, and Michael Plumb.)
- Join AHSA. Membership fees are $70 for people over eighteen and $46 for people under eighteen. Members receive an AHSA book every two years and *Horse Show Magazine* ten times a year.
- Consider membership in the United States Pony Clubs if boarding a pony at home. There are more than 600 Pony Clubs in the United States.

Judging — Cherry Hill's Perspective

Cherry Hill chose the traveling life that is required for anyone devoted to the career of judging. She attained a degree in animal science from Iowa State University, attended the judging school at Washington State University, and then served as an apprentice judge. Because of her education, horse experience, initiative, and impartiality, she is a judge in demand. Cherry says that an industrious, qualified judge can judge a show a week if that much involvement is desired, even though many shows last several days. Most breed shows pay around $300 a day plus expenses.

A person can make an adequate living as a judge, but Cherry is also a versatile horsewoman. For ten years she served as an instructor at several universities in the United States and Canada. Today, she judges at various breed shows, is a seminar speaker, trains, and shares her expertise with thousands of readers as an author of twelve books and innumerable magazine articles.

Becoming a Judge — How to Do It

If life on the road as a judge sounds appealing, read horse publications (many post show schedules), study the show schedules, discover who the judges are, and give them a call. Some will be too busy to talk with you, but if you are sincere, communicate well, and can demonstrate the characteristics listed in the checklist, you are sure to find a mentor.

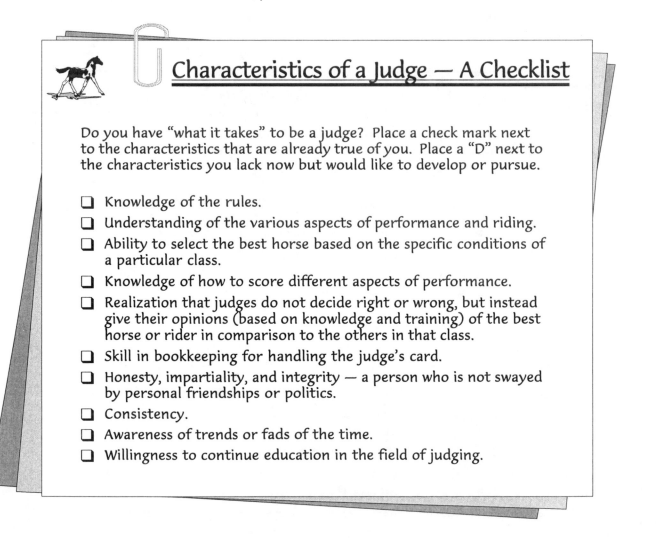

Characteristics of a Judge — A Checklist

Do you have "what it takes" to be a judge? Place a check mark next to the characteristics that are already true of you. Place a "D" next to the characteristics you lack now but would like to develop or pursue.

❑ Knowledge of the rules.
❑ Understanding of the various aspects of performance and riding.
❑ Ability to select the best horse based on the specific conditions of a particular class.
❑ Knowledge of how to score different aspects of performance.
❑ Realization that judges do not decide right or wrong, but instead give their opinions (based on knowledge and training) of the best horse or rider in comparison to the others in that class.
❑ Skill in bookkeeping for handling the judge's card.
❑ Honesty, impartiality, and integrity — a person who is not swayed by personal friendships or politics.
❑ Consistency.
❑ Awareness of trends or fads of the time.
❑ Willingness to continue education in the field of judging.

Becoming a judge can be expensive because as a learner judge you will have to pay your own transportation and expenses — it is a "pay to learn" system. In addition to apprenticing with experienced judges, you can gain skills by attending judging clinics and classes offered through college or university equine programs. For example, Lamar Community College offers an associate degree in horse training and management; Colorado State University has a riding instructor training program and a horse training program; and the private school, University of Findlay, in Ohio, offers an equestrian program in which students train 350 horses for the public each year.

Judging seminars are offered by a variety of organizations. For example, in 1997 the National Horse Show Commission and the Tennessee Walking Horse Breeder's and Exhibitors' Association co-sponsored a seminar for prospective new judges that included sessions on conformation judging, gait analysis, lameness, show ring image, equitation, reining judging, Western riding, showmanship, and halter. The seminar included the judging of four live classes and presented information on how to become a licensed judge.

To locate additional training opportunities, contact boarding facilities, equestrian schools, veterinarians, tack and feed stores, breed and sport organizations, your college extension service, and the state horse council. Horse expositions and events often have booths of information regarding clinics. Here are some other things you can do to build your judging skills.

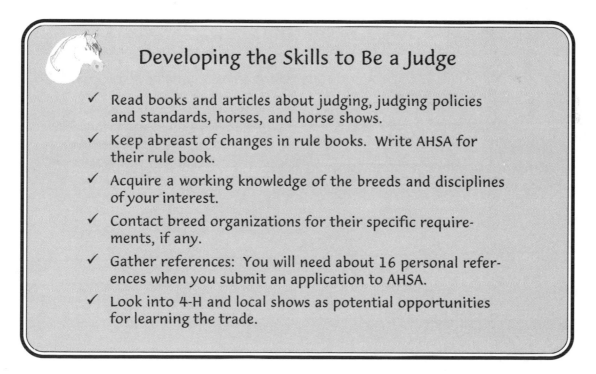

Developing the Skills to Be a Judge

✓ Read books and articles about judging, judging policies and standards, horses, and horse shows.

✓ Keep abreast of changes in rule books. Write AHSA for their rule book.

✓ Acquire a working knowledge of the breeds and disciplines of your interest.

✓ Contact breed organizations for their specific requirements, if any.

✓ Gather references: You will need about 16 personal references when you submit an application to AHSA.

✓ Look into 4-H and local shows as potential opportunities for learning the trade.

RESOURCES

American Horse Show Association (AHSA). 202 E. 42nd Street #409, New York, New York 10017-5876. (212)972-2472. Offers a manual and information on judging.

Colorado State University. Equine Science Program, Fort Collins, Colorado 80523. (970)491-8373.

Community colleges, colleges, and universities. See Chapter One for college directories.

Findlay, University of. 1000 North Main Street, Findlay, Ohio 45840-3695.

Hill, Cherry. P.O. Box 140, Livermore, Colorado, 80536.

Horse Industry Directory. American Horse Council. 1700 K Street NW, Suite 300, Washington, D.C. 20006. (202)296-4031. Lists 133 breed registries and associations, and veterinary schools in the United States, many of which have equine courses with judging classes.

Johnson, Bob. HCR 82, Box 83B, Lemon, South Dakota 57638. (605)374-5733.

Lamar Community College. 2401 South Main Street, Lamar, Colorado 81052. (719)336-2248, extension 140.

National Horse Show Commission (NHSC). P.O. Box 167, Shelby, Tennessee 37160. (615)684-9506. Makes rules, licenses judges, and sanctions affiliated horse shows; furnishes affiliated horse shows with a list of qualified judges and their level or area of judging expertise.

North American Equine Services^SM. Dave Johnson. 35644 N. 11th Avenue, Phoenix, Arizona 85027-8704. (602)582-8635. *davidj@goodnet.com.*

Triangle Bar Quarter Horses. Doug Kafka. P.O. Box 5, Granite Canon, Wyoming 82059.

United States Pony Club. 4071 Ironworks Pike, Lexington, Kentucky 40511. (606)254-7669. *http://www.horseworld.com/uspc/index.html.*

White-Mullin, Anna Jane. *Judging Hunters and Hunter Seat Equitation.* Trafalgar Square Publishing, North Pomfret, Vermont (1992).

White-Mullin, Anna Jane. *Winning: A Training and Showing Guide for Hunter Seat Riders.* Trafalgar Square Publishing, North Pomfret, Vermont (1993).

Chapter Seven

Stables and Riding Instruction

Owning, operating, and working for a stable or boarding facility are popular professions in the horse industry. Boarding facilities range from mere pasture land to luxurious facilities that combine boarding and instruction. Likewise, stables can rent out horses for people to ride on near-by trails, or offer instruction in outdoor riding arenas, or provide much more elaborate accommodations that incorporate specialized programs requiring the expertise of full-time instructors.

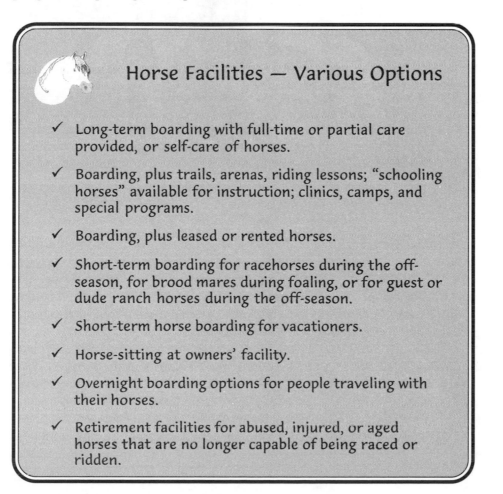

Horse Facilities — Various Options

✓ Long-term boarding with full-time or partial care provided, or self-care of horses.

✓ Boarding, plus trails, arenas, riding lessons; "schooling horses" available for instruction; clinics, camps, and special programs.

✓ Boarding, plus leased or rented horses.

✓ Short-term boarding for racehorses during the off-season, for brood mares during foaling, or for guest or dude ranch horses during the off-season.

✓ Short-term horse boarding for vacationers.

✓ Horse-sitting at owners' facility.

✓ Overnight boarding options for people traveling with their horses.

✓ Retirement facilities for abused, injured, or aged horses that are no longer capable of being raced or ridden.

BOARDING FACILITIES AND STABLES

As cities close in on the country, the space for keeping horses at home is diminishing. Many city people, out of necessity, seek a place to board their horses. Facilities that offer country to ride in, an arena, and instruction are a plus for many of these people. Options range from pasture land rented out for a minimal fee, to full-service operations. Fees range from $25 to more than $300 a month.

Running a Horse Facility — Is It for You?

Horses can be very hard on a facility. Upkeep of fences, stalls, buildings, and equipment are an on-going process. As with any business, you can depreciate your equipment and many expenses can be tax deductible, which can help out financially. You need to have good liability insurance coverage for both horses and patrons. A time-management consideration if you are running a boarding facility is that people will stop by to see their horses when it is convenient for them, and many will want input from you during their visit.

Talk to someone in the business — many people are very willing to share their experiences with others. Annette Turno is one such person.

Starting a Stable from Scratch — the Turnos' Experience

Annette Turno claims that if *Mommy* and *Daddy* were her first words, then *horse* was her third word. Her dream of owning a horse didn't come true until she was seventeen. When she looked at her first horse and realized it was hers, she promised herself she would never be without a horse again. So far, twenty years later, she has kept that promise.

Annette successfully competed in horse shows, earned an associate degree in veterinary technology, and used that degree to become a licensed veterinary technician in South Carolina. But her dream went beyond owning a horse.

Annette and Don Turno with multi-champion Arabian, Skywatch Shamal, at Turnabout Stables.

She wanted to open a boarding stable of her own — a place where horses would have quality board and care, clean stalls, a work-out ring, trails, and a turn-out area. She lived modestly and scrimped to save enough to start a stable. When she met her husband, Don, she found that he too shared her dream. They both sold their homes, started a savings account together, and in 1996 they purchased 60 acres of land, built a very small house, a very large barn, and began a business of their own.

Their future goals include trail rides, family horse outings, pony rides, birthday parties, lessons, and horse drawn carriage rides in downtown Aiken, South Carolina. Aiken is an extremely horsey town that is full of polo, Thoroughbred racing, and hunter jumper, eventing, and dressage training centers.

The Turnos strive to make their new business their primary source of income. Sacrifice, careful planning, strict budgeting, and continuous financial analysis have contributed to their success so far. They realize there is still much work in store for them, but they also believe that any dream worth having is worth the sacrifice.

Running a Large Multi-Purpose Facility

Just fifteen miles south of Colorado Springs, Colorado, situated on 87 acres, sits Five Star Ranch and Equestrian Center. This deluxe facility that accommodates 200 horses features 125 12-by-12-foot heated indoor stalls; 5 15-by-30-foot foaling stalls; 2 huge heated indoor arenas; a 47-foot and a 50-foot indoor round pen; 8 full-care pastures; turnout pens; 3 outdoor arenas; a therapeutic bath walker; indoor washing facilities; and a blanket cleaning unit.

The year of 1998 marks the opening of the first full breeding season under the management of Brad Ray, M.S. In this newly renovated training and breeding facility, Brad plans to concentrate on a quality state-of-the-art breeding program using the most recent advancements in equine reproduction technology. He anticipates performing fifteen to twenty embryo transfers and breeding up to 200 mares in 1998. Services include stallion and brood mare management, artificial insemination; semen collection, cooling, shipping, freezing; breeding soundness evaluations; and behavior training.

Five Star changed hands in September of 1996. The new owners are receptive to horses of all breeds and trainers of many disciplines. They offer hunter/jumper schooling and training in dressage, as well as instruction for Western riders. Experienced resident and outside trainers are available. The versatile facility is used for horse events of all kinds. A newly remodeled home provides a restful guest house for clinicians, judges, and guests, and it lends itself to executive retreats, receptions, and reunions.

The new owners of Five Star have been involved with horses since their youth. Luis Praxmarer, owner of the Munich, Germany, subsidiary of the American firm META Group, and Sabine Gurich travel back and forth from Germany several times a year. Since the purchase, they have invested nearly $2 million in the ranch and have plans to invest another $2 million in the next several years.

The owners plan to continue the renovations of pastures and to develop 30 additional turnout runs, landscaping, fencing, and perhaps an eventing course. Five Star's farm philosophy calls for a first-class facility that meets all horse owners' needs, including breeding, boarding, and training. For example, they have several mares boarded that are in foal. The owners ride them, taking advantage of Five Star's training services. They will have their mares foal at Five Star and then breed them again at the facility. Some will use shipped or frozen semen.

With 125 stalls, boarding comprises a major part of Five Star's income. The fees reflect the quality of the facility — $295 per month for indoor stalls (this includes daily cleaning and two feedings a day), and $15 for a 30- to 45-minute optional grooming session. Turnouts run $40 per month and pasture $150 per month. Brad Ray says, "Visitors are welcome."

Operating Children's Day Camps

Paint Horse Stables, located inside Cherry Creek State Park near Denver, Colorado, is owned and operated by Bob Hantschel. The stable is a concession inside the park, and the horses, buildings, and equipment are owned by Paint Horse Stables. More than 3,500 acres of land and 1,000 acres of water make it a perfect location for renting out horses for trail rides and boarding horses, which were the original emphases of the business.

Today, day camps for children are a growing part of Paint Horse Stables. Each year additional camps are added as the demand increases. Paint Horse Stables also offers Pony Pals, a youth riding club for children seven years and older, riding lessons for youth and adults, pony rides for younger children, hayrack rides led by Belgian draft horses, and catered horseback and hayrack rides. In addition, they provide hayrack wagons for parades, office parties, church outings, and neighborhood events. Trail rides are offered throughout the year as the weather permits. Several wranglers are hired year round, with the numbers increasing during the summer to accommodate the children's day camps. Bob owns about 50 horses and boards an additional 26.

Another Approach to Horse Camps

Jim and Kris Cooper, owners of Anchorage Farm, in Pine, Colorado, began their business in 1967 as a boarding and training facility. While continuing to train horses and to board as many as 22 horses, this family-owned and -operated business responded to clients' requests and now runs a variety of camping programs.

One of the programs, called After School at the Stable, offers group lessons, study time, and an opportunity to help in the stables to receive credit for future lessons. After-school pick up is an added amenity. Anchorage Farm riding camps include: Little Kids Camp for five- to seven-year-olds, four-day Trail Camp for anyone over the age of eight, four-day pack trips for children and adults, and a four-day Dressage Camp. A bed and breakfast — for horses and people — complete with trail-riding options, is also available.

Children love horses and being out of doors. More and more parents are seeking horse-related activities for their children. Combine this trend with the growing population of adults who want to ride horses, and you may find a role in fulfilling the increasing demand for stables, boarding facilities, and camping programs in your area.

RIDING INSTRUCTION

Equestrienne, teacher, trainer, stable hand, manager, counselor, coach, encourager, confidant, and *friend* are all terms that apply to riding instructors. You can qualify to be a riding instructor through college horsemanship classes and equestrian schools, and by working for camps, stables, and ranches. Even though certification is not required, it is highly recommended because certification programs focus on protecting riders against injury and accidents. Attaining a credential also lends credibility to your qualifications as an instructor.

Certification can be acquired in several ways. The Horsemanship Safety Association (HSA), organized in 1964 by Betty Bennett and the late John Bennett, offers a 40-hour comprehensive clinic leading to instructor and trail guide certification. Clinic participants are judged on their personal horsemanship skills, evaluated according to their teaching techniques with child riders, and graded on a written examination. More than 3,000 participants in the program have become certified instructors. Re-certification is required every three years. HSA training provides the industry with instructors who are aware of safe horsemanship techniques.

The Association for Horsemanship Safety and Education, incorporated in 1967 as a nonprofit organization, also trains riding instructors and trail guides. Each year they offer 80 to 100 clinics throughout the United States and in Canada and Australia. Four levels of trail certification are provided along with instructional workshops on horse packing, trail riding, and other topics. They also have materials, publications, and manuals for trail-ride guides, instructors, and riding students.

Incomes for riding instructors vary greatly. Fees for private lessons range from $10 to $60 for a one-hour lesson, but some highly qualified instructors with national status charge as much as $100 a lesson. Expenses depend on the type and size of the facility; if the facility is owned, rented, or leased; the income and aspirations of the clientele; and whether students are instructed on their own horses or on horses provided by the riding instructor. Many instructors supplement their income by training, boarding, judging, coaching students at horse shows, and conducting clinics.

Characteristics of a Riding Instructor

How many of the following traits are true for you? Place a check mark next to the characteristics that you already have and a "D" next to the skills you lack now but would like to develop or pursue.

- ❏ Experience riding horses, preferably most of your life, and the desire for continued hands-on contact with horses.

- ❏ An impressive record of success in participating in horse competitions.

- ❏ Experience as a student with an outstanding riding instructor.

- ❏ Excellent communication skills with both people and horses.

- ❏ Expertise in instructing and teaching.

- ❏ Honesty.

- ❏ Good organizational skills (and effective time-management skills that can accommodate telephone time, canceled lessons, and parent input).

- ❏ Desire to work out of doors.

- ❏ Ability to be self-employed.

Instructor Extraordinaire — Laurie Krause

Laurie Krause embodies all of the characteristics presented in the instructor checklist. Laurie has a lifetime of experience in the saddle. She grew up riding hunter jumpers and in the 1970s she added Quarter Horses to her experience. She has advanced through the amateur ranks to a professional level, obtained a degree with a teaching emphasis, acquired experience as a rider and trainer on the show circuit catering to a high-income clientele, taught at the university level, judged horse shows nationally and internationally, and acquired the background and knowledge to run her own business.

Laurie Krause with student and assistant Tana Buckner.

Soon after she obtained a bachelors degree in physical education and a teaching certificate from Colorado State University, she translated her teaching expertise to riding instruction and horse training. For years she prepared, hauled, and exhibited horses for owners, coached riders, showed horses, and judged, spending most of her time on the road.

In 1983 she joined the staff of the equine science program at Colorado State University as a riding instructor, guest speaker in classes, and advisor. In 1987 she left CSU and returned to private instruction, this time instructing and training from her home. Today she seldom travels the show circuit with clients' horses. She boards and trains horses and works with students one to three times a week, depending on the riders' preferences. Laurie is also a certified judge with the American Quarter Horse Association and the Palomino Horse Association, but these days she limits her judging to shows in and around her home. Although many of these shows last only a half-day and pay less than $200 a day, they give her the opportunity to be around young people and practice a skill she loves. (For more information about judging, see Chapter Six.)

Currently, besides training, instructing, and judging, Laurie does volunteer horse work (she is currently the director of the Greeley Saddle Club). She also leads clinics locally and nationally, and foals out mares on her facility. Her facility is located in Eaton, Colorado, where she has a large outdoor arena, six indoor 8-by-10-foot stalls, two foaling stalls, a pasture, and several outdoor runs. While snowfall is not unusual in the winter, it melts quickly, which allows Laurie to instruct and train year round. Her location is easily accessible to riders from the neighboring towns of Greeley, Fort Collins, Ault, and Kersey.

Laurie has enjoyed all the stages of her career, but she feels instructing, training, and judging are her special niche. For someone considering this aspect of the industry, she offers suggestions and comments that appear on the next page.

Tips from the Experts —
Laurie Krause, Instructor, Trainer, Judge

- When you seek an internship, if possible visit the facility — telephone or letter contact does not always provide enough information for you to assess the working conditions.

- Your first job may serve as a "reality check" for the long hours and "grunt work" required in entry-level positions.

- Match your operation to the capital you have to invest — size and luxury are not as important as maintaining a clean, neat facility.

- Hard work is a key factor for success. If you have a bad experience, don't give up — there are many wonderful people in the industry.

- Be dedicated to your clientele — you are more than an instructor to them.

- Allow time for stable and arena preparation and maintenance, and telephone time for scheduling and consulting with riders and parents.

- High-income clientele usually have expensive horses, equipment, and clothing, as well as the finances to travel, and they usually want the instructor or trainer to accompany them or their horses.

- Instructing middle-income students often affords you the opportunity to be at home more, and it can be just as profitable.

- Assess and meet your clients' needs and schedules. Instructional schedules must be arranged around the students' schedules, which means instructing after school, evenings, weekends, and school vacation time.

- Don't become possessive. You put a lot of energy into your clients, and watching them move on to another instructor can be difficult. Don't take it personally — it is part of the industry.

- Be approachable when working in public or showing, and you will acquire new students and jobs.

- Parents seek a calm, stable, level-headed instructor who uses only clean language.

- Hours vary greatly, from twelve-hour days in the summer months to slack time in the winter.

- Activities range from mucking stalls, listening to clients' concerns, helping children develop a positive self-concept, to actual teaching.

- Be realistic — this is not the type of career you should enter for the money, but you do need to make a living. Approach it as a business.

- Adjust your expenditures to compensate for slack periods and no shows. Assess your fees according to your expertise, ability to produce the promised skills, and what the market in your location will bear.

- Take care of yourself — prepare physically, as any athlete would, by drinking lots of water, eating healthy food, and getting adequate sleep.

- Be aware of the materialistic aspects of the horse industry — it is easy to get caught up in the desire for better horses, trainers, and fancy equipment.

- Pay attention to your emotional, social, and spiritual needs. Schedule fun and recreational time for you and your family, and attend to your spiritual life.

THERAPEUTIC RIDING INSTRUCTION

In the 1950s, it was discovered that horseback riding improves muscle tone, balance, posture, coordination, strength, and flexibility. Riding also helps develop a better emotional and psychological outlook on life. Many horse enthusiasts claim that when they are feeling down, with body aching and a headache that just won't go away, all they have to do is head for the barn, saddle a horse, and within an hour they feel great.

Riding a horse stimulates the same muscles as walking, and therefore it can serve as a therapeutic technique for people with impaired mobility. With this in mind, it is easy to see how the relationship between a horse and a rider can also help psychologically, mentally, and emotionally disabled people. Riding requires concentration and discipline, which can lead to a relationship between the horse and rider that transfers over to the rider's relationship with other people.

When the benefits of riding for physically, mentally, and emotionally disabled people were recognized, therapeutic riding programs began to appear. In 1969, the North American Riding for the Handicapped Association (NARHA) was formed to promote the recovery of individuals through horseback riding. The organization also supports research and trains and certifies riding instructors.

For the skilled horse person who has a special interest in working with people with physical and emotional needs, NARHA offers unique and enriching volunteer opportunities, and a limited number of paid positions. At more than 600 centers, 30,000 riders take part in programs that include 1,250 instructors, 34,000 volunteers, 3,800 individual members, 840 licensed therapists, and 4,500 therapy horses.

There is a growing need for therapeutic riding services. Many of the 600 centers have client waiting lists during the riding season. NARHA offers educational and networking assistance for individuals interested in starting up a therapeutic riding center. They offer a *Start-Up Packet* for $10 that includes information on budgets, personnel, facilities, insurance, funding, equipment, and samples of required federal, state, and NARHA forms.

Nora Fischbach, program director for Special Equestrian Riding Therapy, Inc., and a member of NARHA, conducted a survey in California of therapeutic riding programs. She discovered that the average pay for program directors is $25,000 a year and instructors' average pay was $10 an hour. However, there are also all-volunteer programs throughout North America.

If a therapeutic riding program is accredited by NARHA, instructors must be registered and certified through them. Certification requires passing a written test and a video practical test of the instructor's actual instruction. Training classes are available across the country. Contact NARHA for more information.

RESOURCES

Anchorage Farms. Jim and Kris Cooper. 12889 Parker Avenue, Pine, Colorado 80407.

Association for Horsemanship Safety and Education. 5318 Old Bullard Road, Tyler, Texas 75703. (800)399-0318. *http://www.cha-ahse.org.*

Five Star Ranch and Equestrian Center. Owners: Luis Praxmarer and Sabine Gurich. General Manager: Brad Ray. 18850 Midway Ranch Road, Pueblo, Colorado 81001. (719)382-5601. Fax: (719)382-7561.

Horsemanship Safety Association (HAS)/American Riding Instructors Certification Program. Betty Bennett-Talbot. 517 Bear Road, Lake Placid, Florida 33852-9726. (941)465-1365. (800)798-8106.

Krause, Laurie. 19037 Weld County Road 74, Eaton, Colorado 80615.

North American Riding for the Handicapped Association (NARHA). P.O. Box 33150, Denver, Colorado 80233. (800)369-7433. *http://www.narha.org.* Offers educational resources on starting and maintaining successful riding programs for the handicapped, and a list of centers by state for those interested in volunteering or in paid instructor positions.

Paint Horse Stables. Bob Hantschel. 4201 Parker Road, Aurora, Colorado 80014.

Special Equestrian Riding Therapy. Nora Fischbach, Program Director. Agoura, California. (818)776-6476. *http://www.instanet.com/~sert.*

Turnabout Stables. Annette Turno. 142 Dalmatian Drive, Aiken, South Carolina 29803. (803)593-3473.

U.S. Stabling Guide. 5 Barker Street, Pembroke, Massachusetts, 02359. (800)829-0715. lists 750 stables, ranches, equestrian centers, and bed and breakfasts.

Windes, Vina. "Five Star Creates a Buzz." Maverick Press. 220 Livestock Exchange Building, 4701 Marion Street, Denver, Colorado 80216. (888)310-7770. E-mail: *maverickpress@worldnet.att.net.*

Chapter Eight

Horse Vacationing

Long work days. Community, church, or social activities. Children's sports. Dance groups. Horse shows. Rodeos. Then that wonderful reprieve: vacation! Does that sound familiar? These days, everybody is seeking the ideal vacation — the perfect respite from responsibility and stress-filled days that will sustain them for one more year.

There are nearly as many horse vacation options as there are types of people looking for them. There are extravagant resorts with plush accommodations, which offer riding packages along with fine dining, golf, fishing, yachting, saunas, whirlpools, and a country club atmosphere. There are small rustic working ranches that afford opportunities to ride, round up cattle, mend fences, and be a part of the cowboy world. Pack trips with outfitters offer access to hunting, fishing, photography, and hiking spots that can best be reached by horse or on foot. And there are opportunities that fit about every horse experience in between. To meet the growing demand for vacation facilities that provide horseback riding opportunities, competent, energetic owners and employees are needed.

DUDE RANCHES AND GUEST RANCHES

Dude ranches and guest ranches originated in the mid-1800s when ranchers opened their homes to guests who wanted to visit the real West. The concept grew, and today such ranches, most of which are located west of the Mississippi River, have become cherished summer vacation destinations. It is estimated that 300 to 500 dude ranches and guest ranches exist in the United States.

Employment opportunities are many and varied. Ranches may be totally owner-operated, or they may hire staff numbering up to 100 employees. An average-size ranch can accommodate 42 guests, and has a staff of 24.

Staff positions depend on facilities, geographical location, and the target clientele. Some ranches with resort, lodge, or modern cabin facilities offer riding opportunities along with tennis, golf, and other social activities. Other ranches feature restored historic log homes, rustic cabins, bunk houses, and camping facilities, and offer programs that revolve around horses, trail rides, camp rides, and riding lessons.

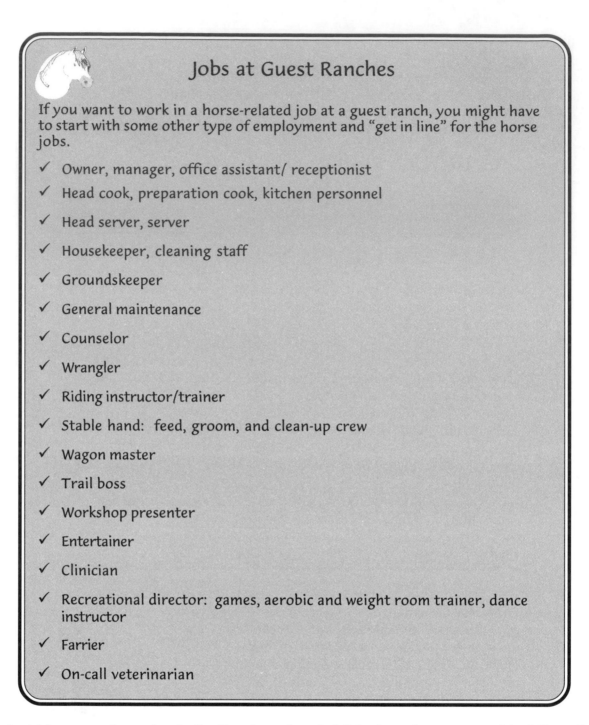

Jobs at Guest Ranches

If you want to work in a horse-related job at a guest ranch, you might have to start with some other type of employment and "get in line" for the horse jobs.

- ✓ Owner, manager, office assistant/ receptionist
- ✓ Head cook, preparation cook, kitchen personnel
- ✓ Head server, server
- ✓ Housekeeper, cleaning staff
- ✓ Groundskeeper
- ✓ General maintenance
- ✓ Counselor
- ✓ Wrangler
- ✓ Riding instructor/trainer
- ✓ Stable hand: feed, groom, and clean-up crew
- ✓ Wagon master
- ✓ Trail boss
- ✓ Workshop presenter
- ✓ Entertainer
- ✓ Clinician
- ✓ Recreational director: games, aerobic and weight room trainer, dance instructor
- ✓ Farrier
- ✓ On-call veterinarian

Activities range from simple family-oriented and child-oriented programs with daily trail rides to actual cow-calf operations. Some may include other packages, such as hunting, fishing, hiking, rafting, or skiing. Accommodations for weddings, corporate retreats, seminars, and clinics are specialties offered by still others. Some ranches offer video and game rooms, guided and do-it-yourself trail rides, riding lessons, Western dancing, square dancing, water sports, tennis, golf, and weight training programs, complete with teachers and trainers. The only limit seems to be the imagination.

Because guest ranches differ so greatly in the focus and variety of activities they offer, it is important that a prospective employee carefully research the types of horse opportunities ranches provide. Keep in mind that it may be necessary to get your foot in the door and work your way up to a horse-related position.

If your career goal is to eventually own and operate a ranch, then summer employment on a variety of ranches may be the best way to start. Ranches also provide wonderful employment opportunities for people who are merely seeking a summer change of pace. Most jobs are seasonal. Some ranches located in temperate climates stay open year round.

Educational requirements depend on the specific job. Most ranches offer hands-on training. The more horse experience and education you have, the better your chances to be hired as a wrangler, counselor, or stable hand. Riding instructor and trainer positions often require the additional experience of working directly with a reputable trainer and/or a degree or certificate reflecting that level of education and experience.

Dude Ranchers Association

At times, the quest for that perfect niche in the equine industry may become frustrating and seem beyond your reach. Words of advice from Bobbie and Jim Futterer are, "Don't give up." For nearly 25 years, as they vacationed at ranches throughout the West, they aspired to own a dude ranch of their own some day. Jim, a retired army clinical psychologist, and Bobbie, a former legal secretary, researched the possibilities and began to feel that the financial investment was beyond their reach. Unwilling to give up their dream, they kept on searching. When the directors of the Dude Ranchers Association decided to retire, Jim and Bobbie applied for the job and were accepted.

The Dude Ranchers Association was formed in 1926 to preserve the wonders of the West for all the visitors who longed to experience the adventure, beauty, and romance of the West. With more than 100 members, the association is the largest in the guest ranch industry. The member ranches range in size from accommodations for 10 to 120 guests. A typical season, due to seasonal weather patterns, is 18 weeks. Approximately 30 ranches operate for extended seasons of six months or more, and most offer other packages, such as hunting and snow sports.

Guest Ranches — Numbers and Finances

Only ranches that meet the requirements set forth by the Dude Ranchers Association may become members. These criteria include guidelines for exemplifying the Western ranch ideal of hospitality and having an ample, well-maintained horse program, including riding instruction. Member ranches are also expected to have access to plenty of land that will accommodate a full-scale horse program.

Average Guest Ranch Income Estimate

Avg. Ranch Capacity	Length of Season	Occupancy Rate	Total Guests
36.2 X	18 weeks X	76.8%	= 500.4

Ranch Guests Served	Average Price	Reduced Rate for Children and Friends	Avg. Gross Income
500.4 X	$1,076 X	80%	= $430,830

The rates of the member ranches vary from $500 a week to $2,135 a week, based on double occupancy. Jim has compiled some figures to aid prospective owners.

As the table shows, $430,830 is the average gross income per season for an average guest ranch of 36 guests. While the figure seems sizable, it is important to take into consideration the costs. Guest ranches are not get-rich-quick operations, and initial investments are substantial.

Purchase of an existing ranch is estimated to run $2 million and up. A realistic down payment for a ranch is $500,000. If you are considering purchasing raw land and building a new ranch, you will soon discover that land prices are soaring nearly everywhere in the West. Land that has access to public land to use for trail rides and other outdoor activities has become extremely costly. Loans are hard to acquire because on paper most ranches don't appear to be profitable enterprises.

If a ranch is owned out right, the sellers may be willing to finance it themselves. Others may carry an assumable note. Still other ranches may require total refinancing. New owners need approximately five to seven years to break even financially. Consequently, substantial capital reserves are essential. New owners should plan on sustaining themselves for those years.

To calculate a guest ranch's income for the first season, you must remember that 40 to 80 percent of the original ranch's clientele consists of repeat customers. Many old guests will stay loyal to the previous owners and seek a new vacation spot when ownership changes. Filling those vacancies will take effective advertising and marketing skills.

Cherokee Park Ranch

Christine and Dickey Prince were raising Tennessee Walking trail horses in Tennessee, when, in 1992, they vacationed with their four children at Cherokee Park Ranch in Livermore, Colorado. After this first dude ranch vacation, they knew what direction they wanted their lives to take. They contacted a realtor and began searching for a guest ranch to purchase. Dude ranches come on the market regularly and that first year they looked at thirteen ranches.

While continuing their search, the Princes economized, but one expense they continued was spending their summer vacation at Cherokee Park Ranch. This 300-acre historical ranch borders Roosevelt National Forest and Colorado Division of Wildlife lands, offering ranch guests access to an additional 600,000 acres of land. Cherokee Park Ranch became the standard they used as they looked for a ranch to purchase. When ranches within their price range didn't meet their expectations, they became discouraged. In 1996, a ranch came on the market that came close to measuring up. They began the paper work and shared their good news with the owners of Cherokee Park Ranch, with whom the Princes had become good friends. A few days later they were informed that their friends were selling the Cherokee Park Ranch. Were they interested? The answer was an enthusiastic, yes.

Within months, the Princes had packed up, left Tennessee, and begun their first season as dude ranch owners. The Princes were fortunate. One of the former owners stayed on during the season — a season booked to capacity. The guests found very few changes and began to bond to the new owners.

As members of the Dude Ranchers Association and the Colorado Dude and Guest Ranch Association, the Princes follow specific rules and regulations, but during the off-season, they are free to pursue other ventures. Some ranches merely close, some provide pack trips. In the fall, the Princes and a neighboring cattle rancher offer two cattle drives for more experienced riders, and they work full days in the saddle doing real ranch work.

Cherokee Park Ranch accommodates 42 guests. When the ranch opens in early May, the guest list is usually at about a third of capacity, but all 24 of the staff members are at the ranch to

Staff Positions at Cherokee Park Ranch

✓ Ranch manager. Year-round, full-time employee, oversees the ranch 24 hours a day, lives at the ranch. Skills include: ranch management and horse experience, business management, and people skills. Receives room, board, a vehicle, and a salary in the $800 to $1,000 a month range.

✓ Wranglers. Seven wranglers are hired each year. Required: experience working with horses and people skills. On the average, dude ranches employ one wrangler for every six guests, so many wrangler positions are available at ranches throughout the country. Returning qualified staff are given job selection preference.

✓ Head counselor and children's counselors. One head counselor and four children's counselors. Second only to wrangler positions in popularity, these employees spend time each day on horseback as they accompany children on rides.

✓ Maintenance crew. Seasonal employees in charge of maintaining grounds, cabins, rooms, pool.

✓ Head cook, preparation cook, and head server.

✓ Servers/housekeepers. Dual position employees serve tables and also clean guests' rooms each day. On Saturdays at 10:00 A.M. they work frantically to prepare all the rooms for the next set of visitors who will arrive around 3:00 P.M.

✓ Secretary. Runs the office, and handles phone calls, clerical work, and guests' questions.

✓ Visiting farrier. Shoes 68 head of horses each summer and fall for $30/head plus room and board while he is at the ranch.

✓ Veterinarian. A very important person to the ranch, who also happens to be Dickey Prince's brother.

begin their training. Training for the full capacity months of June, July, and August is important, and the early season provides a perfect time for that.

Compensation for seasonal staff includes room and board, $425 a month, and a share of the gratuities. As a result of these gratuities, in June 1996, Cherokee Park Ranch employees received an extra $700; in July they received $825 extra; and in August the figure jumped to around $1,000.

Jobs at Cherokee Park Ranch are similar to those at most ranches, although the numbers vary, as do some of the titles. Because Dickey Prince continues to work outside the ranch, a full-time, year-round ranch manager is employed at Cherokee Park Ranch. However, approximately 80 percent of dude ranches in the Dude Ranch Association are owner-operated and do not hire ranch managers.

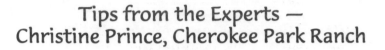

Tips from the Experts — Christine Prince, Cherokee Park Ranch

If you would like to own or manage a guest ranch, here are some suggestions.

- Study and experience the dude ranch culture.

- Research all aspects of the business by talking to owners: liability insurance, recordkeeping, obvious and not-so-obvious costs, staffing needs, and winter procedures. Don't leave anything uncovered.

- Acquire the business skills needed to keep financial, reservations, and repair records.

- Have personnel skills for training and managing people from widely varying backgrounds.

- Learn how to calculate expenses for all your overhead: advertising, supplies, feed and food, equipment, electricity, propane, firewood, maintenance and repair costs, etc.

- Utilize management and organizational skills for scheduling programs and meals.

- Love horses, people, and the out-of-doors. Understand that this is a physically and emotionally demanding business. Twelve-to fourteen-hour-days are the norm.

- Maintain a quality program. Initiate change slowly and in response to guest input.

Golden Hills Trail Rides and Resort

Guests have the option of bringing their own horses to the Golden Hills Trail Rides and Resort in Raymondville, Missouri. This resort has tent sites and other camping facilities, pull through RV sites, lodging, a dining hall that seats 1,200 people, 585 boarding stalls, and 30 rental horses. The resort offers riders 140 miles of trails, as well as another 40,000 acres of adjacent land owned by a timber company. People can choose to participate in organized trail rides or do-it-yourself trail rides.

Golden Hills also offers riding and horsemanship clinics, overnight cattle drives, a fleet of wagons and stagecoaches, a boot and saddle shop, an exercise room complete with aerobic instructors and trainers, and dance lessons. The resort uses farriers and veterinarians on an on call basis.

The competition for jobs at guest ranches is tough. However, even though a job might not offer hands-on horse experience, it can be an effective stepping stone for moving into a wrangler or counselor position in the future. And most ranches allow their employees to have access to the horses on days off and during free time.

WAGON TRAINS

Relatively few commercial wagon train operations exist today. However, interest in all aspects of the historical Old West seems to continue to build, and wagon trains are a very important part of that history. If you have investment capital, a desire for adventure, and excellent business acumen, they may be an enterprise worthy of consideration.

Opportunities to work on or run wagon trains are limited, but their appeal to the public is great. Because wagon trains are, like parades, fun to simply watch, they offer many income-earning possibilities for photographers, writers, concessions, and support enterprises. Consult the Internet, magazines, newspapers, and breed publications for information about commercial and commemorative wagon trains.

Flint Hills Overland Wagon Train Trip

Ervin E. Grant was one of two people who originated Flint Hills Overland Wagon Train, which offers daily and overnight weekend wagon train trips. During the first years of operation, they only conducted about four rides per season with twenty or thirty people each. They continued to offer rides because of the appreciation voiced by people who enjoyed this unique opportunity. By 1997, functioning as a corporation with eighteen stockholders, they had scheduled more than 30 trips, and the trips were generating a profit.

Designed to recreate the simplicity of frontier life and pioneer travel, trail riders are invited to bring their own horses and join the trek. The staff consists of the stockholders. If additional wranglers and wagon masters are needed, they are hired on a contract basis.

Oregon Trail Wagon Train

Kevin and Connie Howard are the second generation in the Howard family to operate the Oregon Trail Wagon Train, located in Bayard, Nebraska. In addition to wagon train treks, nightly outdoor cookouts include a fifteen-minute wagon ride, a steak dinner, and campfire sing-along. Three-hour Chimney Peak tours offer a longer wagon ride coupled with an opportunity to learn about the Oregon Trail. Living history programs, given to school classes, include a tour of authentic log cabins, viewing of artifacts, meeting a pony express rider, wagon rides, and homemade sour dough bread cooked over a campfire. During the winter there are indoor prime rib dinners.

The truly adventurous can vacation along the old Oregon Trail on a one-, four-, or six-day wagon train trip, complete with pony express mail service, a mock Indian attack, a council with a Native American chief, artifact searches, black powder rifle demonstrations and participation, and lots of history.

During the summer months, the Howards employ fifteen full-time people who are versatile enough to cook, split wood, work as wranglers, and generally help wherever needed. A wagon master versed on the history of the Oregon Trail shares stories as he leads the wagon train. Year round there are three full-time staff. Oregon Trail Wagon Train is basically a family owned and operated business. Most of the employees are local people and friends who return year after year.

Wagon Trains as Commemorative Events

Charitable organizations, cities, counties, and states may plan a wagon train to commemorate a special occasion or to raise special funding. An example is the Shasta Valley Wagon Train out of California that sponsored a fundraising wagon train in August 1997 to raise money for Stable Hands Riding Program for Disabled and Abused Children.

In 1986, Doug Kafka (see Chapter Six) hitched a team of horses to a twenty-foot Conestoga wagon and joined the Sesquicentennial Wagon Train that toured every major town in Texas. Sponsored by Wrangler Jeans and U.S. Tobacco for $150,000, he and his partner traveled the full 3,600 mile trek across Texas. With a budget of $3 million, the Wagon Train Association, formed for this special event, employed 63 people, including managers, nurses, teachers, mail deliverers, water wagon drivers, cooks, veterinarians, and farriers. In addition, many sponsors, such as Wrangler Jeans, contracted with cowboy teams to run their wagons.

HORSE CAMPS FOR YOUTH

Summer and camp just seem to go together. Add horses and kids and you have a combination that's hard to beat. Youth camps range from after-school camps offered seasonally and children's day camps (see Chapter Seven), to weekend camps, and camps with sessions lasting one to six weeks. Some cater exclusively to horseback riding and instruction, and some combine other horse opportunities. The popularity of camps is due in part to the increased problems children experience today — many parents view camp as a way to help their children face stresses in life, and to have a good time, too.

Jameson Ranch

In the southern Sierra Nevada Mountains near Glennville, California, Jameson Ranch provides an atmosphere where everyone works and plays together. Under the direction of Ross and Debby Jameson, the camp offers two-week sessions to 40 boys and 40 girls throughout the summer. Children sleep outside under the stars (or under a canopy if the weather dictates). During the day they enjoy crafts, drama, riflery, gardening, hiking, and cookouts, but horse-related activities are the priority. Children may attend one or more sessions in Western and bareback riding, herding cattle, mail delivery by pony express (for the more experienced riders), recreational riding, trail riding, gymkhana games, wrangling, and vaulting (gymnastics on the back of a moving horse).

Counselors serve in several capacities, helping out wherever needed. Counselors and campers alike tend to the garden, care for the horses, and help maintain the ranch. The ranch also employs kitchen helpers and one full-time assistant director who receives room and some board plus a salary. The senior summer staff earn room and board plus a salary of $2,200 for the June to September season.

Cheley Colorado Camps

Cheley Colorado Camps, founded in 1921, are still run by the Cheley family. Don and Carol Cheley are dedicated to making a difference in the lives of children. They offer two one-month sessions, with 490 children at each session. One-third of the programs revolve around horses — camp outs with horses, trail rides (as long as seventeen miles), horseback riding, grooming, feeding, identifying illnesses, such as founder and thrush, and doctoring horses.

These camps provide excellent opportunities for summer employment with hands-on experience with horses. More than 200 staff positions are available each season at Cheley Colorado Camps, offering an opportunity to work in the beautiful mountains adjacent to Rocky Mountain National Park. Staff are paid $1,250 for the nine-week season plus room and board. The jobs at horse camps for youth and the jobs at dude ranches and guest ranches are usually quite similar — ranch manager, counselors, wranglers, cooks, servers/housekeepers, maintenance crew, office staff, nurse, farrier, and veterinarian. At Cheley Colorado Camps, nearly 200 counselors live in cabins with the campers, and those with special skills — in horsemanship, hiking, backpacking, archery, riflery, etc. — are very much in demand. General counselors, hired for their versatility and broad range of skills, fill in wherever they are needed. Counselors have a unique opportunity at Cheley Colorado Camps because they get to lead rides, instruct riders, and care for horses, and thus gain a great deal of hands-on horse experience.

In addition to the summer camps, the Cheleys maintain a staff of 60 to work in a camp for severely burned children. This camp is co-sponsored by the Children's Hospital in Denver. Two family camps follow at the end of August and, in September, in conjunction with nearby schools, sixth-grade classes attend Outdoor Education Camps.

Don Cheley feels that there is always a need for more quality camps that offer children a dude ranch type experience minus the parents. Although many people are competing for the money available for children's activities, a quality camp is highly valued by parents as a healthy alternative to malls and computer games.

Tips from the Experts — Don Cheley, Cheley Colorado Camps

If you're considering opening a camp, here are some pointers.

- A camp is more of a lifestyle than a profession.
- Unless a facility is already developed, the initial investment is high.
- Camps usually run only two or three months a year — a very limited time to earn a yearly income.
- Be sincerely interested in children, and be sensitive to the growing needs of children as you design your programs.
- Have a strong work ethic — work days are long and demanding.
- Research federal, state, and local regulations and requirements needed to become an approved camp.
- Consult the American Camping Association, and state and local health departments for guidelines.

American Camping Association (ACA)

Being involved with a horse camp for children can be rewarding in many ways. You get the chance to experience the world of horses, and you see how your personal efforts can make a difference in a child's life. Kathy Henchey of the American Camping Association (ACA) knows first hand the impact such programs have on children. Her son attended horse summer camps for four years, and the experience helped him discover his consistent desire to work with horses. She also points out that counselor/wrangler jobs are wonderful for résumé references and for helping young adults further evaluate their career objectives.

At the President's Summit for America's Future, ACA made a commitment to increase the number of children who have a camp experience by 15 percent, which represents an additional 810,000 campers nationwide. To do that, additional counselors will be needed. Likewise, new quality camps will be welcome additions. Call ACA for information and guidelines on setting up a camp.

Working at a Horse Camp

Counselor salaries are often paid by the season. They range from $1,000 to $2,500, depending on the location of the camp and the duration of the season. Camps that offer weekend and afternoon programs often pay minimum wage. Higher hourly rates depend on positions and expertise. Camp director salaries range from $600 to $1,600 a month.

Educational requirements for camp positions are similar to those for employees at dude ranches and guest ranches. People with horse experience and formal training are given first options for counselor, wrangler, and riding instructor positions. Priority consideration is given to people with a sincere love for children, the energy to share that love all summer long, and a desire to make a difference in children's lives. Couple those qualifications with a strong work ethic, the ability to get along well with people, flexibility, and a positive attitude and you have a perfect applicant who is highly sought after. A camp counselor is a combination of friend, mentor, teacher, coach, confidant, parent, and minister — a person who constantly helps a child succeed and feel worthwhile.

With 500,000 staff members employed at more than 8,500 camps across the country, the employment opportunities are immense. For listings of camps, consult the resources at the end of this chapter.

TRAIL RIDING

Dude ranches, camps, and wagon trains are just a few of the ways people seek the cowboy adventure. Many people also enjoy trail riding. This creates a demand for businesses that offer a variety of riding choices. Trail riding operations range from "bring your own horse" to horse rentals. Rides vary in duration from one hour, to a day, overnight, or a week or more. Competent wranglers, packers, cooks, stable hands, entertainers, farriers, wagon masters, overnight guides, day guides, workshop presenters, and trainers are employed by these organizations.

Trail Ride Businesses — Variety and Specialization

Canyon Trail Rides is a trail ride concession owned and operated by Pete and Keela Mangum and family. They and their cowboys have been guiding riders through Zion, Bryce, and Grand Canyon National Parks for more than 20 years. With 300 head of horses, their wranglers take riders of all ability levels on daily excursions. They also have a seven-day Western Horseback Ride Adventure.

Some businesses like Diamond B Appaloosa Ranch, northeast of Spokane, Washington, combine trail riding with other horse-related enterprises. Appaloosa horses are bred and raised at the Diamond B, and the ranch hosts the Mount Kit Carson School for Horses, which trains all breeds of horses.

Zane and Sandra Spang of Cheyenne Trailriders Ranch began offering specialized trail ride packages in 1992 on the Cheyenne Reservation adjacent to Custer National Park in Montana. The 444,000 acres of the Northern Cheyenne Reservation offers such variation in terrain as river land, hills covered with pine trees, and prairie land. Born and raised on the reservation, the Spangs have always enjoyed horses and sharing their land and heritage with friends. After hosting many large trail rides for friends, the Spangs set up their own commercial trail riding business.

Zane, a transition counselor for Dull Knife Memorial College, is an advocate of education. Combining his background in horses and education with the availability of reservation land, much of which has never been traversed by auto, he and Sandra created specialty rides for young people. The first ride, conducted for Montana Educational Talent Search, a subsidiary of the Montana University System, was nonprofit. Children from all over the state gathered at Cheyenne Trailriders Ranch. The purpose of the ride was to encourage children to consider careers in math and science. Along the trail, as riders stopped to rest, workshops were given by individuals in math- and science-related disciplines. Campfire entertainment included a Cheyenne storyteller, a country western sing-along, and clown dancers.

Zane and Sandra developed other theme rides for children that met with success, and now the approach is offered to business organizations as well. Custom packages from one-hour to several days are offered for one to twenty riders at a time. Courses in Northern Cheyenne history, culture, and ethnobotany can be added to the program. Wagons are available for those who prefer not to ride. The Cheyenne encourage the Spang's program and individuals appreciate the opportunities it affords for side businesses and tourism.

The Spangs began with seven horses and have increased to seventeen. Often more horses are needed, so Zane and Sandra have encouraged Zane's brother and several friends to set up their own businesses from which the Spangs contract horses and wagons for their larger rides.

Persistence, combined with creativity, initiative, sacrifice, and hard work have been key factors to finding a successful niche in the horse industry. In 1996 the Spangs conducted sixteen commercial rides with guests from as far as France, England, and Scotland. They also conducted several nonprofit rides. On the big rides they have as many as 75 guests with 25 to 30 employees traveling along as wagon master, wranglers, cooks, counselors, and workshop presenters. Most of the employees are hired by the ride. Workshop presenters are hired for their qualifications in their special areas.

Plans are in the offing for purchasing a sleigh and extending the season. During the last five years profits have been reinvested in the business, and Zane and Sandra's goal is to build the business to the point where it is their primary source of income.

OUTFITTERS

Accessing the back country by horseback, whether for hunting, fishing, photography, hiking, or camping is the specialty of outfitters. Outfitters range in size from one-man operations to large businesses that hire several guides, packers, cooks, and wranglers.

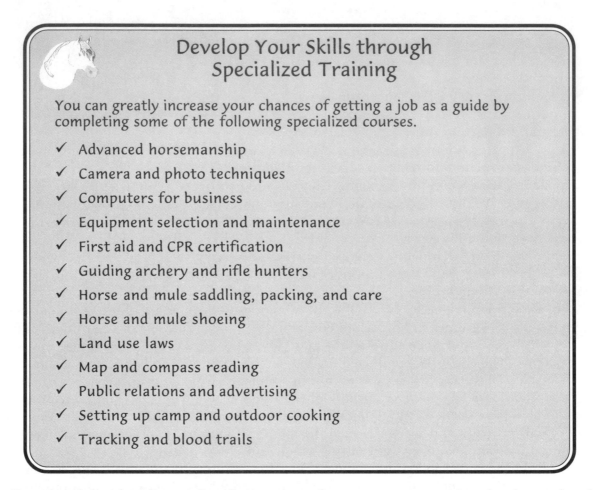

Develop Your Skills through Specialized Training

You can greatly increase your chances of getting a job as a guide by completing some of the following specialized courses.

- ✓ Advanced horsemanship
- ✓ Camera and photo techniques
- ✓ Computers for business
- ✓ Equipment selection and maintenance
- ✓ First aid and CPR certification
- ✓ Guiding archery and rifle hunters
- ✓ Horse and mule saddling, packing, and care
- ✓ Horse and mule shoeing
- ✓ Land use laws
- ✓ Map and compass reading
- ✓ Public relations and advertising
- ✓ Setting up camp and outdoor cooking
- ✓ Tracking and blood trails

Because of the abundance of outfitters across the county, a moratorium has been placed on forming a new business. To become a new owner, it is necessary to buy an existing business. Yet, good, qualified guides are always in demand, and as Bill Guth of Flying Resort Ranches and Guide Schools states, "The guide of today is the outfitter of tomorrow. The outfitting business is wide open for new, innovative, and experienced people."

Guiding is a physically demanding occupation that is usually seasonal, but it does provide priceless experiences, lasting friendships, and an opportunity to work in the back country. It is not a lucrative business, and the new man on the block will usually start out in a lower income range. Starting salaries range from $650 to $1,000 a month plus room and board. The more experience, the higher the earnings. Some guides earn $2,500 a month plus benefits.

With more than 2,500 outfitters in the country, it is no wonder that the possibilities within the profession are unlimited. There are lodges, resorts, and guest ranches that provide the opportunity to pack into remote areas to hunt and fish, or to take a "photographic safari." And there are outfitters who concentrate entirely on big game hunts.

Becoming an Outfitter or Guide

Outfitter setting out with pack team. Photo courtesy of Erv Malnarich, ELM Outfitters.

Although a college degree in wildlife or a similar field is not required for outfitters and guides, many have opted to gain such a degree. Other courses in such areas as business, wildlife management, computers, public relations, and communications are helpful. Some guides and outfitters have achieved their education through experience or on-the-job training. Practical horse experience is required for anyone who plans to lead pack trips and guide hunters from horseback.

Guide schools that provide specialized training as well as job placement opportunities have gained popularity over the last 30 years. When Erv Malnarich was guiding in the back country of Idaho in 1959, the incompetence of several guides disturbed him. He discovered that other outfitters had similar experiences. Guides who would guide, help with chores around camp, dress, skin, and cape animals, and demonstrate other necessary skills were in short supply. Erv decided to develop a written course and follow-up schooling to educate and train competent guides.

Today Erv's course is used as a prerequisite for several guide schools. Erv is the administrator of ELM Outfitter and Guide Training, Inc.; author of a training course entitled, *Outfitters and Guide Bible*; and the originator of Big Game Outfitters and Guides Training Schools in America. Along with his course, he conducts personal training and advises people who are seeking appropriate schools. Upon graduation from a school, Erv assists graduates in finding job placements.

In his 35 years in this profession and with a list of 2,500 outfitters, Erv has successfully placed 100 percent of the graduates who seek jobs.

Tips from the Experts — Erv Malnarich, Outfitter/Educator

Here are some recommended schools. (Contact information for each appears in the Resource section at the end of this chapter.)

- Bald Mountain Outfitters, Inc.
- Dave Hanna: Outfitter and Guides Training School
- Elk Mountain Guides and Outfitter School
- Flying Resort Ranches: Outfitter and Guide School
- Royal Time Guide School
- Tim Doud's Bliss Creek: Professional Wilderness Elk Guides and Packers School
- World Class Outfitting Adventures

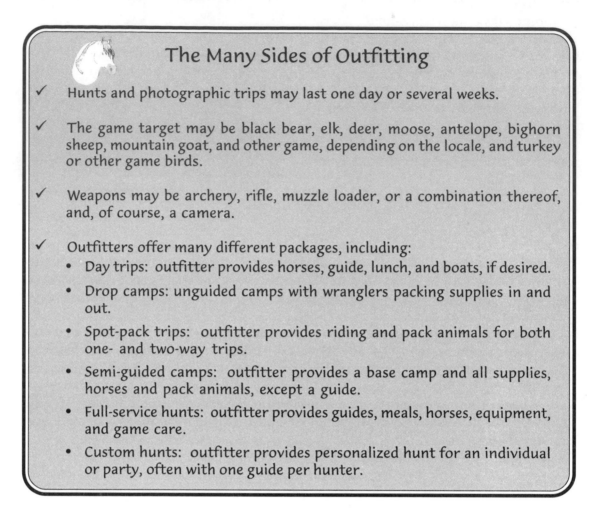

The Many Sides of Outfitting

✓ Hunts and photographic trips may last one day or several weeks.

✓ The game target may be black bear, elk, deer, moose, antelope, bighorn sheep, mountain goat, and other game, depending on the locale, and turkey or other game birds.

✓ Weapons may be archery, rifle, muzzle loader, or a combination thereof, and, of course, a camera.

✓ Outfitters offer many different packages, including:

- Day trips: outfitter provides horses, guide, lunch, and boats, if desired.

- Drop camps: unguided camps with wranglers packing supplies in and out.

- Spot-pack trips: outfitter provides riding and pack animals for both one- and two-way trips.

- Semi-guided camps: outfitter provides a base camp and all supplies, horses and pack animals, except a guide.

- Full-service hunts: outfitter provides guides, meals, horses, equipment, and game care.

- Custom hunts: outfitter provides personalized hunt for an individual or party, often with one guide per hunter.

CONCLUSION

Most dude ranches and guest ranches, wagon trains, youth camps, trail rides, and outfitters are seasonal in nature. However, if you aspire to a full-time horse career, the horse vacation industry offers hundreds of horse-related jobs that can give you irreplaceable experience. The pay is often low, but room and board are usually part of the package. An additional advantage is that recreational activities outside of the place of employment are usually limited, which makes it easier to save your meager wages. These jobs also provide experience, background, and contacts for people who want to become owners, full-time operators, managers, directors, or outfitters.

Resources

Guest Ranches and Dude Ranches

American Outdoor Adventures Service. *http:www.america-outdoors.com*. Lists guest ranches, working ranches, dude ranches, lodges, outfitters, and guides for big game pack trips.

Blood Horse: The Source, The. P.O. Box 4710, Lexington, Kentucky 40544-4710. (800)582-5604. Comprehensive directory of Thoroughbred Owners and Breeders Association. Includes travel and tour companies.

Cherokee Park Ranch. Christine and Dickey Prince. 436 Cherokee Hill Drive, Livermore, Colorado 80536. (970)493-4726.

Dude Rancher Association Directory. Jim and Bobbie Futterer. P.O. Box 471, La Porte, Colorado 80535-0471. (970)223-8440. *http://www.duderanch.org. duderanches@compuserve.com.* Free guide lists more than 100 dude ranches in twelve Western states and two Canadian provinces.

Golden Hills Trail Ride and Resort. 19546 Golden Drive, Raymondville, Missouri 65555. (800)874-1157.

Horse Lovers Vacation Guide. Riding Vacations, Inc. P.O. Box 502, Richfield, Ohio 44286-0502. (216)659-6007. Has 32 categories of horseback riding vacations and bring-your-own-horse vacation spots. Price: $10.

Horse and Rider magazine. 1597 Cole Blvd., Suite 350, Golden, Colorado. (800)829-3340. January 1998. Pages 74-77.

Guest Ranch Guide. *Horse and Rider.* January 1998. Pages 74-77. Subscriptions: (800)829-3340.

Internet: Call up Dude Ranchers Association, Equine Travelers of America, and Kilgore Ranch Vacations, which will link to others, or using a search engine, call up Dude Ranches, Guest Ranches, Horse Vacations, Pack trips, Guides, and Hunting Trips.

Kilgore, Gene. *Ranch Vacations: The Complete Guide to Guest Ranches and Resorts, Fly Fishing, and Cross Country Skiing.* John Muir Publications. P.O. Box 613, Santa Fe, New Mexico 87504. *http://www.ranchweb.com.* Lists ranches, ranch camps for children, annual Western events, top PRCA rodeos, wilderness pack trips, workshops, and wagon train adventures. Web page includes ranch and dude ranch associations, employment opportunities, travel agencies, and current ranches for sale.

Overnight Stabling Directory and Equestrian Vacation Guide. Equine Travelers of America, Inc. P.O. Box 322, Arkansas City, Kansas 67005-0322. (316)442-8131. Includes layover locations as well as vacation spots, trails, bed and breakfasts, vacation attractions, motels, and other services. Updated annually.

Record Horseman Equine Directory and Vacation Guide. P.O. Box 1209, Wheat Ridge, Colorado 80034. (303)425-5777. Fax: (303)431-8911. Free directory features horse-related equine businesses, products, and vacation spots.

State and Canadian province ranching associations and tourism offices provide lists within individual states:

Alberta Country Vacation Association. Box 396, Sangudo, Alberta, Canada TOE 2A0. (403)785-3700.

Arizona Dude Ranch Association. P.O. Box 603 K, Cortaro, Arizona 85652.

British Columbia Guest Ranch Association. P.O. Box 4501, Williams Lake, British Columbia, Canada. (800)663-6000.

Colorado Dude and Guest Ranch Association Vacation Guide. P.O. Box 300, Tabernash, Colorado 80478. (970)887-3128.

Idaho Guest and Dude Ranch Association. John Muir, IGDRA Secretary, 7600 E. Blue Lake Road, Harrison, Idaho. (800)VISIT-ID.

Montana Big Sky Ranch Association. 1627 West Main Street 434, Bozeman, Montana 59715.

Supernatural British Columbia Guest Ranch Association Directory. Tourism British Columbia, 117 Wharf Street, Victoria, British Columbia, Canada V8W 2Z2. (800)663-6000.

Western Horseman. Box 7980, Colorado Springs, Colorado 80933-7980. (800)877-5278. Each year the magazine devotes the February issue to more than 400 horse vacation spots listed by state.

Western Horseman Buying Guide. P.O. Box 7980 Colorado Springs, Colorado 80933-7980. (800-874-6774). Lists products and services, with a section on horseback vacations. Price: $4.95.

Wagon Trains

Flint Hills Overland Wagon Train. Ervin S. Grant. P.O. Box 1076, El Dorado, Kansas 67042.

Kafka, Doug. Triangle Bar Ranch. P.O. Box 5, Granite Canon, Wyoming 82059.

Kilgore, Gene. *Ranch Vacations: The Complete Guide to Guest Ranches and Resorts, Fly Fishing, and Cross Country Skiing.* Lists several wagon trains.

Oregon Trail Wagon Train. Kevin and Connie Howard. Route 2, Box 502, Bayard, Nebraska 69334. (308)586-1850.

Horse Camps for Youth

American Camping Association (ACA). *Guide To Accredited Camps.* Kathy Henchey. 5000 State Road 67 North, Martinsville, Indiana 46151-7902. (765)342-8456. (800)428-CAMP. *http://www.aca-camps.org.* Lists more than 2,200 camps accredited by ACA. Price: $16.95. Also available: a free directory of employment opportunities. Web page lists camps by state and activities and current job opportunities.

Breed associations. Some associations have lists of camps run by members.

Camping Magazine. American Camping Association, 5000 State Road 67 N, Martinsdale, Indiana. 46151-7902. (317)-342-8456. Informative articles on running camps plus a classified section of camps for sale and help wanted.

Cheley Colorado Camps. Don Cheley. P.O. Box 6525, Denver, Colorado 80206. (800)CAMP FUN.

Horseplay Magazine. "Horseplay's Camp Guide and Directory." February 1998. (301)977-3900. Pages 45-49.

Internet: Using a search engine, call up Camps, American Camps, Camp Jobs, and Horse Camps.

Jameson Ranch. Ross Jameson. P.O. Box 459, Glennville, California 93226. (805)536-8888.

Kilgore, Gene. *Ranch Vacations: The Complete Guide to Guest Ranches and Resorts, Fly Fishing, and Cross Country Skiing.* John Muir Publication, P.O. Box 613, Santa Fe, New Mexico 87504. *http://www.ranchweb.com.*

Western Association of Independent Campers (WAIC). P.O. Box 23657, Tempe, Arizona 85285-3657. (800)787-WAIC. Lists more than 40 accredited camps that meet nearly 250 stringent standards. Not all camps offer horseback riding.

YMCA. Check with your local YMCA for children's camps.

Trail Riding

Aadland, Dan. *Frommer's Horseback Adventures.* Howell Book House, Macmillan Inc., 1633 Broadway, New York, New York 10019. (800)428-5331.

Canyon Trail Rides. Pete and Keela Mangum. P.O. Box 128, Tropic, Utah 84776.

Cheyenne Trail Rides. Zane and Sandra Sprang. Box 206, Ashland, Montana 59003. (406)784-6150. Diamond B Ranch. *appaloo@cet.com.*

Dickerman, Pat. *Adventure Travel North America.* 7550 E. McDonald Drive, Suite M, Scottsdale, Arizona 85250. (800)252-7899.

Endurance News. American Endurance Ride Conference. 701 High Street, #203, Auburn, California 95603-4727. (916)823-2260. *aercmiki@aol.com.*

Hancock, Jan. *Horse Trails in Arizona.* Golden West Publishers, 4113 N. Longview, Phoenix, Arizona 85015. (800)658-5830. 602-265-4392.

Horse Industry Directory. American Horse Council. 1700 K Street NW, Suite 300, Washington, D.C. 20006. (202)296-4031. Lists trail organizations, the newsletters of which can provide contacts and resources.

Internet: Using a search engine, call up Trail Rides.

Mouchet, Paulette. *Horseback Riding Trails of Southern California, Volumes I and II.* Crown Valley Press, Box 336, Acton, California 93510-0336. (805)269-1525).

Robinson, Betty. *A Guide to Horse Trails in Arkansas.* Equestrian Unlimited, Box 225, London, Arizona 72847. (501)293-4642.

Sacks, Arthur. *World-Wide Riding Vacations: The Complete Traveler.* 2425 Edge Hill Road, Huntington Valley, Pennsylvania, 19006. (215)659-3281. Lists riding vacation spots around the world. Price: $14.

Saddle Up! A Guide to Planning the Perfect Horseback Vacation. Equus USA. Route 7, Box 124MU, Santa Fe, New Mexico 87505. (505)982-686. (800)982-6861.

U.S. Stabling Guide. 5 Barker Street, Pembroke, Massachusetts, 02359. (800)829-0715. Lists 750 stables, ranches, equestrian centers, and bed and breakfasts.

Western Horseman. Box 7980, Colorado Springs, Colorado 80933-7980. (800)877-5278. Each year the magazine devotes the February issue to more than 400 horse vacation spots listed by state.

Whoa Guide to Ranch Recreation in Wyoming. Box 40048, Casper, Wyoming 82604. (307)237-3526.

Outfitters

Bald Mountain Outfitters. P.O. Box 754, Pinedale, Colorado 82941. (307)367-6539.

Board of Outfitters. Department of Commerce. 111 N. Jackson, Helena, Montana 59620-0513. (406)444-3738.

Colorado Outfitters Association. Box 1304, Parker, Colorado 80134. (303)841-7760.

Tim Doud's Bliss Creek: Professional Wilderness Elk Guides and Packers School. 326 Diamond Basin Road, Cody, Wyoming 82414. (307)527-6103.

Elk Mountain Guides and Outfitter School. 2301 San Juan Avenue, La Junta, Colorado 81050. (719)384-0223.

ELM Outfitter and Guide Training. Erv Malnarich. P.O. Box 267, Corvallis, Montana 59828. (406)961-3603.

Flying Resort Ranches: Outfitter and Guide School. Bill Guth. RR1 Box 225-10, Salmon, Idaho 83467. (208)756-6295.

Dave Hanna's Outfitter and Guides Training School. P.O. Box 3832, Jackson Hole, Wyoming 83001. (307)733-5065.

Idaho Outfitters and Guides Association. Box 95, Boise, Idaho 8370. (800)847-4834.

Idaho State Outfitters and Guides Licensing Board. 1365 North Orchard, Room 172, Boise, Idaho 83706. (208)327-7380.

Internet: Call up *huntinfo.com/O&G.htm* for a list of outfitters and agents.

North American Association of Pack and Trail Operators. Box 223, Paynesville, Minnesota 56362. (320)243-7250.

Outfitters and Guide Registration. 1560 Broadway Suite 1340, Denver, Colorado 80202. (303)894-7778.

Royal Time Guide School. P.O. Box 129, Drummond, Montana 59832.

Sports, outdoor, recreation, trade, and horse conventions, shows, magazines, and publications.

State Board of Outfitters and Professional Guides. 1750 Westland Road, Cheyenne, Wyoming 82002. (800)264-0981.

State fish and game or wildlife departments.

World Class Outfitting Adventures. P.O. Box 351, Arlee, Montana, 59821. (800)203-3246.

Chapter Nine

Working as a Farrier

The farrier serves the horse industry in ways beyond the application of horseshoes. Expert, well-trained farriers are always in demand. A farrier's job requires a special blend of science, art, personal relations skills, physical stamina, and personal motivation. It is a job that varies daily, affords the opportunity to work outdoors, and requires a great deal of hands-on experience with horses. A farrier is afforded the privilege of providing comfort to one of the world's favorite creatures. Farriers can schedule their own hours and vacation time, and to a certain degree they can choose their work conditions and clientele. Farriers have some latitude in determining their fees because they are their own bosses and their own best employees.

No formal certification or registration is required in the United States, although many farriers join local, national, or international organizations that provide limited tracking of the number of farriers in the field. Several studies indicate that there are 30,000 to 50,000 farriers in the United States.

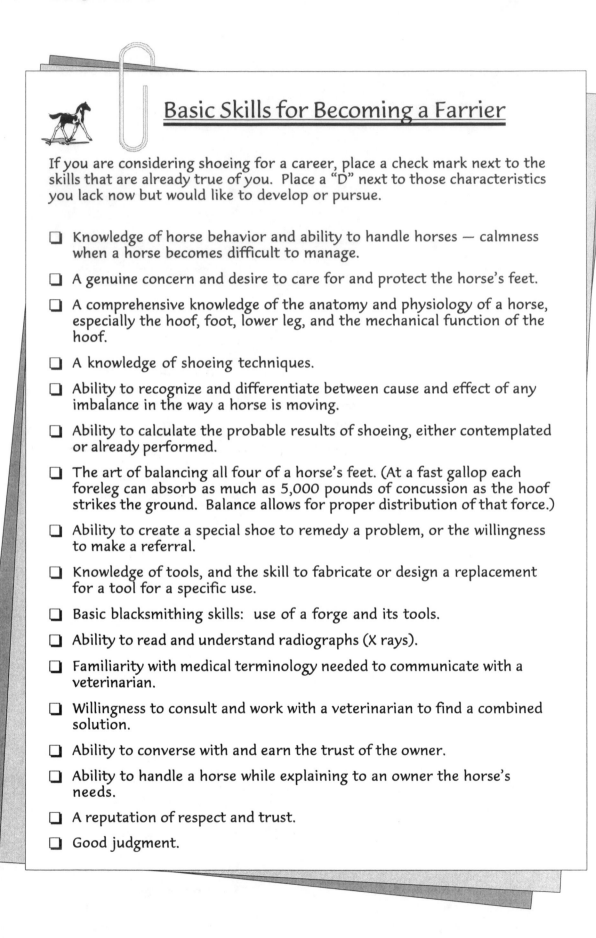

Basic Skills for Becoming a Farrier

If you are considering shoeing for a career, place a check mark next to the skills that are already true of you. Place a "D" next to those characteristics you lack now but would like to develop or pursue.

❑ Knowledge of horse behavior and ability to handle horses — calmness when a horse becomes difficult to manage.

❑ A genuine concern and desire to care for and protect the horse's feet.

❑ A comprehensive knowledge of the anatomy and physiology of a horse, especially the hoof, foot, lower leg, and the mechanical function of the hoof.

❑ A knowledge of shoeing techniques.

❑ Ability to recognize and differentiate between cause and effect of any imbalance in the way a horse is moving.

❑ Ability to calculate the probable results of shoeing, either contemplated or already performed.

❑ The art of balancing all four of a horse's feet. (At a fast gallop each foreleg can absorb as much as 5,000 pounds of concussion as the hoof strikes the ground. Balance allows for proper distribution of that force.)

❑ Ability to create a special shoe to remedy a problem, or the willingness to make a referral.

❑ Knowledge of tools, and the skill to fabricate or design a replacement for a tool for a specific use.

❑ Basic blacksmithing skills: use of a forge and its tools.

❑ Ability to read and understand radiographs (X rays).

❑ Familiarity with medical terminology needed to communicate with a veterinarian.

❑ Willingness to consult and work with a veterinarian to find a combined solution.

❑ Ability to converse with and earn the trust of the owner.

❑ Ability to handle a horse while explaining to an owner the horse's needs.

❑ A reputation of respect and trust.

❑ Good judgment.

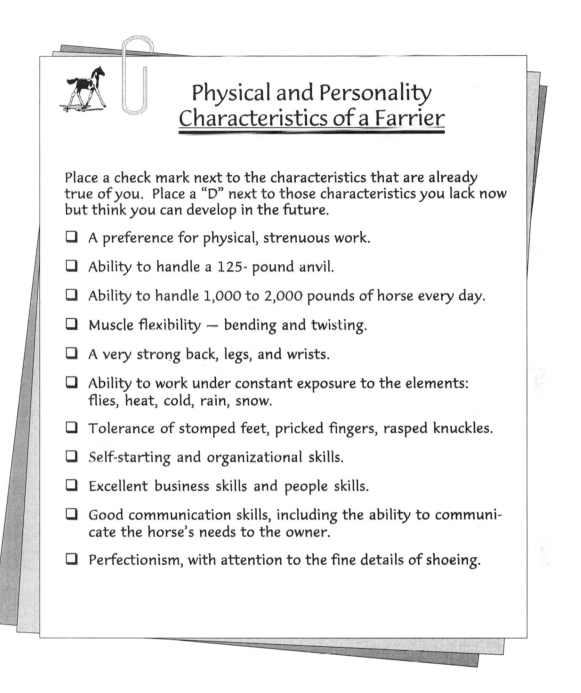

Physical and Personality Characteristics of a Farrier

Place a check mark next to the characteristics that are already true of you. Place a "D" next to those characteristics you lack now but think you can develop in the future.

- ❑ A preference for physical, strenuous work.

- ❑ Ability to handle a 125- pound anvil.

- ❑ Ability to handle 1,000 to 2,000 pounds of horse every day.

- ❑ Muscle flexibility — bending and twisting.

- ❑ A very strong back, legs, and wrists.

- ❑ Ability to work under constant exposure to the elements: flies, heat, cold, rain, snow.

- ❑ Tolerance of stomped feet, pricked fingers, rasped knuckles.

- ❑ Self-starting and organizational skills.

- ❑ Excellent business skills and people skills.

- ❑ Good communication skills, including the ability to communicate the horse's needs to the owner.

- ❑ Perfectionism, with attention to the fine details of shoeing.

THE FARRIER PROFESSION

No standard criteria exist for becoming a farrier. Some farriers grew up around horses and through observation, hands-on training, and practice established their careers. Others chose a school, acquired training, served as apprentices, and then entered the industry. Still others combined these two methods and acquired certification through an organization with established testing procedures and levels.

Horseshoeing is one of the most physically demanding, on a sustained basis, of all horse-related professions. Prior to making the decision to become a farrier, you should speak with several working farriers about the profession's physical demands and the personality traits needed to be successful.

95

Income Expectations of Horseshoeing

Farriers are considered self-employed business people. Fees, inventory, and supplemental sources of income are at the farrier's discretion, which causes considerable variations in income levels. The November 1996 issue of the *American Farriers Journal* reported the results of a survey of 554 part- and full-time farriers. Some of the findings are listed here.

1995 Farrier Income Levels

Average Income
Full-time farriers:	$54,666
(28% of these also earned income from other sources)	
Full-time farriers earning more than $70,000 — 22%	
Full-time farriers earning less than $ 9,999 — 2%	
Part-time farriers:	$16,888

Regional gross incomes:
Far West	$46,828
Southwest	$42,263
West	$32,728
Central	$44,700
Northeast	$51,378
Southeast	$44,285

Farrier's Rates

	Average Fee
Full-time farriers:	
Trimming 4 hooves	$19.78
Setting 4 keg shoes	$60.31
Plus applying 2 pads and packing	$16.78
Trimming and resetting 4 shoes	$56.38
Trimming, and making/setting 2 bar shoes	$72.78
Trimming, and making/setting 4 handmade shoes	$92.20
Average total fee per horse	$34.16

Part-time farriers:	Somewhat lower in all categories, compared to full-time farriers

Profile of the Average Farrier

Full-time farriers:

average 32 horses in a 45-hour work week	
travel an average of 439 miles/week	
charge extra for miles traveled	15 %
work out of a truck	96 %
work out of an in-house facility and a truck	32 %
work entirely out of an in-house facility	4 %
are under 40 years old	42 %
are between 40 and 59 years old	54 %
are 60 years old or older	4 %
have a high school diploma	96 %
have a two-year college degree	23 %
have a four-year college degree	19 %
have a master's degree	5 %
have a Ph.D. or doctorate	1 %
have farrier school training	72 %
served as apprentices	53 %
practice therapeutic shoeing	96 %
continue to attend clinics	69 %
continue to attend workshops	35 %
continue to attend seminars	26 %
work in consultation with veterinarians on hoof cases	56 %

The Business of Being a Farrier

Farriers are self-employed businesspeople who are responsible for the following:

✓ Insurance: vehicle, health, disability, liability

✓ A vehicle that serves as a mobile shop

✓ Adequate inventory

✓ Continuing education — through clinics, seminars, publications

✓ Keeping abreast of new innovations by testing new products

✓ Securing a client base

✓ Collecting and paying bills

✓ Keeping tax records and filing quarterly and year-end statements

✓ Efficient time management: setting appointments, allocating time for work and travel

✓ Retirement

THE FARRIER AS BUSINESSPERSON

Capital Outlay

As your traveling shop, your vehicle is your first and most essential capital outlay The cost of the truck depends on whether you want a new truck or are able to purchase a good used one. Additional basic equipment is not extremely expensive and, once again, prices depend on your ability and willingness to purchase quality used equipment.

Rich Reuter compiled the following list of basic equipment necessary to effectively start up a business. The prices are based on the lower average. For instance, a good quality driving hammer runs $100, but you can still get the job done with a $19 hammer. Also included here are items you need to have in your inventory, but the size of your inventory really depends on the accessibility of your supplier; that is, you don't need to keep huge quantities on hand if you can get them immediately and at a reasonable cost from your supplier.

Start-Up Equipment and Supplies for a Farrier Business

Equipment		Items in Inventory		Other Tools
Anvil	$350	Keg shoes	$250	Drill press
Anvil stand	85	Nails	40	Arc welder
Foot Stand	45	Assorted pads	50	Bench belt sander
Anvil hardy (cutoff)	25	Misc. items:	150	Pad cutter
Apron	85	hoof repair		Band saw
Driving hammer	30	hoof packing		Tap and die set
Rasps (2)	35	pine tar		Oxygen and welding set
Handles (2)	9	thrush medicine		
Rounding hammer	30			
Hoof knife	15			
Sharpener	12			
Clinch block	14			
Clinchers	50			
Clinch cutter	14			
Nippers	75			
Nail Puller	40			
Hoof gauge	35			
Dividers	9			
Nail nippers	28			
Propane forge	400			
Fire tongs	25			
Pritchel	20			
Pulloffs	45			
Tool box	80			
Totals	$1,556		$490	

FARRIER SCHOOLS AND ORGANIZATIONS

There are more than 60 farrier schools in the United States and Canada. The lengths of courses vary from one-day refresher classes to one-year comprehensive programs. If you are considering embarking on a farrier career, you should check several programs and then select a program that best meets your personal needs. Several excellent sources for locating farrier schools are listed in the Resources section at the end of this chapter.

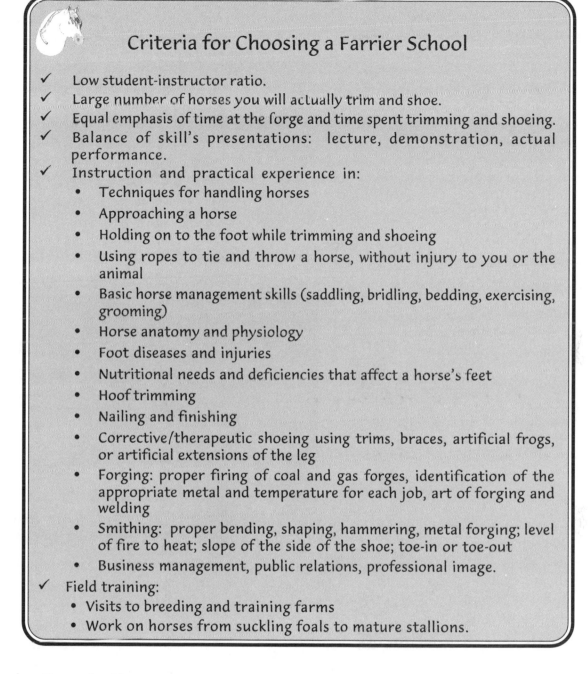

Criteria for Choosing a Farrier School

✓ Low student-instructor ratio.

✓ Large number of horses you will actually trim and shoe.

✓ Equal emphasis of time at the forge and time spent trimming and shoeing.

✓ Balance of skill's presentations: lecture, demonstration, actual performance.

✓ Instruction and practical experience in:

- Techniques for handling horses
- Approaching a horse
- Holding on to the foot while trimming and shoeing
- Using ropes to tie and throw a horse, without injury to you or the animal
- Basic horse management skills (saddling, bridling, bedding, exercising, grooming)
- Horse anatomy and physiology
- Foot diseases and injuries
- Nutritional needs and deficiencies that affect a horse's feet
- Hoof trimming
- Nailing and finishing
- Corrective/therapeutic shoeing using trims, braces, artificial frogs, or artificial extensions of the leg
- Forging: proper firing of coal and gas forges, identification of the appropriate metal and temperature for each job, art of forging and welding
- Smithing: proper bending, shaping, hammering, metal forging; level of fire to heat; slope of the side of the shoe; toe-in or toe-out
- Business management, public relations, professional image.

✓ Field training:

- Visits to breeding and training farms
- Work on horses from suckling foals to mature stallions.

Farrier Organizations

A farrier school can provide an excellent base for you to begin a farrier business. However, to adequately understand the many facets of farriering, you need to actually shoe 300 to 500 horses. Apprenticing is helpful in acquiring that experience, and farrier organizations are one way to locate a mentor.

Most states and counties have local organizations of farriers that meet regularly to share experiences, network, learn from peers, and grow in their expertise. In November of each year, the *American Farriers Journal* publishes a special edition of "Farrier Supplies and Services" and, in the 1997 edition, 124 local chapters of the American Farriers Association were listed. Other national and international farrier associations, such as the Brotherhood of Working Farriers, are also listed in the special November editions.

When you select an organization, consider these questions: Are they reputable and respected throughout the farrier industry? What levels of certification do they provide and what are the criteria? What benefits do they offer you — referrals, contacts, publications, clinics, research results?

Jeff Rodriguez, past president of the Rocky Mountain Farrier Association, is a certified journeyman farrier (CJF) with the American Farriers Association. Jeff said that two advantages of being part of a local association are that you become part of a group of experienced farriers who can advise you about running a business as well as shoeing, and the monthly meetings are a great opportunity to network.

Associations also provide clinics and workshops. For example, the Rocky Mountain Farrier Association offers approximately four clinics a year. One annual clinic offers a variety of workshops as well as opportunities for competition.

In the Field — Four Interviews

Farrier and Researcher

Dick Williams is a certified master farrier, tester, and director of the Colorado Farrier Research Lab III for the Brotherhood of Working Farriers, and he has a physics degree. In addition to his full-time farrier employment, Dick works to inform the horse-owning public about the safety issues of horseshoeing and the importance of utilizing a knowledgeable, well-trained farrier. Monthly he offers a clinic at his home for farriers and horse owners to help them understand the many variables at work in shoeing a horse. Dick's lab equipment consists of a computer, about $50,000 worth of horseshoeing tools, a shop with a fully equipped work station, and a 50-yard sand track with an overhead electric-powered

Dick Williams offers a free clinic for horse owners and farriers.

video camera. The camera films horses as they move along the track at various speeds and gaits, enabling Dick to analyze leg and hoof action and impact. Dick's work at the research lab and as a workshop leader is done on a volunteer basis, and is motivated by the desire to give back to the profession that has been so good to him.

Dick says you must charge enough to cover your overhead. You must take into consideration supplies, insurance, vehicle costs, vacation, retirement, and every other possible overhead expense. If you estimate 1,000 horses shod a year, your average income per horse will need to be approximately $47.70 to cover overhead. Beginning farriers may have to charge less, and initially they may not be able to cover all these expenses.

He advises prospective farriers to remember the three things every farrier really needs: a good horse to work on, a safe work area, and a good check in your hand when you leave. More suggestions appear on the following page.

Tips from the Experts —
Dick Williams, Farrier and Researcher

- At the minimum, complete an eight-week course at a reputable farrier school.
- Plan to invest approximately $3,000 in tools and equipment initially.
- Consider an apprenticeship under a reputable farrier.
- Expect lean earnings for at least two years.
- Shoeing tips: Make the horse as comfortable as possible (an uncomfortable horse will fight you). Exhibit patience, don't rush, and be careful not to spook the horse. Use your sixth sense to predict if a horse is going to act up.
- Monitor your working hours. Fatigue can cause injuries. Don't try to shoe more than five or six horses a day.

Farriering as a Second Career

Rich Reuter of Weed, California, retired and sold his auto parts business after 30 years because he longed to be outside working with horses. Now a certified farrier with the Brotherhood of Working Farriers, Rich gained his experience through an apprenticeship. He shoes three to five horses each morning, and he runs cattle and builds horse carriages in the afternoons.

Several times a year Rich attends clinics to improve his farrier skills. He estimates his actual cost of materials for shoeing one horse with standard keg shoes (disregarding truck expenses, fuel, and equipment he already possesses) is about $8.

Farrier and CSU Instructor

Steve Moline just seemed to ease his way into the business. He was brought up around horses and apprenticed at an early age with several farriers. When he was sixteen, he began working as a wrangler for a dude ranch in Estes Park, Colorado, where his responsibilities included shoeing the horses. Apprenticing, he says, has the advantage of allowing the new farrier to conduct a business of his own while accompanying and learning from a more experienced farrier on off days. Also, the apprentice can seek the advice of the mentor when a shoeing concern arises, and the mentor sometimes gives surplus clients to the apprentice. Steve feels that it is important to attend a good farrier school, and that there is no substitute for a lot of hand-on experience.

In 1996, after 24 years in the farrier business, Steve took a position at Colorado State University where he heads up the year-long farrier school. The program includes shoeing 126 head of horses plus more than 100 mares in the breeding program. Because most of the shoeing horses are donated, only 1 out of 15 horses is sound. Consequently, the need for and opportunity to do therapeutic work is extensive.

Steve offers much of the same advice as Dick Williams, and also states that anyone who doesn't take into account retirement is a fool, and anyone who doesn't consider vacations important will burn out, which makes that person a bigger fool. Health and liability insurance are essential. A vehicle is costly: if it's new, you have payments; if it's used, you have repairs; if the vehicle is in the shop, you lose that day's income. Your time is valuable — make your appointments as you leave a job; otherwise you will spend hours on the phone. Buy one tool a week. And finally be very aware that only veterinarians can legally make diagnoses.

Farrier, Professor, Speaker, Author

The career of Dr. Doug Butler, an internationally known farrier and professor with more than 30 years of practical teaching experience at several universities, offers another perspective on the unlimited opportunities available to a farrier. His ability to simplify detailed information into workable solutions for horse professionals has made Dr. Butler one of the farrier industry's most sought after speakers and best selling authors. He is among the estimated 1 percent of farriers who also have a Ph.D. or doctorate degree (his is in veterinary anatomy and equine nutrition). Dr. Butler is a certified journeyman farrier (CJF) with the American Farriers Association and Fellow of the Worshipful Company of Farriers (FWCF) in England. Only 40 living farriers have the distinction of being classified as an FWCF. This certification is earned by very stringent testing administered by the Worshipful Company of Farriers, which has been in existence since 1356 AD.

Dr. Butler relates that he reluctantly entered college at Utah State University in the fall of 1960 after cowboying at the OT Ranch in Arizona, where he read his first horseshoeing book. His interest sparked, and he applied for and was accepted to the Cal Poly horseshoeing school. To graduate from Cal Poly, he wrote as his senior project a book entitled, *Horseshoeing Iron and Forge Work*. This project marked his beginning in the field of publishing and fueled his desire to teach. Today his book *Principles of Horseshoeing II* is the most widely used textbook in the world on the subject of farriery.

Dr. Butler advises farriers to prepare themselves in theory as well as with plenty of practical experience. He says, "Many farriers just plain stop too soon. The competition is incredible in this industry and the physical stamina required is great. A knowledgeable, well-trained farrier will not only have a better chance to achieve, but also a better chance to avoid injury."

He compares farrier education and training to riding great horses: "I've ridden many great horses. The greatest have been those that would not accept much fussing or correction from the rider. They worked and progressed best when you didn't resist them or fight them but worked with them. In fact, I have had four different horses that had seriously hurt or killed people because the people tried to force the horses to do things the horses weren't ready to do. But by working with them and reading them, each horse became great. They could think . . . for themselves, . . . and . . . enjoyed being treated with respect. But they had to be accepted for what they were."

Dr. Butler goes on to say, "A farrier without learning is like an untrained horse. Farrier training is absolutely necessary for success. I believe that small group workshops and one-to-one training with highly skilled farriers will allow us to return to the roots of learning this craft. It is essential that basic skills are mastered before a farrier can progress on to higher levels."

Dr. Butler believes a lifelong commitment is necessary to achieve success in farriery. As he says, "Farriery is easy to learn, but hard to master. It takes discipline, desire, and determination to constantly improve oneself, to have the knowledge necessary to promote and ensure the welfare of the horse."

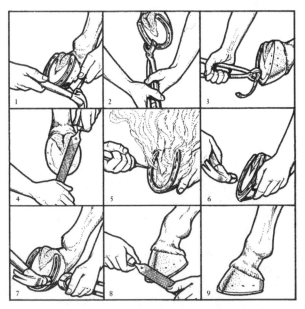

NOT JUST FOR MEN

According to Bill Laste, associate editor of the *American Farriers Journal*, women comprise approximately 8 percent of the American Farriers Association membership. Jeff Rodriguez, past president of the Rocky Mountain Farrier Association, says that, at any given time, his organization has 6 to 15 women members out of approximately 100 members. Unfortunately, he says, women have to be better than their male counterparts if they plan to succeed in this male-dominated career. One key to their success, Jeff says, is to join an organization and link up with open-minded and supportive farriers in the organization.

Linda Browneller, certified farrier.

Linda Browneller did just that. Linda's horse consistently pulled shoes, sometimes as often as six times per shoeing cycle. She loved to ride her horse regularly, but since it was difficult to get her farrier to return each time the horse pulled a shoe, she found herself unable to ride for days at a time. She wondered if she could learn to shoe her horse herself and started reading extensively, acquiring detailed knowledge on the anatomy and physiology of a horse's hoof.

Linda joined the local Rocky Mountain Farrier Association and was encouraged by the warm reception she received. Experienced farriers (including Jeff Rodriguez) allowed her to accompany them on calls and willingly shared their expertise with her. Linda fell in love with the business. She enjoyed being outside, working with horses, and meeting fellow farriers, as well as new clients. Her initial fear of being shunned because she was a woman disappeared quickly, and she discovered that many clients, in addition to the farriers, were kind and friendly to her. Some clients even said that their horses were men-haters, and preferred a woman farrier.

After three years of studying and working with successful farriers, Linda became a certified farrier. She now runs her own practice three days a week. Two days a week she travels with other farriers to acquire more skills. Her goal is to obtain her certified journeyman certificate. Her

Achieving Success as a Farrier

Even though farriery has a high attrition rate, thousands of people do achieve success in this field. Success depends on the following.

✓ Suitability for the profession.

✓ Quality work.

✓ A reliable, honorable reputation.

✓ Willingness to work long and irregular hours.

✓ Ability to deal with demanding customers, unruly horses, and undesirable working conditions.

husband and two children are very supportive and proud of her career. A supportive family is essential in this career, according to Linda.

Linda does wish she had started earlier to learn farriery. In her thirties now, she realizes that there is so much to learn and much of that knowledge can only be obtained by actually working on horses. She feels that when she truly understands, it will be time to retire. Meanwhile she plans to continue to learn, shoe horses, and enjoy the profession.

While it takes time to build physical strength and endurance, Linda is still able to shoe three or four horses a day and trim one or two others. If she takes off a few days, she finds she's a little sore the first day back on the job. Her smaller stature makes positioning under the horse easier. Patience and the use of psychology rather than strength when shoeing a horse is helpful when it comes to out-thinking rather than out-muscling a horse. Many clients don't object when she brings her children and the children enjoy the outing.

The farrier business is one of knowledge, skill, and ability. If a woman possesses these skills, she not only receives respect but also a substantial clientele.

NEW FARRIER ON THE BLOCK

The farrier business involves a great deal of loyalty on the part of clients, and the new farrier has to persevere to build a clientele. Richard Klimesh, a certified journeyman farrier in the American Farriers Association, said the neophyte who is trying to establish a clientele may have to shoe horses that established farriers turn down. Often these horses are ill-mannered and even dangerous, but that kind of shoeing is considered part of paying your dues. However, Dick Willams recommends against this type of work as a safeguard to physical safety.

The new farrier may face working conditions ranging from generally miserable to hot rocky hillsides to cold muddy pens. Persistence is needed to gain enough clients so that you can eventually be selective. Attendance at a quality school and apprenticeship with a reputable established farrier will definitely help you build a good reputation.

Studies conducted on farrier drop-out rates indicate that after five years, only 5 to 10 percent of farrier school graduates remain in the business. A main factor accounting for this decrease is the physical demands of the work. However, thousands of people find success as farriers.

FARRIER-RELATED CAREERS

Farriers use their skills in a variety of ways. Some supplement their incomes by working in other jobs, and others seek employment in related fields. Baron Tayler, once a full-time farrier, branched out into manufacturing horseshoes. After years of working as a farrier, he discovered a special design for a shoe that set it apart from others and filled a niche in the market. Today his business continues to grow, and subsequent products designed in response to farrier needs have been added.

Richard Klimesh, a certified journeyman farrier in the American Farriers Association, currently uses his training in a farrier-related business. After studying architecture and advertising design in college, he became a carpenter and cabinetmaker. Then at the age of 28, he decided to pursue farriery, which would allow him more independence yet let him utilize his artistic talents. Even though no formal schooling is required in the United States, Richard enrolled in Olds College in Alberta, Canada. There, along with eleven other students, he studied the farrier trade eight hours a day, five days a week, for four months.

The first year after graduation Richard entered the farrier profession and supplemented his income with carpentry. To keep abreast of developments in the industry, he attended clinics and seminars on horseshoeing and subscribed to horseshoeing trade journals and magazines. For seventeen years, Richard was a full-time farrier but in 1994 he sustained a serious injury to his knee while working on a horse. During recovery, Richard began writing articles for such magazines as *Western Horseman, American Farriers Journal, Anvil,* and *Horse and Rider.* Utilizing his artistic and technical skills he produced a video series entitled, *Horseshoers' Gold.* Today his time is spent developing new videos, writing articles, drawing, illustrating, and taking photographs for books and magazines.

Manufacturing, writing, and video production are only a few farrier-related careers. Farriers can also branch out in: research, development, and sales of farrier products; college or vocational instruction; and even such recreational areas as contest shoeing.

The scope of the farrier business offers many options. Whether you are a woman, full-time farrier, retired business owner, educator, writer, or clinician, exciting career opportunities exist in the world of the farrier.

RESOURCES

American Farriers Association. 4059 Iron Works Pike, Lexington, Kentucky 40511-8434. (606)233-7411. *Farriers@aol.com*. Publishes: *Directory of North American Farrier Schools.*

American Farriers Journal. Magazine of the American Farriers Association. P.O. Box 624, Brookfield, Wisconsin 53008. (414)0782-4480. *Lesspub@aol.com.* A special edition of farrier supplies and services, published each November, includes information on all aspects of the profession. Special edition price: $25.

Anvil Magazine. P.O. Box 1810, Georgetown, California 95634. (916)333-2142. *http://www.anvilmag.com.*

Brotherhood of Working Farriers Association. 14013 East Highway 136, La Fayette, Georgia 30728. (706)397-8047.

Browneller, Linda. 15021 S. Perry Park Road, Larkspur, Colorado 80811.

Butler, Dr. Doug. *Principles of Horseshoeing II.* Butler Publishing. P.O. Box 1390, LaPorte, Colorado, 80536. (800)728-3826.

Coal Creek Forge. Jeff Rodriguez. 456 Coperdale Lane, Golden, Colorado 80403.

Guild of Professional Farriers. David Millwater. P.O. Box 684, Locust, North Carolina 28097. (704)536-0397. *www.horseshoes.com.*

Internet: *www.horseshoes.com* provides a list of more than 60 farrier schools. Profiles of some schools include descriptions of instructors, staff, courses, boarding facilities, costs, and contact data.

Klimesh, Richard. P.O. Box 140, Livermore, Colorado 80536.

Kreitler, Bonnie. *50 Careers With Horses.* Breakthrough Publications, 310 North Highland Avenue, Ossining, New York 10562.

Moline, Steve. 1026 East. 16th Street, Greeley, Colorado 80631. Colorado State University, Fort Collins, Colorado 80523. Equine Science: (970)491-8373.

Reuter, Rich. P.O. Box 507, Weed, California 96094.

Tayler, Baron. Baron Tayler's Journey's End International. 915 S. Cocalico Road, Denver, Pennsylvania 17517. (717)336-3696. *http://www.horseshoes.com.*

Williams, Dick. 2315 County Road 82 E, Livermore, Colorado 80536. (970)484-0757.

World Farriers Association. P.O. Box 1102, Albuquerque, New Mexico 87103-1102. (505)345-7750.

Worshipful Company of Farriers. 37 The Uplands, Loughton, Essex, England IG10 1NQ. 81-508-6242. Fax: 81-502-5237.

Chapter Ten

Horse Racing and Polo

Horse racing and polo are two outstanding sport programs for equine athletes. Both fields offer exhilarating and competitive employment opportunities for the athletic equestrian, as well as support occupations for people who desire to work with and around horses.

HORSE RACING

More than 300 years ago, Arab stallions were bred to England's running horses, and the breeding of the Thoroughbred racehorse was underway. Generations of selective breeding followed, leading to the development of today's tall sleek racehorse — a horse that possesses a special blend of speed and stamina. Horse racing in America developed along with the growth of the colonies, and it has had a tremendous impact on the American economy. Today the racing industry contributes more than 25 percent of the horse industry's total of $25.3 billion worth of goods and services. There are 725,000 horses involved in racing and racehorse breeding, providing positions for 941,000 people in either a professional or volunteer capacity.

Television coverage of racing is well received by the public. The 1997 Kentucky Derby was the highest rated sports program of that weekend, drawing a rating of 7.1 compared to the NBA playoff game on NBC between Phoenix and Seattle with a 4.6 rating. Approximately 6,887,000 households tuned in to the Kentucky Derby. Pari-mutuel betting totaled $51.9 million, and Churchill Downs set a handle record of $82.5 million for the day's program.

The *1997 Jockey Club Fact Book* reveals that the total number of races have declined. In 1989 there were 82,708 races; in 1996 there were 66,308. Still, the foal crop remains level and the purses and handle had their best increases in years. Gross purses in North America, including the United States, Canada, and Puerto Rico, are up 5.2 percent to $897 million. However, fluctuations in the industry are normal. When one region experiences a constant or increase in race attendance, foal crop, purses, and consequently jobs, another customarily suffers.

Controversy surrounds discussions about the direction racing should take, the effects of other gaming (casinos and slot machines at the tracks), and the effects of simulcasting, telephone, and Internet wagering on racing.

Horse racing is many things. To some it is a hobby, to others it is their primary occupation. Other people see horse racing as gambling, entertainment, sport, or a recreational or social outing. To still others, like Ellen Taylor of the Harness Horse Youth Foundation, horse racing means a chance to orient young people to horses, the horse industry, and the role racing plays in that industry.

Types of Races

In the United States, the most common races are flat races, in which a jockey mounts a horse for a race, and harness racing, performed by a driver seated in a horse drawn sulky. The most popular breed of harness racehorse is the Standardbred. The Thoroughbred is usually the first horse that comes to mind for flat racing, but Quarter Horses, Arabians, Appaloosas, and Paints also have their own popular racing circuits.

The Most Common Types of Flat Racing

- ✓ **Stakes races.** Offer the largest purses. Consist of nomination, entrance and/or starting fees, plus money added by the track or sponsor.

- ✓ **Handicap races.** Feature good quality horses. Racing secretary or handicapper assigns weights to horses in an effort to equalize the winning chances of the entrants.

- ✓ **Claiming races.** Constitute approximately 70 percent of all races run. Horses are entered for a specific price and can be purchased or claimed by a licensed owner.

- ✓ **Allowance races.** Generally offer higher purses than claiming races. Weight allowances are assigned based on winnings, or the number or type of wins, over a given period of time.

- ✓ **Maiden races.** Limited to horses who have never won a race. Divided into three categories: Maiden Special Weights, Straight Maidens, and Claiming Maidens.

- ✓ **Trial races.** Designed primarily to determine qualifiers for a final. May or may not have a purse.

- ✓ **Speed index races.** Limited to horses who have never run faster than the speed index or whose last three speed indexes averaged less than the speed index for that particular race.

Harness racing plays a significant role in the racing industry. Across North America more than 300,000 people are employed in occupations related to harness racing. Registered harness horses number 200,000 in North America. Standardbred horses, trained to either trot or pace, are driven by professionals who guide the two-wheeled sulky or horse cart down the track. Twenty-one states and ten Canadian provinces feature harness racing, and these races draw crowds totaling 17 million spectators. Wagers for harness racing exceed $3.5 billion.

Horse Racing Careers — An Overview

Careers in the racing industry vary greatly, depending on the track and the company. Larger tracks and businesses create specialized positions to meet specific needs while smaller ones may combine several positions into one. For specific information on more than 50 careers related to harness racing, the Harness Youth Horse Foundation has published a book entitled, *Careers in the Harness Racing Industry*, along with a video tape. The book lists harness racing associations, tracks, and contact data.

OWNING RACEHORSES AND RELATED PROFESSIONS

Owning racehorses, once considered a privilege of the wealthy, is now open to a broader spectrum of people. Owners take the greatest financial risk. They purchase the horses, hire trainers, pay the bills, and make investment decisions. They may work alone or hire assistants, managers, accountants, lawyers, trainers, and stable hands.

Types of owners include people who: breed and retain ownership of horses; purchase racehorses at sales or directly from a breeder; own one or more horses alone; own one or more horses with a partner; own one or more horses with several other owners; and own one or more horses as part of a syndication.

Claiming a horse is a popular way to enter the field of racing because immediate results are possible. You have the opportunity to race the horse within a week of purchase, as long as down time and more training aren't required first.

One Owner's Story

For seven years after his father's death, Art Costello took over his father's ownership and training of Thoroughbred racehorses. His first step was an apprenticeship followed by successful completion of the Horse Racing Commission Trainer's Test.

Two of Art's inherited horses, Night Breeze and Provit Rosy, were maidens. Acquiring a stall at a major circuit race track for maiden horses is extremely difficult, so Art took his horses to the Caliente Track in Mexico. Night Breeze won her first race. In the second race, she hit a hole, broke her leg, and had to be put down. Provit Rosy placed second in her first race. Two weeks later she came in a winner. Art then applied for and received a stall at Del Mar in California. He began traveling the major circuit. He claimed several horses and did well. Bond Rulla, claimed by Art for $16,000, won in excess of $100,000 and qualified for the Gold Cup in Arizona. Art trained his own horses as well as those of several other owners.

Finding the right jockey was a major concern for Art. As an owner and trainer of a small stable, he didn't have his own personal jockeys. Consequently, he carefully observed the style of each horse and sought the best jockey for that horse. Sometimes he used agents and other times he approached established jockeys directly. If they didn't have a mount for a particular race, they were usually willing to ride one of Art's horses.

Careers Related to Horse Racing

- ✓ Breeder. See Chapter 5.
- ✓ Racehorse owner.
- ✓ Breeding farm management/administration.
- ✓ Trainer.
- ✓ Race track management personnel.
- ✓ State veterinarian.
- ✓ Racing veterinarian or assistant.
- ✓ Equine dental technician.
- ✓ Farrier.
- ✓ Clocker, race timer, identifier, and security control.
- ✓ Track maintenance crew.
- ✓ Race track stable personnel.
- ✓ Harness racing driver.
- ✓ Jockey.
- ✓ Jockey agent.
- ✓ Jockey valet.
- ✓ Exercise rider.
- ✓ Groom.
- ✓ Hot walker.
- ✓ Outrider and pony riders.
- ✓ Jockey room custodian.
- ✓ Bloodstock agent.
- ✓ Handicapper.
- ✓ Training center manager.
- ✓ Racing commission executive managers, staff, and members.
- ✓ Equine laboratory technicians and technologists.
- ✓ Investigative agents and/or government licensing clerks.
- ✓ Television announcer.
- ✓ Pari-mutuel department personnel. (Located at the track and at off-track betting sites, this department constitutes the main source of income for the tracks.)
- ✓ Simulcasting personnel. (Simulcasting is the simultaneous transmission of a race to other tracks, fair grounds, and betting facilities.)
- ✓ Telephone wagering personnel.
- ✓ Interactive wagering personnel. (Users watch and wager on races through cable television and a remote control.)
- ✓ Internet wagering with cable television.
- ✓ Totalizator tote company personnel.
- ✓ Journalist. See Chapter Fourteen for details.
- ✓ Photographer. (Hired by the track to take winner circle and publicity photos.)
- ✓ Freelance artist/photographer. (Breeders, owners, and fans seek quality pictures of their horses.)
- ✓ Appraiser and consultant. See Chapter Fifteen.
- ✓ Insurance agents and brokers. See Chapter Fifteen.
- ✓ Sales, claiming and syndication agents.
- ✓ Transporting horses to and from the race track. (Done by trainers or companies that contract to transport horses by truck or air.)
- ✓ Race breed registries. See Chapter Thirteen.
- ✓ Racehorse adoption programs. (Mostly volunteer nonprofit organizations.)
- ✓ Museum personnel.

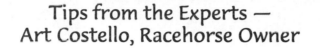

Tips from the Experts — Art Costello, Racehorse Owner

■ Understand clearly your own motives for getting into the racehorse business.

■ Remember that it is a demanding and financially risky business.

■ Continually evaluate your own business. Practice good business and recordkeeping skills. Know the competition.

■ Understand that initial investments for stall webbing, bandages, and supplies can cost $40,000.

■ Be prepared for the emotional and financial costs of accidents.

■ Understand the expense of year round travel for you, the horses, tack, and equipment.

■ Be aware that some horses do not travel well and need time to recuperate.

■ Develop good communication skills for dealing with track officials, agents, employees, and the public.

Owning Racing Quarter Horses

Participating in the Quarter Horse racing industry is not as costly as being involved in Thoroughbred horse racing. A good Quarter Horse racehorse can be purchased for $5,000 to $10,000. Quarter Horse racehorse breeder Ray Wardell (see the section on breeding racehorses in Chapter Five) estimates that it takes about $600 to a $1,000 a month to run a horse. Training fees run from $15 a day to around $40, with the highest fees in California. Some years you can make good money, and Ray supposes there are people who make money year in and year out, but he doesn't know of any.

He justifies his involvement in racing by the money earned from breeding and selling horses, and he feels it is good business for him to diversify. Although Ray's primary focus is market breeding, he also races, trains, and sells horses (sometimes acting as an agent selling horses for a commission). Whenever he hauls his own horses to breeding farms, races, and horse sales, he looks for opportunities to haul other people's horses. This helps others and also provides Ray with some supplemental income. For more information about breeding, see Chapter Five.

Agents

To qualify to be an agent, a college degree in business and marketing along with extensive knowledge of handicapping and the Thoroughbred market are helpful. Agents are paid on a commission basis and annual income usually begins in the $30,000 to $40,000 range with potential earnings of up to $200,000.

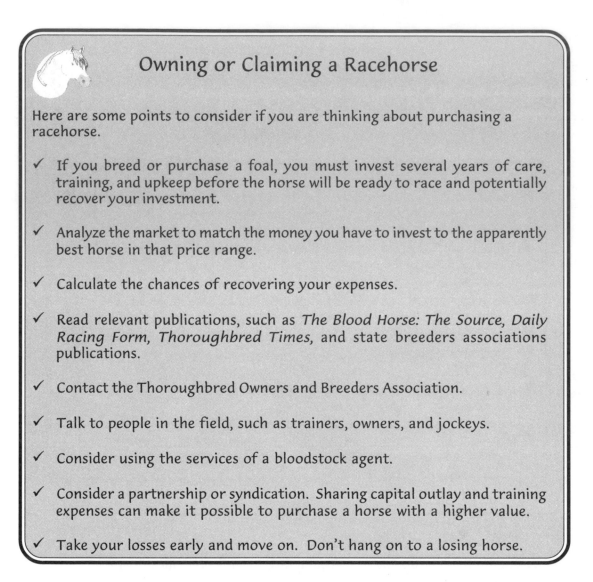

Owning or Claiming a Racehorse

Here are some points to consider if you are thinking about purchasing a racehorse.

✓ If you breed or purchase a foal, you must invest several years of care, training, and upkeep before the horse will be ready to race and potentially recover your investment.

✓ Analyze the market to match the money you have to invest to the apparently best horse in that price range.

✓ Calculate the chances of recovering your expenses.

✓ Read relevant publications, such as *The Blood Horse: The Source, Daily Racing Form, Thoroughbred Times,* and state breeders associations publications.

✓ Contact the Thoroughbred Owners and Breeders Association.

✓ Talk to people in the field, such as trainers, owners, and jockeys.

✓ Consider using the services of a bloodstock agent.

✓ Consider a partnership or syndication. Sharing capital outlay and training expenses can make it possible to purchase a horse with a higher value.

✓ Take your losses early and move on. Don't hang on to a losing horse.

Bloodstock agent. Bloodstock agents act as brokers for buyers and sellers of, primarily, Thoroughbred racehorses. They perform appraisals, pedigree research, and analysis. In addition to making arrangements for breeding, these agents also prepare horses for sales (including conducting advertising campaigns) and contract for horse transportation. Accounting records, insurance, and arrangements for legal advice are also provided.

Sales, claiming, and syndication agent. Roger Thomas was working in a retail business when a friend asked if he wanted to go in partnership on a racing Quarter Horse. Roger said, "Sure," and that marked the beginning of his enthusiasm for racing. Soon thereafter, he helped his parents purchase, claim horses, and select suitable races. He had several contacts with the Mayberry family, which has been in the racing business since before the turn of the century, with a Kentucky Derby winner dating back to 1902. When the Mayberrys offered him a position, he gladly accepted. Unlike most agents, Roger represents the trainer instead of the owners. He works as a liaison between the Mayberrys and owners in purchasing foals, claiming horses, and selecting appropriate races. His day begins at 5:00 A.M., with afternoons spent at the track. He tapes every race, studies the horses, and makes decisions about which horses to claim and in which races to run the horses. A knowledge of handicapping is essential. Forming a syndication of multiple owners that provides finances for more expensive horse purchases is also part of his job.

Harness Racing Drivers

Drivers are responsible for guiding, maneuvering, and prompting a horse during a race to maximize its performance. They must be in good physical condition, have quick reflexes, courage, common sense, and a competitive spirit. Weight, a concern for jockeys, is not a critical factor for drivers. Catch drivers are people who drive for several trainers. Some drivers also maintain training stables.

To qualify to be a harness racing driver, you must pass a medical, written, and performance exam. For more detailed information about becoming a harness racing driver, contact the U. S. or Canadian Trotting Association.

Jockeys

Pound for pound, jockeys are considered among the world's finest athletes. They need the strength to control a force ten times their size, and the courage to face the possibility of injury every time a horse breaks from the starting gate. The weight of the jockey has always been considered critical to winning, and in the early days many jockeys were young boys. Because some lost their lives racing, the English Parliament, in co-sponsorship with the Jockey Club, passed a law that established a jockey weight limit of 77 pounds. However, it wasn't until the Education Act was passed that children under the age of twelve were prohibited from racing. Today U.S. racing associations will not license a jockey who is under the age of sixteen. Legitimate race tracks require jockeys to have a license.

Stories of jockeys. Floyd Campbell is still active as a jockey. He has been a jockey for more than 30 years, which places him in a unique position because most jockeys retire by the time they are 35. Floyd rides almost exclusively for Quarter Horse trainer Bob Johnson. They travel among tracks in Minnesota, Idaho, Utah, and Wyoming. Floyd exercises most of the horses himself so he can get to know the horses better. He seldom receives a mount fee, but due to his skill and win record, he gets first choice of horses.

Floyd believes the most important skills in winning a race are to learn to sit very still, to not over-ride the horse, and to allow the horse to do what he was trained for and wants to do — run and win. A highlight in Floyd's life was being cast in the movie, *Buffalo Soldier*.

Gary Baze, West Coast regional manager for the Jockeys' Guild, spent 25 years as a jockey before moving into his current career. Gary's father was a trainer and his uncle was a jockey. By the time Gary was nine years old, he was galloping horses and hoping he would stay small enough to become a jockey. Gary began by mucking stalls and hot walking and exercising horses. At the age of sixteen he acquired his first mount.

Income depends on individual success. Gary estimates that only 5 percent of jockeys make a good living ($150,000 and up). About 30 percent make enough to pay their bills ($40,000 to $50,000). The rest need another source of income.

Most trainers pay a jockey a mount fee ranging from $20 to $50. With a good agent and win record, a jockey can get a mount for most of the eight to ten races run in a day. Out of the jockey's 10 percent of the earnings, the jockey pays his agent and valet, purchases equipment, and usually rents an apartment for the season. Some jockeys travel and live in a recreational vehicle.

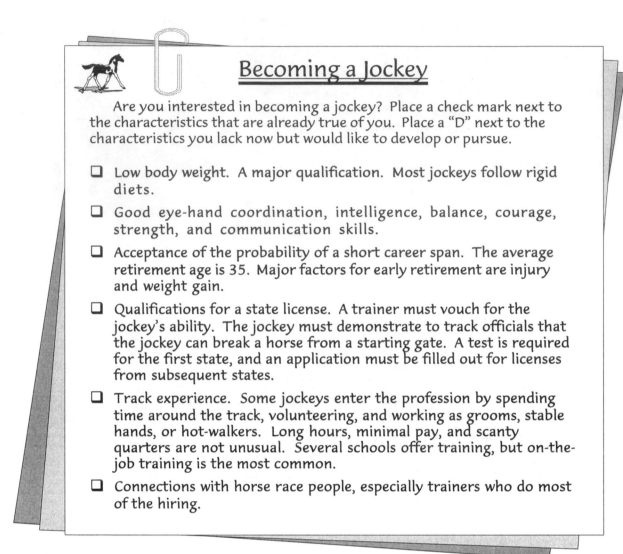

Becoming a Jockey

Are you interested in becoming a jockey? Place a check mark next to the characteristics that are already true of you. Place a "D" next to the characteristics you lack now but would like to develop or pursue.

❑ Low body weight. A major qualification. Most jockeys follow rigid diets.

❑ Good eye-hand coordination, intelligence, balance, courage, strength, and communication skills.

❑ Acceptance of the probability of a short career span. The average retirement age is 35. Major factors for early retirement are injury and weight gain.

❑ Qualifications for a state license. A trainer must vouch for the jockey's ability. The jockey must demonstrate to track officials that the jockey can break a horse from a starting gate. A test is required for the first state, and an application must be filled out for licenses from subsequent states.

❑ Track experience. Some jockeys enter the profession by spending time around the track, volunteering, and working as grooms, stable hands, or hot-walkers. Long hours, minimal pay, and scanty quarters are not unusual. Several schools offer training, but on-the-job training is the most common.

❑ Connections with horse race people, especially trainers who do most of the hiring.

In his current position, Gary travels to tracks in California, Washington, Montana, Idaho, and Nevada for the Jockeys' Guild. He functions as a go-between for jockeys and management, stewards, and insurance companies.

The Jockeys' Guild represents approximately 800 active member jockeys. The guild works to assure jockeys' safety, and helps members file accident reports and process and receive equitable insurance settlements. The guild also represents jockeys' interests by promoting and developing legislation. In addition to employing lawyers and accountants who assist the guild throughout the country, approximately fifteen people also work as office managers and staff, regional representatives, *Jockey News* publication staff, and legal action personnel. They sponsor the Disabled Jockey Fund for members who are permanently disabled due to racing accidents.

Jockey and Racehorse Support Personnel

Jockey agent.   These agents work to procure the best mounts for their jockeys, and they keep track of the mounts each jockey is committed to ride. Jockey agents often work at the track.

> ## Tips from the Experts — Gary Baze, Retired Jockey and Jockeys' Guild Manager
>
> - You have to win in order to make money.
>
> - A six-day work week is not unusual.
>
> - Accidents are common. Often one horse clips another horse's heels in front of him. The horse automatically goes down and the jockey is thrown.
>
> - Travel becomes a way of life, varying with the number of tracks in the vicinity and the duration of a track's race season. Having a gypsy mentality is definitely an asset.

Jockey valet. One valet usually assists four jockeys, and is responsible for keeping track of each jockey's wardrobe and equipment, laying out clothes, carrying tack, and, sometimes, saddling the mount. Jockey valets are usually paid by the track management and also receive 10 percent of their jockeys' earnings.

Exercise rider. This job provides excellent training experience for advancement to the position of jockey. Exercise riders must be proficient riders with the ability to properly pace a horse, and with knowledge of a horse's physical capabilities, muscles, and respiratory system. One rider can exercise as many as 20 horses. Trainers and farm managers usually set a weight limit of about 135 pounds for exercise riders. Exercise riders are customarily hired by racehorse trainers and receive a salary ranging from $10,000 to $20,000. Housing is furnished, in addition to 1 percent of the trainer's 10 percent of the purse.

Groom. Working as a groom requires long irregular hours, but the job provides hands-on experience for aspiring jockeys, drivers, and trainers. Salaries plus 1 percent of the trainer's 10 percent of the purse range from $10,000 to $25,000 per year with board and benefits sometimes included. Traditionally employed by a trainer, the groom is responsible for: the daily care of three to six horses, including brushing, bandaging, monitoring medication, cleaning tack, and mucking out stalls; and managing turn-out. Some grooms are also expected to exercise ride, instruct, and assist in training.

Hot walker. This person cools the horse down after a race and is usually paid a minimal fee on a per horse basis. Many trainers now use hot walker machines.

Outrider and pony riders. One outrider leads the parade to the track and the other follows the parade. They protect the jockeys and assist if a jockey falls from a horse. Pony riders ride alongside the jockeys as they enter the track.

Jockey room custodian. This person maintains the jockeys' locker room.

Statue at Kentucky Derby Museum depicts 1997 Kentucky winner Gary Stevens who rode Silver Charm.

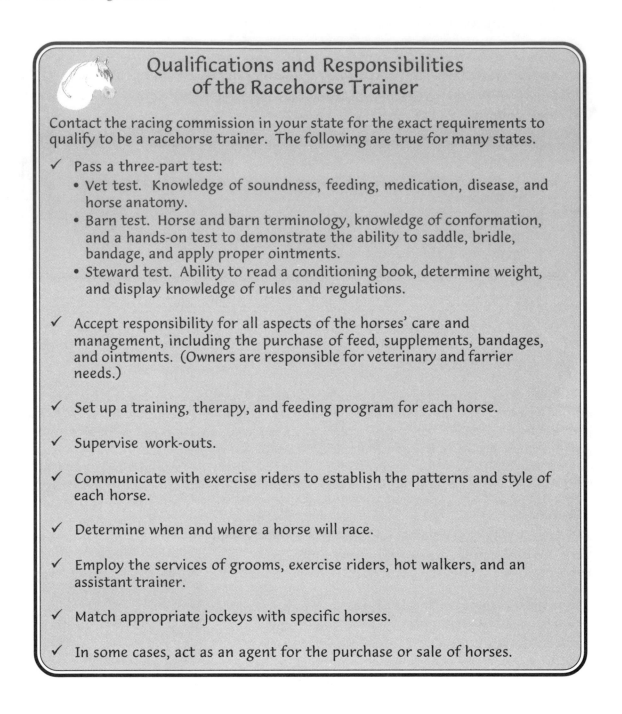

Qualifications and Responsibilities of the Racehorse Trainer

Contact the racing commission in your state for the exact requirements to qualify to be a racehorse trainer. The following are true for many states.

✓ Pass a three-part test:
  • Vet test. Knowledge of soundness, feeding, medication, disease, and horse anatomy.
  • Barn test. Horse and barn terminology, knowledge of conformation, and a hands-on test to demonstrate the ability to saddle, bridle, bandage, and apply proper ointments.
  • Steward test. Ability to read a conditioning book, determine weight, and display knowledge of rules and regulations.

✓ Accept responsibility for all aspects of the horses' care and management, including the purchase of feed, supplements, bandages, and ointments. (Owners are responsible for veterinary and farrier needs.)

✓ Set up a training, therapy, and feeding program for each horse.

✓ Supervise work-outs.

✓ Communicate with exercise riders to establish the patterns and style of each horse.

✓ Determine when and where a horse will race.

✓ Employ the services of grooms, exercise riders, hot walkers, and an assistant trainer.

✓ Match appropriate jockeys with specific horses.

✓ In some cases, act as an agent for the purchase or sale of horses.

Racehorse Trainers. Detailed information about becoming a horse trainer and running a training facility is presented in Chapter Six. Criteria for qualifying to be a racehorse trainer vary from state to state, so you should check with your specific state's racing commission. For harness racing training requirements, contact the U.S. or Canadian Trotting Association.

Race Track Management and Related Personnel

Management. Administrative personnel deal with staff, horse people, fans, and regulatory commissions; make decisions about the overall operation of the track, and ensure that all parts of the track complex run efficiently. To do so, they must have a thorough knowledge of racing and excellent administration skills.

Accountants/controllers oversee the track's financial records. The public relations, publicity, and marketing staff members promote the track to increase attendance, stimulate interest in racing, and educate the public, while maintaining communication with the media. Wagering systems computer operators keep track of all wagering, and other computer operators enter other pertinent data.

The racing secretary has the important responsibility of overseeing the day-to-day operations of the track. This person supervises race officials during a race; fills the scheduled races; writes up all the races for the meet; and takes charge of figures, weights of handicaps for races, and setting up scratch time.

The paymaster of purses is responsible for all financial receipts and disbursements, such as the purses; nominating and entry fees; claiming money; and jockey fees and fines. The paymaster also keeps records of all on-track accounts, transactions, and assignments of interest, partnerships, registration of agents, and lease agreements.

The program director oversees the printing of the daily program, works under the supervision of the racing secretary, performs research on eligibility, and examines folder accuracy for past records of wins and for trainer and owner verification. The program director clocks test runs, draws horses for their races, prepares the official records of each race, enters the data in the computer, and transmits the data to New York for verification. (Harness racing data is transmitted to the United States Trotting Association.)

Judges. Racing commission judges are official representatives of the commission, who regulate and govern races and participants and issue penalties. Judges who report to the racing commission judges include: patrol judges, who watch the progress of the race from various vantage points to spot rule violations, lameness, broken or missing equipment; paddock judges/equipment judges, who verify that the equipment used is the same as that previously listed and approved, inspect horses, and supervise paddock security; and placing judges who work in a station above the finish line, declare the order of finish, post the information on the tote board, and dispatch photographs to the stewards for official rulings in case of disputed finishes.

Video race patrol. These technologically oriented employees need a knowledge of television production, racing, and video equipment. They are responsible for videotaping races for fans viewing the actual race or simulcasts, videotaping many angles of the race for the judge to examine when inquiries are made, and preparing closed circuit television programs with race features, handicapping commentaries, and race highlights. Many are contract personnel.

Photo finish operator. Trained in the use of a camera and photo finish equipment, these operators photograph the finish line.

Simulcasting director. This position requires a thorough knowledge of all racing disciplines, including harness racing. Responsibilities include assisting in the establishment contracts with other race tracks and off-track betting sites and developing contracts, rules, and regulations concerning simulcasting.

Track announcer. While watching the race from a strategic point above the track, the announcer provides a detailed running commentary on the race and provides information regarding authorized race changes. A knowledge of racing, a good voice, enthusiasm, sharp memory, and keen eyes are key qualifications.

Clerk of course. This clerk maintains the records of registration and eligibility certificates, checks foal certificates, verifies ownership of horses, transfers certificates on claimed horses, views the progress of a race, records details of horses' performances, and provides information to the program director.

Clerk of scales. The key responsibility of this clerk is to weigh in jockeys after the race to ensure that the correct weights are carried. At smaller tracks the clerk may serve as a clocker.

Starter. The starter assumes control of the runners and riders at the gate to make sure all the horses are lined up, standing easy, and ready. He ensures that all horses receive a fair and equal start and oversees any problems, such as tack adjustments or withdrawals.

Steward. These state licensed officials protect the public from illegal procedures, govern the rules of racing, nominate horses for drug testing, levy fines, suspend licenses, serve as the final authority on photo finishes, exclude individuals from the race track if necessary, and hold inquires when needed.

Clocker. The clocker times workouts and races.

Official race timer. This person maintains and runs the automatic teletimer.

Identifier. The lip tattoos of horses are checked to ensure that they correspond with the horses' registration papers.

Track maintenance crew. This crew oversees the constant upkeep of the track and facilities.

Security control. Charles Stoeckle and his department provide a good example of race track security control. As captain of security at Arapahoe Park in Colorado, he hires fourteen employees who must be 21 years old and have no traffic or felony records. On-the-job training is provided. This department's responsibilities include: maintaining security and control between and on race days; and securing and patrolling the stable, pari-mutuel, and public areas.

Race track stable superintendent. Keith Hilaman, a 72-year-old race track veteran, is the stable superintendent for Arapahoe Park, which houses 1,450 horses. Keith has been an owner, stable hand, clerk of scales, patrol judge, and steward. In the 1960s he was a partner in the construction of Ohio's first Quarter Horse race track. The stable superintendent's responsibilities include assigning horses and trainers to stalls, and overseeing horse placement to ensure that stalls are utilized effectively and efficiently.

Handicapper. Possessing a thorough knowledge of pedigree, training, race record, jockey suitability, race conditions, the horse's conformation and temperament, the handicapper ascertains if a horse is outclassed or not in a particular race. Full-time salaries range from $22,000 to $28,000 per year plus benefits. Seasonal handicappers are hired by many tracks.

Television announcer. The rise of ESPN coverage provides a variety of television-related positions. Horse expertise and a degree in television communication are assets.

Training center manager. Manager responsibilities vary but usually include the overseeing of track maintenance, therapy barns, and track machinery.

Racing commission executive managers, staff, and members. While management and staff positions are normally salaried, members are usually volunteers.

Investigative agent and government licensing clerk. These employees work with race track managers and the racing commission to maintain a smooth and effectively run race program. Federal and state personnel work at the race tracks in a variety of capacities, including: accountants who oversee payments and disbursements of pari-mutuel handle for taxes, and verify bets and pay-out prices; personnel who check for applicable licenses and proper fingerprinting; and technicians who supervise the collection and analysis of blood.

Lobbyist. Lobbyists establish and/or promote legislation related to the horse race industry.

Simulcasting. The simultaneous transmission of a race to other tracks, fair grounds, and betting facilities provides a variety of positions, including production and publicity jobs.

Race Track Veterinarian and Related Personnel

State Veterinarian. Dr. John Zisk ran his own private veterinary practice while he served as the state veterinarian in the Wagering Division of the Florida State Regulation Commission. As a state veterinarian at Tampa Downs, his pre-race duties included inspecting the horses and collecting and testing blood samples. After the races, he evaluated the horses' health and examined them for injuries. Another responsibility was working with owners and trainers on legal drug and medication administration. (See also the U.S. Department of Agriculture section in Chapter Seventeen.)

Race track veterinarian assistant. Many track veterinarians have assistants who help in examining horses prior to races, providing basic care, and assisting in administering drugs and surgery.

Equine dental technician. This person works with the veterinarian to provide proper dental care.

Farrier. Many tracks have on-site farriers who are specially trained in shoeing racehorses.

Equine laboratory technicians. These technicians are responsible for analyzing blood and urine samples to identify possible health problems and to ensure that prohibited drugs have not been administered.

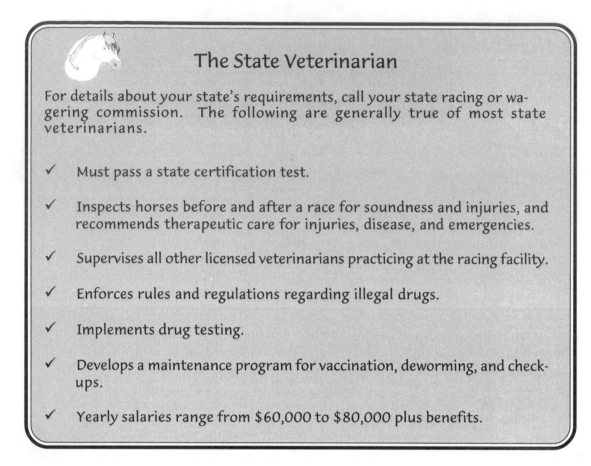

The State Veterinarian

For details about your state's requirements, call your state racing or wagering commission. The following are generally true of most state veterinarians.

✓ Must pass a state certification test.

✓ Inspects horses before and after a race for soundness and injuries, and recommends therapeutic care for injuries, disease, and emergencies.

✓ Supervises all other licensed veterinarians practicing at the racing facility.

✓ Enforces rules and regulations regarding illegal drugs.

✓ Implements drug testing.

✓ Develops a maintenance program for vaccination, deworming, and check-ups.

✓ Yearly salaries range from $60,000 to $80,000 plus benefits.

Horse Race Betting

Pari-mutuel is a French term meaning betting amongst yourselves, not against the house. Pari-mutuels are located at the track and at off-track betting sites. Because a percentage of every dollar bet goes to the track, towards purses, and for taxes, the pari-mutuel betting department constitutes the main source of income for the tracks. Winning bettors receive 82 percent of the wagers; 18 percent is divided and distributed evenly among the state, the horsemen for purses, and the track. The track percentage is then divided between the host track and the off-track site.

Pari-mutuel manager. Jim Olsen, pari-mutuel manager at Arapahoe Park, worked his way up through the system. He supervises an assistant manager, 60 ticket counter employees, and several money room employees. Most work three days a week during the season. Some also work the ticket windows and money room during simulcasts. Manager responsibilities include: overseeing all departments and employees; maintaining security; collecting and disbursing the money wagered; and displaying odds and payoffs.

Pari-mutuel clerk. A clerk may sell and cash wagers through pari-mutuel machines or work in a booth taking check and credit card payments.

Money room personnel. All the money wagered and paid out is handled by these employees.

Telephone wagering. In 1997 more than 100,000 Americans bet over $8.1 million a week over the phone in the six states with legalized telephone wagering operations. (Pari-mutuels and telephone wagering are legal in some states. Regulations may vary). A player in a state that legally offers telephone accounts must first choose a betting organization and establish an account.

Interactive wagering. The first phase of interactive wagering was introduced by On Demand Services Technology and the Jockey Club in early 1997. Users watch and wager on races through cable television and a remote control. New positions for innovative employees become available as the technology of interactive wagering changes.

Internet wagering. IWN is an interactive wagering network that predicts Internet wagering will carry horse racing into the twenty-first century, bring a new vitality to racing, and attract young adults to racing. Challenges exist, however, on political, managerial, regulatory, and technical fronts.

Association and Organizational Positions

One racing organization that employs a variety of personnel is the United States Trotting Association. Formed in 1938, the association licenses owners, trainers, and officials, and formulates rules for and ensures the integrity of harness racing. Nearly 80 people are employed by the association as clerical workers, computer programmers, public relations and licensing professionals, and human resource personnel. Salaries range from $15,000 to $100,000 plus a full package of benefits. Experience in harness racing and with the Standardbred horse is desirable but not a necessity.

Although racing organizations may not require managers to have a background in racing, such experience can definitely be an advantage. Fred Noe, executive vice president of the United States Trotting Association, is a horse owner who participated as a driver in a few amateur races. His background and education in finance, manufacturing, and marketing along with his past history of leadership excellence were his key qualifications.

One of Fred's challenges is keeping the harness racing industry headed in a positive direction through marketing and public relations. According to Fred, the harness racing industry is changing rapidly. Today the industry especially needs individuals who are committed to excellence and are highly motivated toward success, who have the ability to forge bonds between widely disparate groups.

Fred Noe, Executive Vice President of the United States Trotting Association.

121

Museum Careers

These museums are dedicated primarily to the Thoroughbred racing industry: National Museum of Racing and Hall of Fame, Kentucky Museum and Horse Park, Kentucky Derby Museum, and National Horse Racing Museum.

National Museum of Racing and Hall of Fame. Field Horne, curator of the National Museum of Racing and Hall of Fame and a 23-year museum veteran, believes the scarcity of racehorse museums severely limits employment opportunities. He says he was in the right place at the right time with the qualifications of a master's degree in museum studies, and experience in the museum profession. His responsibilities include: the installation, development, procurement, and maintenance of exhibits, the care of museum objects, and recordkeeping.

The National Museum of Racing and Hall of Fame has approximately fifteen positions, none of which require horse background. For people interested in equine-related museums, Field Horne suggests they research opportunities in rodeo, draft horse, or breed association museums.

Kentucky Museum and Horse Park. The Kentucky Museum and Horse Park is the largest equestrian museum in the world, with camping facilities, carriage rides, horse shows, and educational programs. The museum employs about 90 full-time employees and seasonal employment climbs to 150 workers. The museum is a state institution and salaries are based accordingly. Starting salaries are approximately $20,000 with the first raise after six months and additional raises at one-year increments, reaching the $30,000 plus range. The benefits are very good.

Originally from Kentucky, Bill Cooke returned to Lexington during the development of the Kentucky Museum and Horse Park and was able to get in on the initial stages of the operation. As museum director, he realized that museum visitors needed more time to read the abundance of text that accompanies the exhibits. In 1995 he developed a free 500-page Internet museum: *http://www.imh.org*.

Typical Jobs in an Equine-Related Museum

- ✓ Director, assistant director, development director.
- ✓ Education curator.
- ✓ Visitor services employees.
- ✓ Public relations personnel.
- ✓ Clerical.
- ✓ Librarian.
- ✓ Carriage drivers.
- ✓ Top horse riders.
- ✓ Horse show performers.
- ✓ Manager and equine seminar leaders.
- ✓ Head of maintenance and assistants.
- ✓ Gift shop employees.

Educational Opportunities in the Horse Racing Field

Educational requirements are as diverse as career options. On-the-track programs and apprenticeship programs are considered excellent preparation for many racing industry jobs. People fortunate enough to grow up in the industry have a definite advantage.

Most colleges offer business, management, journalism, and other related programs that provide one dimension of the educational background needed for many positions. Equine and animal science programs are offered at many universities, colleges, and community colleges. See Chapter One for suggested equine-related educational programs.

Education and Training Related to Horse Racing

✓ Agricultural Training Institute, Ohio State University, Wooster Campus. One of the only schools with a specific program on the Standardbred horse.

✓ Handicapping sessions. Offered by the *Daily Racing Form* in conjunction with race parks.

✓ Owner workshops. Sponsored by tracks for current and prospective owners on many informational topics, including claiming.

✓ Thoroughbred Owners and Breeders Association (TOBA). Offers ownership clinics and instructional clinics on creating a business, business evaluation, broodmare and foal pedigrees, and tax and legal issues pertaining to the horse industry.

✓ Race Track Industry Program (RTIP), University of Arizona. Bachelor of Science program emphasizes the pari-mutuel racing industry with course work in horse science, animal racing laws and enforcement, marketing, and management of racing animals.

✓ The Writers Project. Unique creative writing program encourages writers to use horses and horse people as subjects. Contact the American Quarter Horse Association, Churchill Downs, Jockey Club, or Thoroughbred Racing Communications.

RACE HORSE ADOPTIONS

What happens to horses after their racing careers are over? Many are retrained for rodeo events, such as barrel racing, others are kept for pleasure horses, breeding stock, or used in other competitive sports. Still others are adopted. If you would like more information about race horse adoptions, check out the organizations and web sites listed in the Resources section at the end of this chapter.

POLO

The Game

This 2,500-year-old game is fast, rough, and dangerous. It is played on a ten-acre grass field with the dimensions of 300 yards by 160 yards. There are six periods, called *chukkers*, which are seven minutes long. A team is made up of four players with assigned positions and handicaps. Handicaps, which reflect the players' abilities, are designed to allow players of diverse skill levels to combine their talents and be competitive. To participate in the sport, a player must have a handicap assigned by the United State Polo Association.

Known as the Game of Kings, polo is still played by royalty, but the key participants are successful athletes who are drawn by the speed and intense competition of the game.

United States Polo Association

The United States Polo Association (USPA) was formed in 1890 to advance the interests of polo clubs. The goal of USPA is to maintain the growth of this sport that has endured world wars, national conflicts, and economic depressions. USPA also sets handicaps, reviews and establishes rules, and sponsors tournaments. In conjunction with the Polo Training Foundation, USPA provides educational materials and facilities, and multilevel umpire and player clinics. USPA membership exceeds 3,400 amateurs and professionals from all levels of commitment to the sport and all walks of life, including people in industry, homemakers, physicians, television celebrities, ranchers, college students, and retirees. Ten percent of the players are women. There are approximately 225 polo clubs in the United States. Twenty-five high schools and colleges offer polo clubs for their students.

USPA Executive Director, Owner, and Player

George Alexander accepted the position of executive director of USPA after serving on the board for many years. He is a college graduate with a degree in business, a former business owner, a polo pony owner, and owner of the Blackberry Polo Club, a recreational club for amateurs. According to George, club membership fees make it possible to maintain this club. George enjoys playing polo four days a week and feels polo is a great sport, but he recommends that people take up polo for the love of the sport, not for money. Only a small number of participants make a living. Unless people have a polo legacy coupled with unique native ability that enables them to make it to the very top, they will not make a good living. Some players may be able to make a modest living by earning around $2,000 a game. Only the top 5 percent of players advance above that income. In most states, the polo season only lasts from three to eight months. This is a short time to make enough money for an entire year.

George suggests obtaining a good education, finding a good job, and then looking for an opportunity to play. Managerial positions are available in about 50 percent of the clubs. The other clubs are small owner-operated clubs. Other positions include farm managers, stable managers, instructors, grooms, and exercise riders. Managers typically maintain the fields and set schedules. Perhaps a dozen of the 225 clubs are large enough to have an administrative manager with a support staff.

The Polo Profession

Entering polo is costly. Beginning players should consider contacting polo clubs in their area. Most offer lessons that cost from $20 to $80 an hour. For beginners, one or two horses are usually sufficient and can be purchased for $3,000 to $5,000 each. Other expenses include feed, stabling, farrier and veterinary fees, lessons, equipment, and membership in the USPA ($150). Advancement from the beginner status entails the purchase of several more horses of increased value ($5,000 to $10,000), and perhaps the services of a groom.

According to the USPA, players working their way up to the professional ranks may be able to earn enough to support a family, and advanced professional polo players earn a significant income reaching into the hundreds of thousands. A player who advances to the professional ranks may be recruited by a team sponsor for as much as $50,000 per tournament. The majority of polo professionals also train horses for themselves and for selling. It is not unusual for a professional to have seven to twenty playing polo ponies with several other green polo ponies in training. Four to eight polo ponies are used per player in each game.

Team sponsors frequently run a stable of 10 to 60 polo ponies valued at more than $10,000 each. They may recruit players who have their own horses or provide horses for their players with wages adjusted accordingly. One full-time groom for every six horses is normally employed at around $1,500 a month plus expenses.

USPA employs ten people, including administrators, professional umpires, and field representatives for collegiate and scholastic programs.

According to the USPA, polo is experiencing a rapid rate of growth in the United States and worldwide. If the game interests you, call the USPA for a list of clubs near you, then visit several clubs or college programs and talk with people in the field.

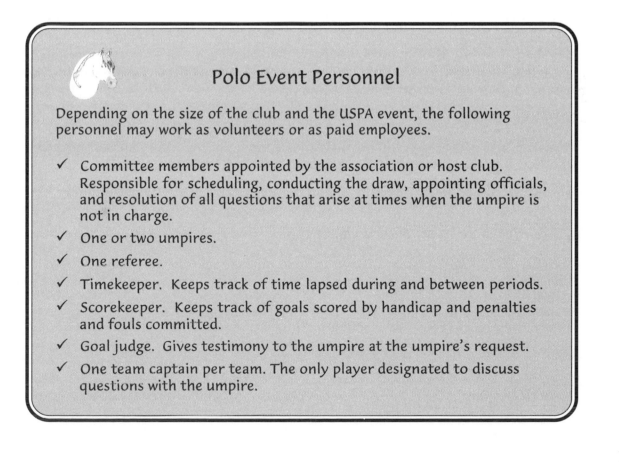

Polo Event Personnel

Depending on the size of the club and the USPA event, the following personnel may work as volunteers or as paid employees.

- ✓ Committee members appointed by the association or host club. Responsible for scheduling, conducting the draw, appointing officials, and resolution of all questions that arise at times when the umpire is not in charge.
- ✓ One or two umpires.
- ✓ One referee.
- ✓ Timekeeper. Keeps track of time lapsed during and between periods.
- ✓ Scorekeeper. Keeps track of goals scored by handicap and penalties and fouls committed.
- ✓ Goal judge. Gives testimony to the umpire at the umpire's request.
- ✓ One team captain per team. The only player designated to discuss questions with the umpire.

RESOURCES

Racing Industry Scholarship Resources

Scholarships for those seeking equine-related careers are also described in Chapter Two.

Equine School and College Directory. Harness Horse Youth Foundation, 14950 Greyhound Court, Suite 210, Carmel, Indiana 46032-1091. (317)848-5132. *hhyfetaylor@iquest.net.* Lists scholarship sources, contact information, the number and amount of the scholarships awarded, and the requirements.

Harness Tracks of America. 4640 E. Sunrise, Suite 200, Tucson, Arizona 85718. (520)529-2525. Offers $15,000 in annual college scholarships to sons and daughters of drivers, trainers, breeders, caretakers, and young people actively engaged in harness racing.

Race Track Industry Program (RTIP). University of Arizona. Office of Student Financial Aid, Tucson, Arizona 85721. (520)621-1858. Funds are available for University of Arizona students. In 1997 the tuition plus estimated expenses for lodging food and books was approximately $6,550 for residents and $14,000 for non-residents per year.

Adoption Resources

California Equine Retirement Foundation. *http://www.viper.net/~syscip/cerf/* .

Days End Farm Horse Rescue. *http://www.bcpl.lib.md.us/~gharris/days.html.*

Standardbred Equestrian Program. *http://www.ustrotting.com/equest/equest.html.*

Standardbred Retirement Foundation. *http://www.harnesshorse.com/srf.html.*

United States Trotting Association. Karen Beach and Sara Short. 750 Michigan Avenue, Columbus, Ohio 43215. (614)224-2291, extensions 3260 and 3226. Provides a list of groups that match retired horses with adoptive owners.

Racing Resources

American Quarter Horse Association. Michael Cusortelli, Racing Information Coordinator. P.O. Box 200, Amarillo, Texas 79168. *http://www.aqha.com/racing.*

Arizona, University of. Race Track Industry Program (RTIP). Educational Building #69, Tucson, Arizona 85721. (520)621-5660. *http://ag.arizona.edu/rtip.*

Baze, Gary. 10528 SE 250th Place, Kent, Washington 98031. *Gbaze1025@aol.com.*

Blood Horse, The. 1736 Alexandria Drive, Lexington, Kentucky 40504. (800)866-2361. Publication of Thoroughbred Owners and Breeders Association. Other reference materials include:

Blood Horse Auctions. A recap of Thoroughbred bloodstock sales. Price: $40.

Blood Horse Dams Index. Lists broodmares represented at public auctions.

Blood Horse Nicks. A broodmare owner's resource. Price: $40.

Blood Horse Sires. A stallion resource. Price: $24.95.

Blood Horse Source, The. A comprehensive directory of people in horse industry professions from accounting to watering systems. Price: $19.95.

Racing Post: The Turf Directory. International guide to horse racing, includes lists of owners, trainers, jockeys, race courses, racing authorities and officials, stud farms, media, bloodstock agents, and racing results.

Campbell, Floyd. 203 Animas, Trinidad, Colorado 81082.

Colorado Owners and Breeders of Racing Arabians. Nancy Anderson. 7965 W. Trail North Drive, Littleton, Colorado 80125. Fax: (303)791-7118.

Costello, Art. P.O. Box 80387, Rancho Santa Margarita, California 92688.

Daily Racing Form. Peter Berry, News Editor. 2231 E. Camelback Road, Suite 100, Phoenix, Arizona 85016. (602)468-6500. Employees of this publication and with Equibase personnel chart races on race days.

Equibase Company. 820 Corporate Drive, Lexington, Kentucky 40503. *http:// www.equibase.com.* The Thoroughbred industry's official data base for racing information.

Equine Line. The Jockey Club Information Systems (TJCIS). 821 Corporate Drive, Lexington, Kentucky 40503. (606)224-2800. *http://equineonline.com.*

Handicapping sessions. *Daily Racing Form,* Equine Line, and *www.freerein.com/haynet/ shows.html* provide lists of tracks where sessions are offered.

Harness Horse Youth Foundation. 14950 Greyhound Court, Suite 210, Carmel, Indiana 46032. (317)848-5132. Publications available on a donation basis include: *Equine School and College Directory, Studying the Standardbred, Careers in the Harness Racing Industry.*

Harness Racing Museum and Hall of Fame. P.O. Box 590, Goshen, New York 10924. (914)294-6330.

Harness Tracks of America. 4640 E. Sunrise, Suite 200, Tucson, Arizona 85718. Fax: (520)529-3235. *harness@azstarnet.com.*

Hay net. *www.freerein.com/haynet/shows.html.* Web page developed by Karen Pautz lists current horse shows and events, including races and tracks by state, with contact information and racing dates.

Hilaman, Keith, Stable Superintendent. Arapahoe Park. P.O. Box 460370, Aurora, Colorado 80046.

Horse Industry Directory. American Horse Council. 1700 K Street NW, Suite 300, Washington, D.C. 20006. (202)296-4031.

IWN. Martin Schrick, Producer. On-Line Paramutuel Services. 5966 La Place Court Suite 100, Carlsbad, California 92008. (619)930-1101. *Martin@iwnonline.com.*

Jockey Club. 40 East 52nd Street, New York, New York 10022. (212)371-5970. Fax: (212)371-6123 and 821 Corporate Drive, Lexington, Kentucky 40503. (606)224-2700. Fax: (606)2242710. Thoroughbred registry. Maintains and publishes *The American Stud Book.*

Jockey Club Fact Book. Jockey Club. 821 Corporate Drive, Lexington, Kentucky 40503.

Jockeys' Guild. 250 West Main Street, Lexington, Kentucky 40507. (606)259-3211. Represents jockeys in insurance and benevolent matters.

Jockey News. Jockeys' Guild. 250 W. Main, #1820, Lexington, Kentucky 40507. (606)259-3211. Fax: (606)252-0938.

Kentucky Derby Museum. 704 Central Avenue, Louisville, Kentucky 40201. (502)637-1111.

Kentucky Museum and Horse Park. Bill Cooke, Museum Director. 4089 Iron Works Pike, Lexington, Kentucky 40511-8400. (606)233-4303. *http://www.imh.org* and *imh.org/imh/ nmr/nmrmain.html.*

Mayberry Racing Stables. Roger Thomas. P.O. Box 1954, Costa Mesa, California 92628. (888)402-4859.

Millen, Maureen M. *Racehorse Trainers Complete Manual.* International Wholesale Video. Baytown, Texas 77521.

National Horse Racing Museum. 99 High Street, New Market, Suffolk, CB8 8JL, England. 0638-667333.

National Museum of Racing and Hall of Fame. Field Horne, Curator. 191 Union Avenue, Saratoga Springs, New York 40511. (800)562-5394.

Pacific Coast Quarter Horse Racing Association. 4961 Katella, P.O. Box 919, Los Alamitos, California 90720. (714)236-1755. E-mail: *pcqhra@kaiwan.com.*

Thoroughbred Owners and Breeders Association. P.O. Box 4367, Lexington, Kentucky 40544. (606)276-2291. *http://www.toba.org.*

Thoroughbred Owners of California (TOC). *http://www.toconline.com.* An on-line racing guide. Includes information on acquiring a Thoroughbred, licensing, trainers, and farms.

Thoroughbred Racing Communications. Media Update. 40 East 52nd Street, New York, New York 10022. (212)371-5910.

Thoroughbred Times. Mark Simon, Editor-in-Chief. P.O. Box 8237, Lexington, Kentucky 40533. (606)260-9800.

United States Trotting Association. 750 Michigan Avenue, Columbus, Ohio 43215. (614)224-229. *http://www.ustrotting.com.* Publishes *Hoof Beats* magazine and *Hoof Pics* newsletter.

Zisk, Dr. John. P.O. Box 827, Jessup, Maryland 20794.

Polo Resources

Blackberry Polo Club. George Alexander. C/O United States Polo Association, 4059 Iron Works Pike, Lexington, Kentucky 40511.

Browne, Sherry. United States Polo Association. 4059 Iron works Pike, Lexington, Kentucky 40511.

Polo Training Foundation. 4059 Iron Works Pike, Lexington, Kentucky 40511. (888)783-7656.

United States Polo Association. 4059 Iron Works Pike, Lexington, Kentucky 40511. (606)255-0593. (800)232-8772.

Chapter Eleven

Rodeo Professions

Action, danger, extraordinary skill, the thrill of cowboys in action, wild and wonderfully trained horses, bulls, clowns, entertainment, fellowship, food — no wonder thousands of people have discovered the world of rodeo.

Rodeos began back in the 1800s, during the era of the great cattle drives. Seeking relief from hard days on the trail or at the

ranch, hands from various outfits gathered to compete in impromptu roping and riding competitions. These spontaneous gatherings became loosely organized contests, and rodeo was born.

AN ORGANIZATION FOR RODEO COWBOYS

In 1929 rodeo received its first formal recognition when a group of North American rodeo promoters, called the Rodeo Association of America, honored their first annual champion cowboys. In 1936, contestants joined together in the Cowboy Turtle Association (named to reflect the slow process it took to unite). Goals of the organization included acquiring fair prize money, consistent judging procedures, and honest advertising for rodeo. The name changed to the Rodeo Cowboy Association in 1945 and in 1975 the current name of Professional Rodeo Cowboys Association (PRCA) was adopted.

Today PRCA has a membership of more than 12,000 contestants, stock contractors, committee members, and contract personnel. In 1997 PRCA sanctioned approximately 750 rodeos with prize money totaling more than $26 million. The purse at the National Finals Rodeo has increased from the initial $50,000 in 1959 to $3.4 million in 1997. Attendance at National Finals has grown from 47,027 to 170,000.

PRCA sanctions about 30 percent of the rodeos in the United States; 50 percent are sanctioned by smaller rodeo associations and 20 percent are not sanctioned.

PRCA — Leader in Rodeo

PRCA developed a detailed list of rules designed to protect the welfare of animals. While 30 percent of the rodeos in the country are PRCA sanctioned, nearly 80 percent have adopted the PRCA guidelines. These rules are strictly enforced at all rodeos.

Two of the twelve salaried PRCA professional judges, or two contract judges, officiate at all PRCA-sanctioned rodeos. All judges must attend Wrangler-sponsored clinics and have a thorough knowledge of the rule book. It is the judges' responsibility to score all rides, guarantee that all the rules are followed, and ensure that all animals are treated humanely. In addition, each rodeo performance or slack must have an on-site veterinarian to further ensure the compliance of these rules and attend to the welfare of the animals.

PRCA Employment Opportunities

The 65 staff positions at PRCA provide employment opportunities for people with a variety of skills, including public relations personnel, secretaries, accountants, animal welfare control staff, and computer and data entry operators. PRCA personnel work year round providing services essential to running successful rodeos. PRCA manages PROCOM, a computerized telecommunication entry system, which allows cowboys to enter several rodeos by making one call. Some cowboys enter as many as 125 rodeos a year, and this system greatly simplifies the procedure. PROCOM handles an average of 1,918 calls a day or roughly 700,000 calls a year.

Employees of PRCA

Sherry Compton and Melissa Sauer work as media specialists for PRCA. Each year in conjunction with ESPN and Winner Communications, their department produces videos of eleven televised rodeos, including the National Finals Rodeo. Sherry has been with PRCA for eighteen years. Her interest began partly because of her husband Kenny's interest in team roping. He is a Gold Card Member of PRCA and was the original operations manager of the ProRodeo Hall of Fame where he was involved in all aspects of collection and design. Continuing in the family tradition are her son Beau, a first-year member of PRCA, and daughter Courtney. Both compete in team roping.

Melissa, a 1996 Colorado State University equine science graduate, worked for several trainers during school and after graduation, then applied for and received the position at PRCA. With evenings and weekends off, Melissa is able to use the judging expertise she gained at Colorado State University to periodically judge. On some evenings she gives riding lessons.

Although most of Sherry's and Melissa's work is in the office, they both meet rodeo contestants and members, and travel each year to the National Finals Rodeo. Their jobs did not require that they have experience with horses, but their horse backgrounds attracted both of them to PRCA.

A look at the contract employees of PRCA provides great insight into the general subject of rodeo employment opportunities. PRCA issues a yearly *Contract Personnel Directory*, which includes descriptions of contract workers, career titles, and other information.

Terri Greer, formerly the PRCA representative for the Animal Welfare Council, an organization of concerned animal groups, helped found the council in 1995. When Terri joined the PRCA staff she brought with her an equine science degree, background as a professional barrel racer, experience as a manager of a large Thoroughbred farm in California, director of the veterinary hospitals for the Santa Anita Race Track and Hollywood Park Race Track, and director of Rancho Santa Fe Veterinary Hospital in California. It was in this latter position that Terri's involvement with animal welfare began. When the hospital began a search for a race track representative to work in the area of humane treatment of animals and animals rights, Terri's genuine concern and knowledge surfaced. No educational program exists for this position — just experience, personal involvement, research, and initiative.

Several years later when PRCA was looking for someone to represent them in animal welfare issues, Terri provided the perfect match. Her duties included acting as a liaison between the rodeo and other animal rights organizations, attending legislative hearings, researching humane issues, presenting facts, communicating with the media, and writing informative publications. Much of her work involved counteracting accusations of extremist animal rights organizations. Although still actively involved with animal welfare, Terri opened a consulting agency in Texas, Cowboy's Unlimited, where she represents professional rodeo athletes.

PRORODEO HALL OF FAME

The ProRodeo Hall of Fame and Museum of the American Cowboy present a wonderful array of multimedia events depicting the development of rodeo, historic exhibits, art, and displays of the gear of today's cowboy. A Hall of Champions honors athletes and rodeo contributors.

Pat Hildebrand, executive director of the Hall of Fame, has a B.A. and an M.A. in history, with employment experience in historic house museums. Presently there are three other employees in the administrative department: an assistant administrator and two staff in charge of membership and program development, who oversee the Hall of Fame Society and the Associate Member Program. Five employees work in Visitor Services as tour guides and in the museum store. The Hall of Fame completed a $4.4 million expansion in 1996. Plans for staff and program expansion are ongoing.

RODEO AT ITS BEST: CHEYENNE FRONTIER DAYS

Cheyenne Frontier Days is one of many PRCA-sanctioned rodeos, yet it provides a wonderful example of rodeo at its best. Dubbed the "daddy of 'em all," Cheyenne Frontier Days was voted the Best Rodeo by PRCA from 1992 to 1996. The celebrations date back to the 1800s. In 1867, General Greenville Dodge chose Cheyenne for a railroad stop. Thirty years later, when the cattle industry joined the railroad, the town boomed. E.A Slack insisted that this booming town needed a celebration and he solicited the town's support. On September 23, 1897, 4,000 people gathered for festivities, carnival, competition, and money purses. The following year, Buffalo Bill participated in Cheyenne Frontier Days, and a tradition that remains a highlight in Cheyenne life was underway. Today more than 300,000 people gather annually to share in this celebration of the old West, and movie stars and politicians are often numbered among the guests.

Cheyenne Frontier Days provide income opportunities for stock contractors, trainers, clowns, arena workers, concession stand employees, community businesses, farrier and veterinary services. Cheyenne merchants do approximately 25 percent of their yearly business in just ten days. Property owners inflate their leases during the summer rodeo months. The cowboys' purses that started out at $5 each now run as high $10,000.

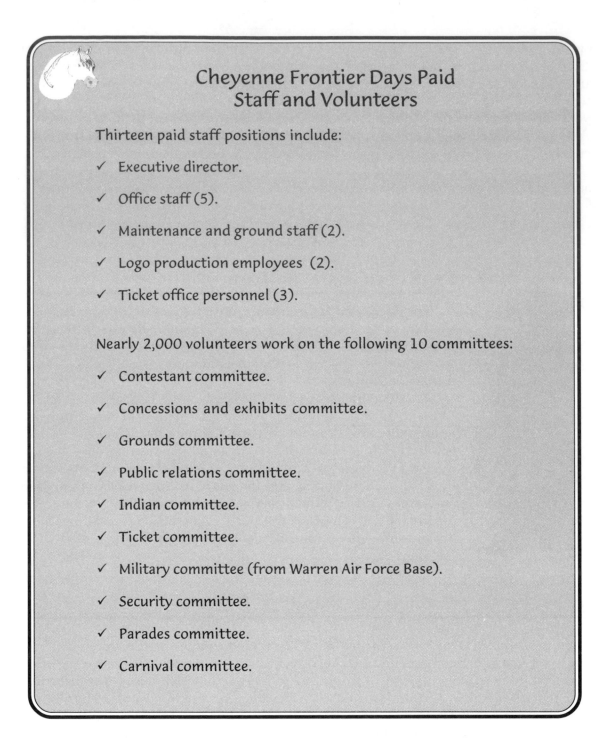

Cheyenne Frontier Days Paid Staff and Volunteers

Thirteen paid staff positions include:

✓ Executive director.

✓ Office staff (5).

✓ Maintenance and ground staff (2).

✓ Logo production employees (2).

✓ Ticket office personnel (3).

Nearly 2,000 volunteers work on the following 10 committees:

✓ Contestant committee.

✓ Concessions and exhibits committee.

✓ Grounds committee.

✓ Public relations committee.

✓ Indian committee.

✓ Ticket committee.

✓ Military committee (from Warren Air Force Base).

✓ Security committee.

✓ Parades committee.

✓ Carnival committee.

Insights from Committee Members

From 1995 to 1997 Phil Van Horn served as the general chairman for the Cheyenne Frontier Days rodeo and celebrations. Over the previous eighteen years, Phil had volunteered on the security committee, and he hasn't missed a year volunteering since. He loves rodeo, loves his community, and willingly pays his own expenses as he volunteers hundreds of hours each year. He feels it is a great honor to be general chairman.

Roger Schreiner, contestant chairman for Cheyenne Frontier Days in 1997, grew up just outside of Cheyenne. As a member of Saddle Tramps, a riding club for youth, he participated throughout his youth in the parades and grand entries. Today, after 20 years of working on various committees, he chairs the contestant committee, which is comprised of 125 volunteers. This committee's responsibilities include hiring clowns, bullfighters, stock contractors, the announcer, collecting entry fees (with the help of PRCA), calculating and distributing purses, organizing the cattle drive, manning all the arena gates, and organizing the Calcutta. The Calcutta is a money raiser that gives spectators an opportunity to bid on projected winners and to win money along with the contestants. Ten percent of the money raised goes to charities.

Roger calculates that from September to January he puts in more than 1,000 hours as committee chairman. Like Phil Van Horn, Roger pays his own expenses. Rodeo and Cheyenne are part of his heritage and the heritage of his country, and he, too, considers it an honor to be a part of the "daddy of 'em all."

Purse Calculation

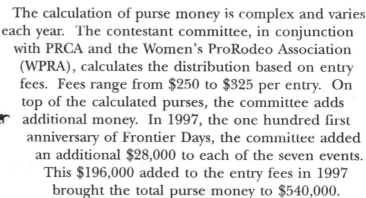

The calculation of purse money is complex and varies each year. The contestant committee, in conjunction with PRCA and the Women's ProRodeo Association (WPRA), calculates the distribution based on entry fees. Fees range from $250 to $325 per entry. On top of the calculated purses, the committee adds additional money. In 1997, the one hundred first anniversary of Frontier Days, the committee added an additional $28,000 to each of the seven events. This $196,000 added to the entry fees in 1997 brought the total purse money to $540,000.

For each event there are two "go rounds" plus the finals. Purses are awarded to the top eight contestants of each go round and to the top four places in the finals. Out of 1,400 entrants, about ten percent, or 140 cowboys, are money winners.

Contestant Selection

Cheyenne rodeo contestants are selected with deference to past world champions, to Cheyenne Frontier Day winners from the past two years, and to top cumulative rodeo money winners as of June 15 of the current year. The remaining entrants' names are placed in the PRCA computer and selected randomly.

Volunteering

Volunteering provides wonderful opportunities to work around rodeo, but the contact with horses is minimal. Roger Schreiner estimates that only six Cheyenne Frontier Day committee people have the opportunity to feed the livestock. Most of the cowboys who work around the stock are hired by the stock contractor or the contestants themselves.

ON THE SCENE — RODEO WORKERS

Announcers

The PRCA directory lists 135 full-time, part-time, and aspiring announcers, all of whom can play an important role in a sport in which 88 percent of the contestants participate with a horse. Basic skills for a rodeo announcer include a knowledge of rodeo, an understanding of events, familiarity with horses, speaking and commentary skills, and the ability to entertain a crowd. If you love and understand rodeo and have a bit of the entertainer and sportscaster in you, this may be just the career for you.

Hadley Barrett, Rodeo Announcer. A successful announcer spends a lot time around horses and must have a thorough knowledge of horses. Hadley Barrett, born and raised on a ranch in Nebraska, now owns and operates this ranch. He also has a small ranch in Kersey, Colorado. He began riding at an early age and has competed in nearly every rodeo event. Hadley not only runs his ranches from horseback, he often announces rodeos from the saddle.

At the age of sixteen, Hadley formed a dance band, Hadley Barrett and the Westerners, and traveled the rodeo circuit simultaneously performing for dances and participating in rodeos. When a friend asked him to fill in as announcer, a combined career of announcer, contestant, and band leader began. As the years progressed, competing and performing took back stage to announcing.

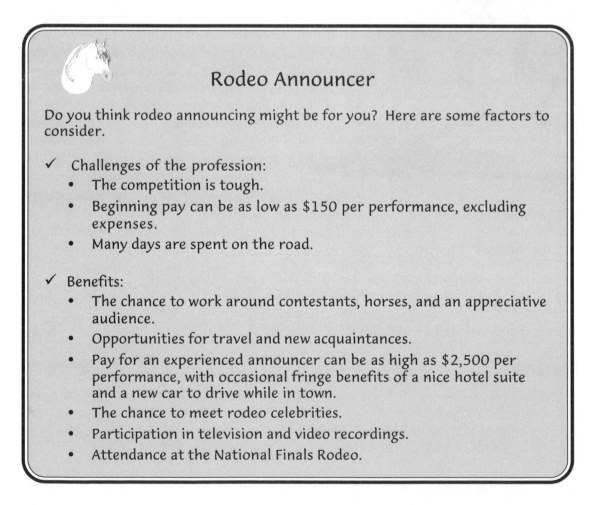

Rodeo Announcer

Do you think rodeo announcing might be for you? Here are some factors to consider.

✓ Challenges of the profession:
  • The competition is tough.
  • Beginning pay can be as low as $150 per performance, excluding expenses.
  • Many days are spent on the road.

✓ Benefits:
  • The chance to work around contestants, horses, and an appreciative audience.
  • Opportunities for travel and new acquaintances.
  • Pay for an experienced announcer can be as high as $2,500 per performance, with occasional fringe benefits of a nice hotel suite and a new car to drive while in town.
  • The chance to meet rodeo celebrities.
  • Participation in television and video recordings.
  • Attendance at the National Finals Rodeo.

Hadley's rewards are many. He is the only person nominated fourteen times for Announcer of the Year. For ten years he served as the television anchor announcer for the National Finals Rodeo. He was selected announcer of the National Finals Rodeo four times, the Canadian Finals Rodeo six times, and the ESPN National Finals Interviewer from 1994 to 1996.

Hadley attributes a great deal of his success to his background as both contestant and entertainer. Spectators wouldn't dispute that, but they would add several other obvious attributes. Whether large or small, Hadley takes each rodeo assignment seriously by spending hours in preparation. He is sensitive to his audience, and realizes that many fans have limited rodeo backgrounds. As he provides information that will not overwhelm the audience, will elicit their attention, and help guests feel they are a part of the event, he is careful not to insult the veteran rodeo fan. When an injury occurs he talks his audience through it in a calm, reassuring manner. His great voice, arena presence, gift of humor, and positive attitude make him a very popular announcer.

Tips from the Experts — Hadley Barrett, Announcer

- Carefully evaluate your rodeo knowledge and communication skills.

- Study and spend time around animals.

- Examine the many facets of rodeo.

- Learn the art of entertaining.

- Attend a rodeo school and/or clinics on announcing.

- Enroll in a drama class or broadcasting school.

- Develop communication skills. Observe successful people in the field and take classes.

- Learn to read without sounding like you are reading.

- Study audiences. Don't assume they are knowledgeable, yet don't offend the knowledgeable.

- Don't overload an audience with information by sounding like a walking rodeo dictionary.

- Poll your audiences. Never assume, even in a place where rodeo is well ingrained, that the audience knows a lot about rodeo.

- Crawl before you walk. If you get ahead of yourself, it will show up. One bad performance stands out more than a dozen successes.

- Don't try to impress others.

Barrelmen, Clowns, and Bullfighters

Horses! Cowboys! Rodeos! They all seem to go hand in hand. Can you imagine a rodeo without cowboys or horses? And can you imagine a rodeo without clowns? These skilled athletes entertain and provide comic relief and that is the side of clowns that spectators see, but rodeo contestants perceive the risks clowns take every time they enter the arena with the cowboys and rodeo stock. Rodeo clowns are there to protect the cowboys.

More than 200 barrelmen, clowns, and bullfighters are listed in the PRCA *Contract Personnel Directory*. Some specialize in one area, and others possess a combination of skills. Individuals set their own rates, which vary from $200 to $1,200 per performance. Expenses are usually the responsibility of the performer and must be calculated into fees. Smaller rodeos usually seek one person with combined bull fighting, barrel, and specialty act skills. There can be one to twenty performances per rodeo. With the increasing popularity of indoor arenas, more rodeos are held during the winter, so more job opportunities exist.

Other rodeo specialty acts include horse, dog, and buffalo acts, trick roping, acrobatics, trick riding, Roman riding, and comedy packages.

Quail Dobbs, **Rodeo Clown**. Quail Dobbs joined the rodeo circuit as a bull rider during his teen years. In 1962 he was working a rodeo in Buffalo, Minnesota, when George Doak encouraged him to get in the barrel. Quail complied and his 33-year career as a rodeo clown began. Each year he takes part in 25 to 35 rodeos. In 1996, at the one-hundredth anniversary of the Cheyenne Frontier Days, Quail was given a special award for having performed 25 consecutive years. Among Quail's other honors are innumerable awards. Four times he has received the Coors Man Can Award, which comes with a $3,000 silver buckle and $10,000 first place purse.

Tips from the Experts — Quail Dobbs, Rodeo Clown

- Attend a good bull fighting school.

- Be competitive and realistic when establishing rates. If rates are too high, you will price yourself out of the market. If rates are too low, you will not be able to make an adequate living.

- Be flexible.

- Acquire a broad base of skills. A bull fighter/ barrel man with an act has a better chance of acquiring a job than one who is specialized.

- Enjoy traveling.

- Love people.

- Plan for your future and retirement.

- As a self-employed person, keep good records.

When Quail began his career, a recommendation by a clown in good standing was required to obtain a PRCA clown card. Today training and certification involve performance and subsequent screening at the bull sale in Las Vegas, membership in PRCA, yearly PRCA dues, and PRCA certification. If laughter, being around cowboys and horses, new adventures, travel, the adrenaline flow that comes from exposure to risk and danger, coupled with the festive environment of rodeo sound exciting, then maybe this is a job for you.

Pickup Men

The pickup man's duties are only slightly less dangerous than those of the rodeo clown, but most spectators don't realize how essential this rodeo hand is. He rides alongside a bucking, kicking bronc, helps the rider to the ground, releases the bronc's flank strap, and gets the bronc back to the catch pen. Sometimes the pickup man has to help free a rider who has been thrown and is hung up in the rigging. All of this is accomplished at a hard run. Pickup men are also responsible for moving bulls back to their pens after they have been ridden (or, more likely, not ridden), which sometimes requires roping the huge animals and dragging them to the pen gate when the bulls will not be driven.

Stock Contractors and Rodeo Producers

There are 71 stock contractors associated with PRCA. Supplying the livestock for the roughstock events (bareback bronc riding, saddle bronc riding, and bull riding) and the timed events (steer wrestling, team roping, and calf roping) are the stock contractors' responsibilities.

Some stock contractors also serve as rodeo producers, which means they handle all aspects of the rodeo, including hiring laborers, promotion, and the production of the opening ceremonies. Establishing a working relationship with the rodeo producer can be very advantageous for a new specialty act, bull fighter, clown, or announcer. The pay may be a little low, but the quantity of performances more than makes up for it.

Harry Vold, Stock Contractor. Rodeo is not only part of America's Western heritage, it is also part of Harry Vold's. As he provides stock for rodeos throughout the country, produces rodeos, and serves as a volunteer on innumerable PRCA committees, he has one key objective: the preservation of the unique place the horse has in American history. Used throughout history for the pony express, cattle drives, farming, and transportation, horses are dear to Harry. At his ranch, an area is set aside as a cemetery to honor special horses and livestock. His home, part of which is a nearly 160-year-old adobe building, tastefully displays mementos of his cowboy career, including the mounted heads of two of his award winning bulls.

The beginning of the Harry Vold Rodeo Company had its roots in Canada in the 1940s when a Montana stock contractor, Leo Cremer, sent a buyer to Canada to purchase horses. Harry was involved in auctioneering and buying and reselling horses. He bucked out horses, bought the best, and resold them to Leo's buyer. Pleased with the stock, Leo eliminated the middle man and dealt directly with Harry. On one occasion when Harry purchased 20 horses for Leo, an outbreak of hoof and mouth disease in Mexico closed not only the Mexican border but all United States borders. Harry was stuck with a truck load of horses. Unable to sell them, he offered the horses to a local stampede (rodeo) to give the horses the chance to buck. Initially the committee refused his offer but by the second day of the stampede it was obvious that the previously contracted horses were road weary. Harry's fresh well-fed horses were substituted. They stole the show. A neighboring town, impressed with the fresh stock, hired Harry and his horses for their rodeo. Harry was now an auctioneer and a rodeo stock contractor. His rodeo businesses grew.

Before establishing a private rodeo company in the states, Harry became a partner in Beutler Brothers Rodeo Company in Elk City, Oklahoma. Soon thereafter the partnership bought out Harry Knight's operation. When complications developed, Harry formed the Harry Vold Rodeo Company, a successful operation that produces or supplies stock for many rodeos.

For 21 years Harry has been the stock contractor for Cheyenne Frontier Days, an honor he doesn't take lightly. Most rodeos buck 20 horses a day — Cheyenne bucks 65. Most rodeos buck 12 bulls a day — Cheyenne bucks 40 or 45. This fast-paced, action-oriented rodeo is the only rodeo for which Harry hires stock subcontractors. More than 1,700 animals are a part of this celebration, including nearly 400 calves, 600 steers, 400 bucking and saddle horses, and 75 parade horses.

In addition to hiring subcontractors, Harry hires about 50 local people to help on feed, sorting, and arena crews, and to help with the overall organization of livestock and events. About seven regular crew members (the livestock superintendent, cowboys, and transport drivers) travel with Harry. Harry prefers to transport the livestock himself, rather than contract out that function. His cowboys know the horses' needs and the best way to position and load them to keep them fit to buck. The crew members who travel to rodeos with Harry make around $25,000 a year each, and they often work other jobs.

Harry's 25,000 acre ranch, located east of Pueblo, Colorado, consists of semi-arid range land

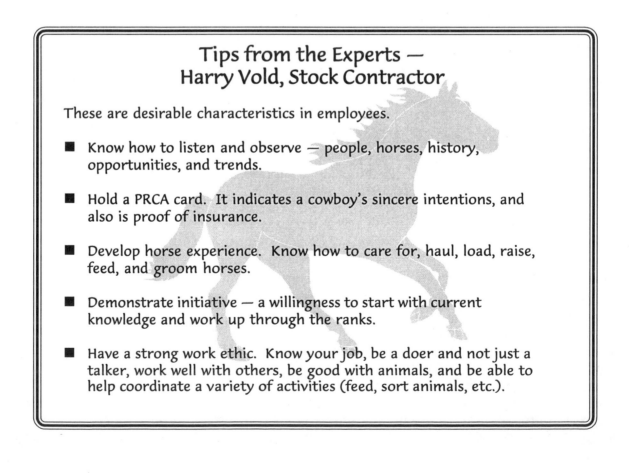

Tips from the Experts — Harry Vold, Stock Contractor

These are desirable characteristics in employees.

- Know how to listen and observe — people, horses, history, opportunities, and trends.

- Hold a PRCA card. It indicates a cowboy's sincere intentions, and also is proof of insurance.

- Develop horse experience. Know how to care for, haul, load, raise, feed, and groom horses.

- Demonstrate initiative — a willingness to start with current knowledge and work up through the ranks.

- Have a strong work ethic. Know your job, be a doer and not just a talker, work well with others, be good with animals, and be able to help coordinate a variety of activities (feed, sort animals, etc.).

ideal for raising rough stock. There is plenty of feed and water. Breeding is done by live coverage. Harry has neighbors who assist with rounding up the stock before a rodeo. A retired person lives on the ranch full time.

Throughout his career, Harry has owned five horses that held Saddle Bronc of the Year titles and he has earned eleven Bucking Stock of the Year awards. He was inducted in the Canadian Hall of Fame, named *Honorable Chief Many Horses* by the Sarcee Indians, received eleven out of fourteen Stock Contractor of the Year awards, and received numerous awards for having top bucking horses at the National Finals Rodeo (elected by peer stock contractors). One of Harry's most meaningful awards came in 1995 when, after previously declining the honor several times because he felt he wasn't worthy, he was inducted into the ProRodeo Cowboy Hall of Fame.

When it comes to animals, Harry is especially proud of Bobby Joe Skoal, a three-time winner of the Bucking Bronc of the Year title. Bobby Joe Skoal was ridden six times by All Round Cowboy of the Year Ty Murray. This horse was bred and raised by Harry, as part of his Born to Buck program. In the early 1970s Harry realized that the bucking horse supply was dwindling. Breeding bucking horses was a relatively novel idea in those days, but Harry bred some of his mares to General Custer who belonged to Mr. Feeke Tooke, a pioneer in the breeding of bucking horses. This successful endeavor was the inception of a winning line of bucking broncs. Today he breeds about 100 mares a year with an average foal crop of 80. Fewer than 30 percent become bucking horses.

Harry's wife, Karen, loves the "cowboy way" as much as Harry. A trick rider herself, she met Harry in the 1970s at a rodeo. Today she travels extensively with him. She says their secluded ranch is the perfect get away, and it also provides excellent facilities for her trick riding schools. Her husband, she says, is in great demand as a rodeo stock contractor, an auctioneer, and PRCA volunteer because he is fair, concerned, honest, and has dedicated his whole life to rodeo.

Other Rodeo Personnel

Rodeo secretaries. Recording contestant times, figuring payoffs, and paying the winning cowboys are among the responsibilities of rodeo secretaries. More than 50 secretaries are listed in the PRCA *Contract Personnel Directory.*

Timers. Several hundred timers, both insured and uninsured, are listed in the directory. Timers keep the official time of the timed events and sound the infamous eight second buzzer in roughstock events.

Chute laborers. Responsibilities are loading the chutes with cattle, steers, calves, broncs, and bulls.

Photographers. The 1997 directory lists 45 photographers.

Permit holders. Applicants for contestant cards must first become permit holders and fill their permits by earning $1,000 (in an unlimited numbers of years) at sanctioned PRCA rodeos. Many PRCA rodeos allow permit holders to compete. In 1995, 3,855 cowboys held permits.

ON THE SCENE — THE CONTESTANTS

Rodeo is one of the fastest growing sports in the nation, and it is the only sport that grew out of the skills required in a work situation. While rodeo is a hobby for most competitors, it is also a career, sometimes a lucrative one, for many cowboys. In 1996, a total of 6,894 contestants competed, which was a 6 percent increase over the previous year. Together, 10,749 permit holders and contestants comprise 65 percent of the PRCA membership.

Top competitors can earn $20,000 to $30,000 at some of the season's riches rodeos with yearly earnings exceeding $100,000 in a single event in a given year. In 1996, the total earnings by contestants were $24,510,585. Prize money was earned by 4,759 contestants, and the average earning was $5,044. The career earnings of Mark Garret, the top bareback rider at the National Finals Rodeo, totaled $586,605, with just his 1996 earnings coming to $139,868. The 1996 bareback rider who ranked at the one-hundredth level earned $5,808.

There is money to be earned — $25.4 million dollars in prize money from PRCA sanctioned rodeos alone — and PRCA rodeos only represent 30 percent of all the rodeos in the country. But it is not easy money. It takes tremendous dedication to be a winner.

Kristie Peterson and Bozo at the Western States Circuit Finals. Photo courtesy of Karen Gleason.

Women and Rodeo

Rodeo is not just a sport for men. In 1948, the Women's Professional Rodeo Association (WPRA) began with 74 members. Today around 2,000 members participate in approximately 780 sanctioned PRCA rodeos, with prize money exceeding the $2.5 million mark.

The Professional Women's Rodeo Association, under the umbrella of WPRA, has approximately 130 members who participate in women's rodeos. Women compete at these rodeos in several timed events and riding competitions similar to the men's, including calf and steer roping and rough stock riding events.

Barrel racing is the only women's event to be held regularly at most PRCA rodeos. The sport demonstrates the skill of the rider working in unison with an exceptionally fast and specially trained horse in a race against the clock. In 1997 Kristie Peterson won her second straight and third overall world title by placing first at the National Finals Rodeo in Las Vegas. Her 1997 earnings were $165,238, bringing her career earnings since 1991 to a total of $694,542.

Part-Time Cowboys

PRCA has twelve regional circuits. The circuit system offers regional and national titles as well as competitions close to home for cowboys who want to compete on the weekends while continuing to work or go to school.

Kelly Wardell, Bareback Bronc Rider

A Bachelor of Science degree in welding and agricultural mechanics may not appear to be a likely background for the bareback bronc rider ranked ninth at the 1997 National Finals Rodeo, but that is the college degree Kelly Wardell earned as he participated in rodeo throughout his college years. His dad, a breeder of racing Quarter Horses, was a rodeo contestant himself, and Kelly figures rodeo is just in his blood.

Among his idols and friends is Joe Alexander, a five-time bareback bronc riding world champion. After Kelly's first encounter with Joe, he knew exactly what he wanted to do. His mom wasn't so sure, but she finally realized Kelly was single minded and gave in. From then on, bareback horses and Kelly have been constant partners. Kelly never had the opportunity to attend rodeo school, but he feels it would have been advantageous.

Riggings, style, techniques, and judges' expectations continually change. The things Kelly learned from the top bareback bronc riders of the past, needed to be replaced with new techniques and strategies. But Kelly was determined. He participated in rodeos as often as he could. For financing, he developed a small business using his welding skills to make spurs, feeders, and breeding chutes. He is in the process of creating a bareback riding machine that accurately simulates an authentic ride. He also works for his dad periodically, at the race track, and in construction.

In 1984, Kelly applied for his Professional Rodeo Cowboy Association (PRCA) permit. With this permit, he needed to earn $1,000 in PRCA sanctioned rodeos to receive his full status card that would allow him to enter any PRCA Rodeo. In February of 1984 he placed in the money, but it was not until October, 1984 that he once again placed in the money.

Many factors go into a win: the luck of the draw, the judges, mental attitude, and ability. Kelly figures that a contestant's worst enemy is his attitude. For seven years, Kelly had pretty lean earnings, which made maintaining a positive attitude difficult. Winning seems to beget winning, says Kelly, but when you feel you must win, the pressure can work against you.

After a seven-year losing streak Kelly was out of money with debts mounting. He decided if he lost at Houston that year, he would quit rodeo. A special golf tournament for cowboys and businessmen was part of the Houston pre-rodeo schedule and that was where Kelly met Gene Grant, the owner of Cadillac Ranch Western Wear. Gene became Kelly's sponsor. That year Kelly finished in the top 30 in the world.

Kelly placed twelfth at the 1996 National Finals Rodeo, earning $67,166, and went on to place ninth at the 1997 National Finals, earning $82,854. An added honor came when the fans elected Kelly as their favorite, and he received the Original Coors Fans' Favorite Cowboy of the Year plaque and a $5,000 bonus.

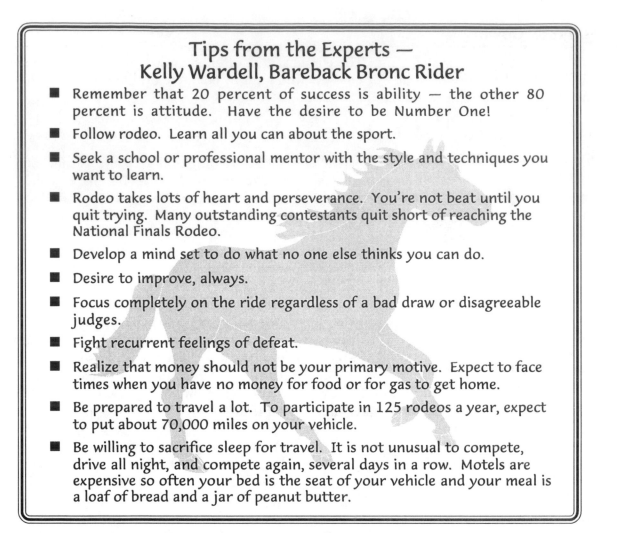

Tips from the Experts —
Kelly Wardell, Bareback Bronc Rider

- Remember that 20 percent of success is ability — the other 80 percent is attitude. Have the desire to be Number One!

- Follow rodeo. Learn all you can about the sport.

- Seek a school or professional mentor with the style and techniques you want to learn.

- Rodeo takes lots of heart and perseverance. You're not beat until you quit trying. Many outstanding contestants quit short of reaching the National Finals Rodeo.

- Develop a mind set to do what no one else thinks you can do.

- Desire to improve, always.

- Focus completely on the ride regardless of a bad draw or disagreeable judges.

- Fight recurrent feelings of defeat.

- Realize that money should not be your primary motive. Expect to face times when you have no money for food or for gas to get home.

- Be prepared to travel a lot. To participate in 125 rodeos a year, expect to put about 70,000 miles on your vehicle.

- Be willing to sacrifice sleep for travel. It is not unusual to compete, drive all night, and compete again, several days in a row. Motels are expensive so often your bed is the seat of your vehicle and your meal is a loaf of bread and a jar of peanut butter.

Kelly is the Cowboy Bareback Bronc Riding Representative to PRCA, a distinction he doesn't take lightly because his fellow cowboys elected him. Kelly will be in rodeo for some years yet. Afterwards, he hopes to open a bareback school with an on-site bunk house and an indoor arena. Today most schools run two to three days, but Kelly hopes to run a week-long school with reasonable rates that will allow more young people to follow their dreams as he pursued his.

Why does Kelly stick with rodeo? He loves the camaraderie with rodeo friends who help each other, share their knowledge, and want their peers to succeed. Every horse, every ride, and every rodeo produce a unique excitement and challenge. And Kelly likes the experience of being on the road. Rodeo is in his blood. Kelly feels he is fortunate to be able to turn his passion into his lifestyle.

CONCLUSION

Rodeo is exciting. The competition, for contestants, stock contractors, specialty acts, and announcers, is great. All participants are self-employed, and must arrange their own benefits, such as vacation, retirement, and insurance. They also have to keep excellent records for tax purposes. There is a financial risk for contestants. Only an estimated 7 to 11 percent are winners at any individual rodeo.

RESOURCES

American Quarter Horse Association. P.O. Box 200, Amarillo, Texas 79168. (806)376-4811.

Barrett, Hadley. 2547 Weld County Road 50, Kersey, Colorado 80644.

Compton, Sherry, Media Specialist. Professional Rodeo Cowboy Association. 101 Pro Rodeo Drive, Colorado Springs, Colorado 80919. (719)593-8840.

Cowboy's Unlimited. Terri Greer. 224 N. Main Street, Weatherford, Texas 76086. (817)341-0703.

Dobbs, Quail. P.O. Box 288, Coahoma, Texas 79511.

Hildebrand, Pat, Executive Director. ProRodeo Association Hall of Fame and Museum. 101 Pro Rodeo Drive, Colorado Springs, Colorado 80919. (719)593-8840.

Internet: For a general search, use a search engine to call up Rodeo.

> American Professional Rodeo Clown and Bullfighter Association. *http://www.prorodeoinfo.com/apb.htm.*
>
> *http://www.gunslinger.com/rodeo.html.* Lists college, local, women's, specialty, and upcoming rodeos that can be directly accessed for specifics, with links to other pages.
>
> Fellowship of Christian Cowboys, Inc. *http://www.geocities.comYosemite/Trails/2976/index.html.*
>
> *http://www.cowgirls.com/dream/jan/rodeo.htm.* Numerous links to rodeo pages.
>
> *http://www.npra.com/frmain.htm.* Lists upcoming events and rodeos, standings and earnings, and links to other rodeo pages.
>
> *http://roughstock.com/wayte.* Lists rodeo-related schools.

Miss Rodeo America. 27906 Cumbers, Pueblo, Colorado. (719)948-9206.

NHSRA Times. 11178 N. Huron Street #7, Denver, Colorado 80234. (303)452-0820. Monthly newspaper of the National High School Rodeo Association.

Partain, Kyle. "NFR First Takes Root in 1958 Meeting." *ProRodeo Sports News.* January 14, 1998. Page 26. 101 Pro Rodeo Drive, Colorado Springs, Colorado 80919. (719)593-8840. Fax: (719)548-4876. *http://www.prorodeo.com.*

Partain, Kyle. "Bozo Doesn't Clown Around at NFR." *ProRodeo Sports News: 1997 Year-End Edition.* December 1997. Page 55. 101 Pro Rodeo Drive, Colorado Springs, Colorado 80919. (719)593-8840. Fax: (719)548-4876. *http://www.prorodeo.com.*

Partain, Kyle. "Kelly Wardell Takes Fans' Favorite Award" *ProRodeo Sports News.* December 17,1997. Page 13. 101 Pro Rodeo Drive, Colorado Springs, Colorado 80919. (719)593-8840. Fax: (719)548-4876. *http://www.prorodeo.com.*

Professional Rodeo Cowboys Association. 101 Pro Rodeo Drive, Colorado Springs, Colorado 80919. (719)593-8840. *http://www.prorodeo.com.* Rodeo schedules, sponsor information, event descriptions, publications are available by mail or on their site. Resources: *PRCA Annual Report; Articles of Incorporation, By Laws and Rules; Committee Guide: Your Handbook for a Successful Rodeo; Contract Personnel Directory; The Cowboy Sport: An Inside Look at Rodeo and Its Roots; Humane Facts: The Care and Treatment of Professional Rodeo Livestock; Media Guide; Rodeo: The Demographics of Professional Rodeo.*

ProRodeo Hall of Fame and Museum of the American Cowboy. 101 Pro Rodeo Drive, Colorado Springs, Colorado 80919. (719)593-8840.

ProRodeo Sports News. 101 Pro Rodeo Drive, Colorado Springs, Colorado 80919. (719)593-8840. Fax: (719)548-4876. *http://www.prorodeo.com.* A weekly publication of the PRCA, with a special year-end edition that summarizes each year's activities.

Rodeo associations (non-PRCA):

American Cowboys Rodeo Association. 6147 W. Farm Road 18, Willard, Montana 65781. (417)742-4587.

American Junior Rodeo Association. 6029 Loop 306 S., San Angelo, Texas 76905. (915)651-2572.

American Professional Rodeo Association. 109 Curtis Avenue, Thorofore, New Jersey 08086. (609)384-1200.

Canadian Professional Rodeo Association. 223 2116 27th Avenue NE. Calgary, Alberta, Canada T2E 7A6. (403)250-7440.

Cowboys Professional Rodeo Association. P.O. Box 1151, Winnie, Texas 77665. (409)296-3255.

International Pro Rodeo Association. P.O. Box 83377, Oklahoma City, Oklahoma 73148. (405)235-6540.

National Intercollegiate Rodeo Association. 2316 Eastgate North. Street, Suite 160, Walla Walla, Washington 99362. (509)529-4402.

National Little Britches Rodeo Association. 1045 West Rio Grande, Colorado Springs, Colorado 80906. (719)576-0900.

National Senior Pro Rodeo Association. P.O. Box 419, Roundup, Montana 59072. (406)323-3380.

Professional Women's Rodeo Association. Route 5, Box 698, Blanchard, Oklahoma 73101.

Women's Professional Rodeo Association (WPRA). 1235 Lake Plaza Drive, Suite 134, Colorado Springs, Colorado 80906. (719)576-0900. *http://www.sanctum.com/rodeo/ wpra.htm.*

Rodeo Video. Box G 412 Main, Snowflake, Arizona 85937. (520)536-7111.

Saurer, Melissa, Media Specialist. Professional Rodeo Cowboy Association. 101 Pro Rodeo Drive, Colorado Springs, Colorado 80919. (719)593-8840.

Schreiner, Roger. 1800 Carey Avenue, Cheyenne, Wyoming 82001.

Van Horn, Phil. Wyoming Student Loan Corporation. P.O. Box 209, Cheyenne, Wyoming 82001.

Vold, Harry and Karen. Harry Vold Rodeo Company, Avondale, Colorado 81022.

Wardell, Kelly. Box 288, Bellevue, Idaho 83313. (208)788-9882.

Chapter Twelve

Horse Selling and Auctioneering

Horse sales take many forms and have many dimensions. Some people supplement their income by selling their own horses via referral, reputation, advertising, and on the Internet. Others, like Charles and Cheryl Weatherell (see Chapter Five), not only breed and train horses but operate a full-scale sales program using videos, photos, magazine advertisements, and attendance at horse expositions to promote their businesses. Still others take their horses to horse sales and auctions where buyers from miles around gather to purchase new stock.

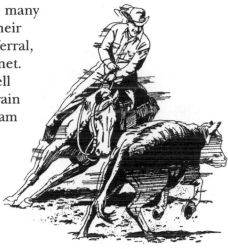

HORSE SALES

A growing trend in the sale of ranch horses is a competition prior to the sale. Sale horses compete in the following categories: handling the feet and ground tying, trailer loading and unloading, pattern work, boxing and fencing a steer, roping and pulling the steer, and working the gate.

Bobby Atwood of Koscuisko, Mississippi, has sold several horses at ranch horse sale competitions. In 1995, he had the top score at the ranch gelding competition in San Antonio. In 1996, three of the top six horses were his. Sale prices are unpredictable: one year the top horse sold for $21,000, but in 1996 the top price was $6,500.

Until about six years ago, Bobby bought, trained, and sold horses for a profit but never set foot in a sale ring. He now views sale rings as great places to obtain top dollar. Ranchers still look chiefly for ranch broke horses, but buyers looking for family horses, show horses, or event horses want top horses that can run, slide, and stop on four feet.

A seller needs to know what a buyer is looking for and Bobby makes it a point to keep in tune with the industry he loves. To prepare for shows, he carefully selects horses. Finding the best mounts for competitions is a challenge. He usually looks for trained horses with cow horse bloodlines (cutting or reining horses with a correctable problem that kept them from the show arena).

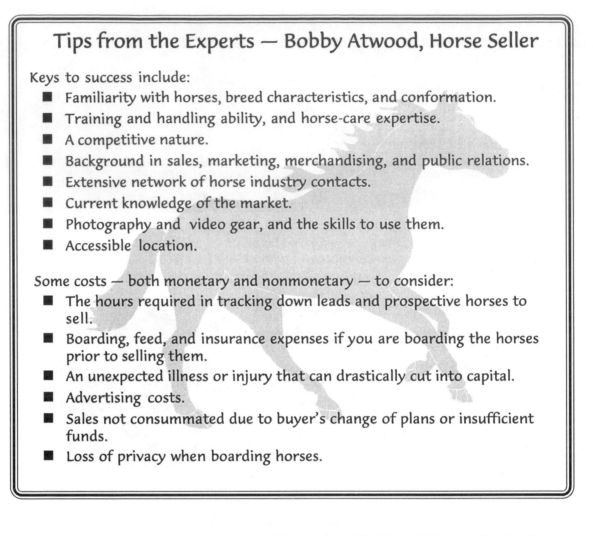

Tips from the Experts — Bobby Atwood, Horse Seller

Keys to success include:
- Familiarity with horses, breed characteristics, and conformation.
- Training and handling ability, and horse-care expertise.
- A competitive nature.
- Background in sales, marketing, merchandising, and public relations.
- Extensive network of horse industry contacts.
- Current knowledge of the market.
- Photography and video gear, and the skills to use them.
- Accessible location.

Some costs — both monetary and nonmonetary — to consider:
- The hours required in tracking down leads and prospective horses to sell.
- Boarding, feed, and insurance expenses if you are boarding the horses prior to selling them.
- An unexpected illness or injury that can drastically cut into capital.
- Advertising costs.
- Sales not consummated due to buyer's change of plans or insufficient funds.
- Loss of privacy when boarding horses.

Today in addition to sale competitions, Bobby works with 30 to 40 horses, buying horses that people have problems with, training the horses, and then carefully matching horses to buyers. The stereotype of the horse trader does not apply to Bobby — he has a reputation as a scrupulously honest, reputable, caring horse seller.

Bobby has a special soft spot for children and he spends time helping children with their horses. When one young boy asked for help training his horse, Bobby and his wife, Janice, spent an afternoon making a video for the boy. Bobby also visits elementary schools to help children understand horses and the horse business. Another new adventure is putting on roping and team penning clinics.

At one of his class reunions, his friends mentioned how fortunate he was to be doing what he always wanted to do. Bobby knows that not everyone is fortunate enough to have their high school dreams come true. Still, the horse sale business is difficult, time consuming, and often risky. Market prices, which follow the economy, tend to fluctuate widely.

AUCTIONEERING

The auction is an increasingly popular method of sale, according to Matthew Kruse of Reppert School of Auctioneering. People enjoy attending auctions, and if properly advertised and attended by buyers, an auction brings in the best dollar value for the product being sold.

There are more than 30 private schools throughout the United States. About ten are classified as National Auction Schools — schools that offer courses that cover all aspects of auctioneering. Other schools offer shorter courses that teach the certification knowledge needed to pass state licensing tests. However, not all states require certification. Check with your state professional licensing agency for specific requirements. The April 1997 issue of *The Auctioneer* contains a list and contact information for international and state auctioneer associations.

Auctioneering skills can be acquired by attending school, and also through an apprenticeship and working for an auctioneering company. National Auction Schools, such as Reppert and the World Wide College of Auctioneers, offer courses lasting ten days to two weeks. Instruction starts at 8:00 A.M. and extends to 9:00 P.M. Tuition is generally under $1,000. Curriculum includes preparation for state testing, instruction on bid calling, running a business, advertising, developing a clientele, clerking, cashiering, setting up a computer program, and running a profitable, organized show.

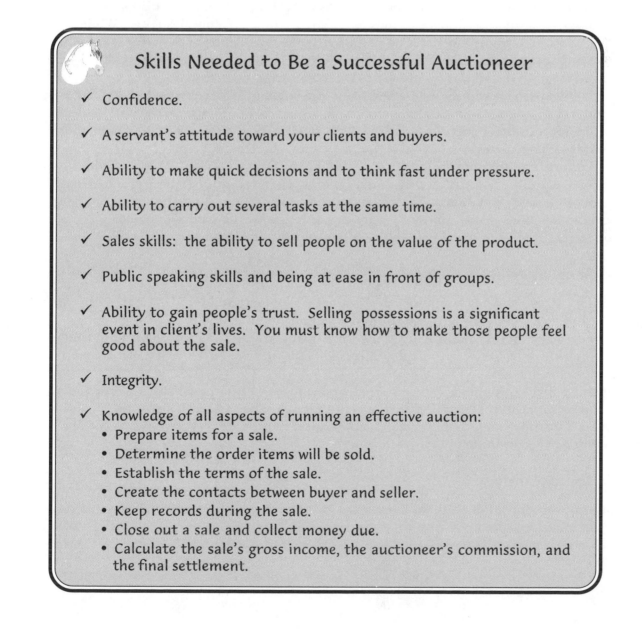

Skills Needed to Be a Successful Auctioneer

✓ Confidence.

✓ A servant's attitude toward your clients and buyers.

✓ Ability to make quick decisions and to think fast under pressure.

✓ Ability to carry out several tasks at the same time.

✓ Sales skills: the ability to sell people on the value of the product.

✓ Public speaking skills and being at ease in front of groups.

✓ Ability to gain people's trust. Selling possessions is a significant event in client's lives. You must know how to make those people feel good about the sale.

✓ Integrity.

✓ Knowledge of all aspects of running an effective auction:
  • Prepare items for a sale.
  • Determine the order items will be sold.
  • Establish the terms of the sale.
  • Create the contacts between buyer and seller.
  • Keep records during the sale.
  • Close out a sale and collect money due.
  • Calculate the sale's gross income, the auctioneer's commission, and the final settlement.

Although specialization is the new trend in auctioneering, good general background in the entire auction industry is helpful. Working initially with a firm that conducts sales in land, estates, livestock, horses, and furnishings can provide that overall background.

The World Wide College of Auctioneering, which began in 1933, has produced several champion livestock auctioneers. As one of the largest auctioneering schools in the United States, it employs three full-time office people and twenty-two instructors. Five instructors specialize in livestock auctioneering. Most of the instructors are full-time auctioneers, and many are graduates of the college who teach primarily to give back to the school that gave them so much.

The World Wide College of Auctioneering holds four yearly terms, which are attended by approximately 75 students; 16 students customarily specialize in livestock and horses. Some students seek full-time careers, some are retirees who want to work part time, and others simply desire new supplemental income.

An Experienced Horse Auctioneer

Bill Addis, president and part owner of the World Wide College of Auctioneering, attests that auctioneering can be a lucrative business. As the third generation in his family to be in the horse industry, Bill found his earnings as a trainer barely matched his costs. While managing a horse farm in the 1970s he managed to save enough money — $685 at the time — to attend auctioneering school. Within ten days of graduation, he earned back his school tuition two times over and was on his way to a very satisfying career.

Today Bill specializes in the sale of Arabians and Arabian/American Saddlebred crosses, and conducts an average of two sales a month. Sales last from one to seven days. While the normal fee for a livestock sale starts at $150 a day and peaks at $575 a day, Bill commands $2,500 a day plus expenses.

Bill's efforts are not only directed to conducting auctions, however. Most of June is spent on the road acquiring livestock for sales and building contacts. At his home ranch, situated on 480 acres in Guthrie, Oklahoma, Bill feeds, trains, and conditions 30 to 100 horses to be sold in upcoming auctions. Four times a year he travels to the World Wide College of Auctioneering in Iowa to teach his skills to other aspiring auctioneers.

Third-Generation Auctioneer

Matthew Kruse and his family recently purchased Reppert School of Auctioneering in Auburn, Indiana. As the third generation in his family to enter the field of auctioning, Matthew explains there is more to auctioneering than learning to chant or be a bid caller, which he says is only 10 percent of auctioneering. Many learned skills and a great deal of knowledge are needed.

Anything that can be sold, can be sold at an auction, says Matthew Kruse. Consequently there is always a need for qualified auctioneers. After you have attended a good auctioneering school and/or served as an apprentice, there are several ways to actually enter the auctioneering business.

Work for a Company

You can work for an established livestock yard or auctioneering company. You may have to start by helping get animals ready, bring them around, or work the ring. Once your initiative and skill are recognized, the doors for bidding are sure to open.

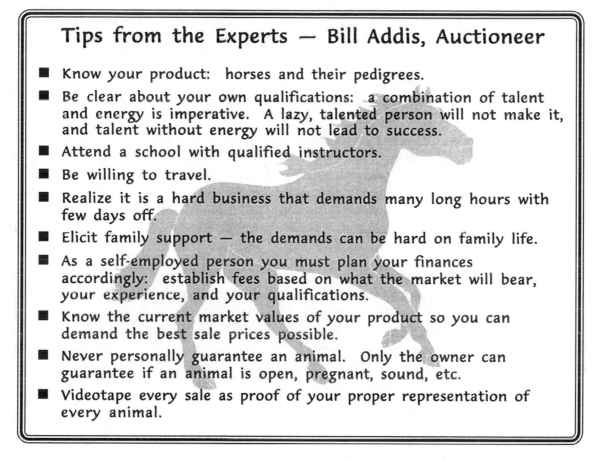

Tips from the Experts — Bill Addis, Auctioneer

- Know your product: horses and their pedigrees.
- Be clear about your own qualifications: a combination of talent and energy is imperative. A lazy, talented person will not make it, and talent without energy will not lead to success.
- Attend a school with qualified instructors.
- Be willing to travel.
- Realize it is a hard business that demands many long hours with few days off.
- Elicit family support — the demands can be hard on family life.
- As a self-employed person you must plan your finances accordingly: establish fees based on what the market will bear, your experience, and your qualifications.
- Know the current market values of your product so you can demand the best sale prices possible.
- Never personally guarantee an animal. Only the owner can guarantee if an animal is open, pregnant, sound, etc.
- Videotape every sale as proof of your proper representation of every animal.

Work as a Self-Employed Auctioneer

You can be a self-employed business person, in terms of taxes, recordkeeping, and operating costs. You will set your own rates. The overhead is minimal: stationery, business cards, a gavel, microphone, and tape recorder. However, a great deal of initiative is needed to meet people; make contacts with horse owners, breeders, ranchers, trainers, and riding instructors; build clientele; and gain the confidence and support of bankers, certified public accountants, and attorneys who deal with livestock owners.

Sponsor Your Own Auction

A facility can be purchased or rented. Livestock can be bought and resold or contracted from owners on a commission of sales basis. Using this approach, the auctioneer is responsible for all aspects of the sale.

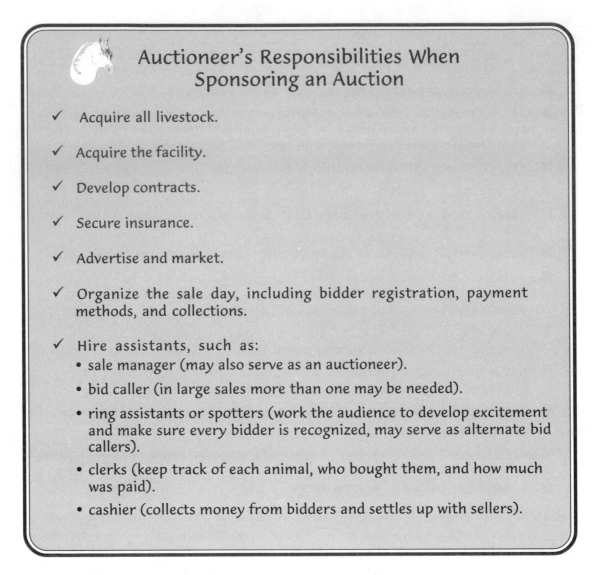

Auctioneer's Responsibilities When Sponsoring an Auction

✓ Acquire all livestock.

✓ Acquire the facility.

✓ Develop contracts.

✓ Secure insurance.

✓ Advertise and market.

✓ Organize the sale day, including bidder registration, payment methods, and collections.

✓ Hire assistants, such as:
- sale manager (may also serve as an auctioneer).
- bid caller (in large sales more than one may be needed).
- ring assistants or spotters (work the audience to develop excitement and make sure every bidder is recognized, may serve as alternate bid callers).
- clerks (keep track of each animal, who bought them, and how much was paid).
- cashier (collects money from bidders and settles up with sellers).

CONCLUSION

People like auctions because they are exciting, says Matthew Kruse. That makes auctioneering a fun, enjoyable, exhilarating, yet demanding career. For those with energy, talent, willingness to travel, motivation to do a good job, and the zeal to learn the trade, the money is there. Beginning auctioneers earn about $150 a day. For the experienced auctioneer who has a good reputation, earnings can run as much as $1,000 a day and more than $100,000 a year.

RESOURCES

Atwood, Bobby. Route 4 Box 92-A, Koscuisko, Mississippi 39090.

Auctioneer, The. 8880 Ballentine, Overland Park, Kansas 66215-1985. (913)541-8084. *naahq@aol.com.* Magazine of the National Auctioneers Association (NAA). April 1997 issue lists international and state auctioneer associations. A special February edition provides data on all NAA members.

Auction Marketing Institute. 8880 Ballentine, Overland Park, Kansas 66215-1985. (913)541-8084. *naahq@aol.com. http://www.auctioneers.org.* Affiliated with the National Auctioneers Association. Holds certification classes at Indiana University for Certified Auctioneer Institute (CAI), Accredited Auctioneer Real Estate (AARE), and Graduate Personal Property Appraiser (GPPA).

National Auctioneers Association (NAA). 8880 Ballentine, Overland Park, Kansas 66215-1985. (913)541-8084. *naahq@aol.com. http://www.auctioneers.org.* Web page has information on affiliate organizations, including state organizations, and how to inquire about scholarship funds.

Reppert School of Auctioneering. Matthew Kruse. Kruse Auction Park., P.O. Box 190, Auburn, Indiana 46706. (800)968-4444.

Weatherell, Charles and Cheryl. CK Ranch. 33525 Wapati Circle, Buena Vista, Colorado 81211. (719)395-8423.

World Wide College of Auctioneering. William Addis, President, and Vicki Flickinger. P.O. Box 949, Dept. WHD, Mason City, Iowa 50402-0949. (515)423-5242. Fax: (515)423-3067.

Chapter Thirteen

Breed Registries and Associations

Over the ages, both natural selection and human-induced selective breeding have produced an estimated 300 breeds of horses. No doubt, nature has played a major role in the development of these breeds, as natural barriers, climatic conditions, and availability of feed influenced their breeding and survival.

Throughout recorded history, certain characteristics in horses have been admired over others. For instance, such ancient civilizations as the Egyptians and Greeks selectively bred horses to acquire the characteristics of strength and speed. Another example dates to 126 BC, when the Chinese Emperor Wu Ti, attracted to the color of the dapple horse of the Persians, offered a substantial amount of gold for some of their horses. When the Persians refused his offer, a year-long war resulted.

BREED REGISTRIES — AN OVERVIEW

Today the many breeds of domestic horses fall into three main categories: ponies, work horses, and recreational horses (sport, race, pleasure, etc.). The *Horse Industry Directory* of the American Horse Council lists 133 breed registries and associations along with contact data, publications, and annual meeting dates. A description of each breed, the latest yearly registration figures, and the total registration figures for listed breeds are included. Small registries, such as the Cleveland Bay Horse Society of North America with three registered horses in the U.S. and the National Native Gaited Horse Registry with nine registered horses in the U.S., are described, as well as the larger registries, such as the American Quarter Horse Association with 2,792,381 registered horses in the U.S. and the Jockey Club executive offices with 1,241,442 registered Thoroughbred horses.

In the 1997 edition of the *Horse Industry Directory*, the sixteen major breed registries from 1986 to 1995 are charted in graph form. For each year the total number of horses registered is cited. The Quarter Horse heads the list with 107,332 horses registered in 1995, a decrease from the 153,773 Quarter Horses registered in 1986. The American Paint Horse Association moved to second place in 1997 with 412,880 registered horses. As of 1995, the total number of horses registered in the sixteen major breeds showed a decrease of 54,279 from 305,456 in 1986 to 251,177 in 1995.

WORKING FOR A BREED REGISTRY

Office sizes and employee numbers for different breed registries vary from those run by volunteers and those with a couple of part-time workers, to registries with personnel numbering in the hundreds. If you are interested in employment with a particular breed, call or write the breed registry to acquire their publication and other information. Most secretaries are friendly and may be able to assist you in making contacts in the industry.

Employment opportunities with breed registries are diverse, not only in responsibility but also in requirements and salary. Educational requirements range from high school diplomas to college degrees. Experience with the breed is an asset but only required for specific jobs. Salaries range from minimum wage to more than $100,000 per year. Likewise, responsibilities range from clerical jobs and office work, to customer relations and management positions. Many positions with registries and associations require office and managerial skills.

To give you an idea of the employment picture of breed registries and associations, seven registries are profiled below.

PALOMINO HORSE ASSOCIATION

Raelene Rebuck, secretary of the Palomino Horse Association, which was founded in 1936, is the association's only paid staff person. As secretary, she is paid hourly. Her hours vary according to the work load. This nonprofit organization publishes a bimonthly newsletter, registers Palominos on the basis of color and conformation, and is dedicated to the promotion of the Palomino horse. Raelene is also dedicated to Palominos and when her husband became president of the Palomino Horse Association, she applied for and received the position of secretary.

Raelene has been a horse enthusiast since she was five years old. Today, she raises, trains, and shows Palominos. It was her love and involvement with horses, especially Palominos, as well as the opportunity to meet other owners from all over the world, that motivated her to apply for this position.

PONY OF THE AMERICAS

Pony of the Americas Club, founded in 1954, is dedicated to the promotion of the Pony of the Americas (POA). The organization maintains a trustworthy stud book for registration and transfer that is accepted throughout the world. The club holds breed promotion sales and shows, and provides an avenue of competition that is friendly and family oriented.

In addition to 40 state POA clubs run by many volunteers, the POA association has four full-time staff people consisting of the registrar, show secretary, executive secretary, and bookkeeper. Salaries range from $15,000 to $30,000 a year. The key qualifications for employment are office and computer skills.

Jean Donley, executive secretary of POA, is also involved in the American Horse Council and American Youth Horse Council Education Committee. She began riding early in life and by high school knew she wanted to work in the horse industry. She graduated from William Woods University in Fulton, Missouri, with a double major in business administration and equestrian science. Jean served as a 4-H leader, a claims analyst with an equine insurance company, and as an admissions counselor for the Equestrian Department of William Woods University, before she began work at the Pony of Americas Club.

Although most of her work is centered around administrative duties and working with people, Jean feels fortunate to be associated with the horse industry. She enjoys attending equine trade shows and related association meetings that draw all the disciplines together, such as Equitana and the American Youth Horse Council Leader Symposium.

PASO FINO HORSE

The Paso Fino Horse Association was formed in 1972. With approximately 6,300 members and registered horses totaling more than 28,000, this registry provides public education about the Paso Fino Horse; regulates matters related to breeding, exhibition, promotion, and improvements of the Paso Fino Horse; and maintains the breed standard.

C.J. Marcello, executive director of the Paso Fino Horse Association, is in charge of the day-to-day operations. A horse owner and breeder for 25 years, C.J.'s original career goal was veterinarian, but Vietnam interfered with his plans. He remained in the U.S. Army for 21 years as an aviator, earned a degree in animal science, and upon retirement from the service joined the staff of nine full-time and two part-time employees of the Paso Fino Horse Association.

Wages for hourly employees of the Paso Fino Association range from $5.15 to $8, and salaried personnel earn from $20,000 to more than $45,000 a year. Requirements vary for each position, and include managerial, computer, telephone, and customer relations skills. Horse experience is not required. Most of the outside committee and show work is accomplished by volunteers.

TENNESSEE WALKING HORSE

Ranked fifteenth among the 133 breed registries in the *Horse Industry Directory* is the Tennessee Walking Horse Breeders' and Exhibitors' Association. Sharon Brandon, who has been the secretary/treasurer since 1966, rode horses as a child and continues to love them — a sentiment that led her to her current position. Her key responsibilities are administration and public relations. She enjoys working in the horse industry, the personal contact with customers, and the friendships that have developed over the years.

Of the 24 staff members, only a few of the Tennessee Walking Horse Breeders' and Exhibitors' Association employees are horse owners. This association's employees perform clerical, computer, accounting, and public relations functions. Youth programs offer photo, essay, and art contests; local 4-H information; and the opportunity to apply for five annual scholarships of approximately $1,500 each.

155

In 1996, 9,450 Tennessee Walking Horses were registered, bringing the total registry, since the organization's inception in 1935, to 305,319. Preserving the pedigree of this purebred horse and overseeing its use are key goals. Members of the Tennessee Walking Horse Breeders' and Exhibitors' Association may register their first foal (if they own the mare at the time of foaling) for free. Additional foals are registered for $30. A fee of $50 is charged for a blood kit. Owners, usually assisted by a veterinarian, extract blood from the horse and mail the kit to one of the two contracted laboratories. DNA Diagnostics Inc./Shelterwood Laboratories is one of those contracted laboratories. (This laboratory is described in the section on veterinary medicine in Chapter Four.)

Staff Positions of the Paso Fino Horse Association

✓ Executive director. Responsible for all day-to-day operations and administration.

✓ Assistant director of operations. Responsible for personnel, automation, finances, supplies, membership, and facilities.

✓ Assistant director of registrations/registrar. Oversees registration, transfers, and blood typing.

✓ Assistant director for marketing. Responsible for promoting the breed.

✓ Show manager. Coordinates regional and national shows and publications; maintains show records and point standings; and acts as a liaison with several committees, principally, the Judges and Stewards and Amateur Owner Committees.

✓ Clerical staff.

✓ Judges.

✓ Stewards.

APPALOOSA HORSE

The Appaloosa Horse Club (ApHC), according to Heather Tiel, marketing associate, is dedicated to collecting, recording, and preserving the history and integrity of this breed; improving and promoting the Appaloosa; and honoring its heritage. Historians believe that the first American Indian tribe to selectively breed horses for the specific traits of intelligence and speed were the Nez Perce of Washington, Oregon, and Idaho. The spotted mounts of these sophisticated equestrians were prized and envied by other tribes. When white settlers came to the northwest Palouse region, they called the attractive spotted horse *a Palouse* horse. Eventually the name was condensed to *Appaloosa*.

In the 1800s, during the Nez Perce War, the tribe fled the U.S. Cavalry. They traveled more than 1,300 miles until they surrendered in Montana. Their surviving horses were relinquished to soldiers, left behind, or given to settlers. Nothing was done to preserve the Appaloosa until 1938 when a group of dedicated horse people formed the Appaloosa Horse Club. The breed grew in popularity and in 1996 ApHC was the seventh largest breed registry in the United States with a total of 581,319 registered horses and 27,640 members. They approved 800 regional shows and 460 Appaloosa races during 1996. There are also 155 regional clubs.

The ApHC has 52 employees, including the chief executive officer, registrar, show department supervisor (show manager), youth coordinator, and director of advertising/marketing. Other employees include editorial and graphic design staff of the *Appaloosa Journal*, management information systems personnel, trail and distance coordinator, and racing coordinator. Knowledge of horses is either required or desired for most positions. Training is provided for some jobs.

Keri Minden-LeForce, show department supervisor for the ApHC, started riding before she could talk. She was in her first parade, decked out in her saddle club colors and chaps, at fourteen months of age. Her memories all center around horse activities of showing, trail riding, junior rodeos, and 4-H. While pursuing a bachelor's degree, she worked part time for the ApHC show manager and youth coordinator. In this position she traveled to the World Championship Appaloosa Show in Fort Worth, Texas. She returned knowing that the traveling life was invented for her. As graduation neared, her boss resigned, and two weeks out of college Keri inherited the youth program.

Tips from the Experts — Keri Minden-LeForce, Show Department Supervisor, ApHC

If you are seeking a career in a breed association:

- Know your horse.

- Know your breed.

- Spend time working on listening skills.

- Seek better ways to do things.

- Keep past mistakes and successes in mind and use them for the association's benefit.

Keri has been with the ApHC since 1992, and she says the greatest challenge she faces is finding a balance between being a wife, mom, and busy professional. Her career is 100 percent horse related, but it also involves financial considerations, organizing and managing events, taking a stand on important issues, talking with customers, traveling to educational symposiums, and seeking ways to make things easier and more financially beneficial for clients. Fitting this into an eight-hour day is impossible. Keri works overtime, travels, and sometimes eats, sleeps, and dreams the business.

Shonda Nelson, ApHC registrar, was born and raised on a cattle ranch in Montana. She gained valuable experience in the horse world as she attended numerous horsemanship clinics, learning from talented horse trainers, and served as Miss Rodeo Montana. She began working with the ApHC in 1994.

The greatest challenge of Shonda's position is the changing industry. Currently the ApHC registers solid-color Appaloosa horses, but in order for a solid, non-characteristic, registered Appaloosa to show, race, or exhibit in ApHC-approved events, the horse must have a CPO (certified pedigree option); that is, the horse's parentage must be verified through DNA genetic testing or blood typing. Other challenges include keeping up with current technology, such as transported cooled semen, frozen shipped semen, embryo transfers, and recent questions regarding cloning.

As registrar, Shonda is responsible for registrations, transfers, breeding programs, genetic testing, stallion breeding reports, and descriptions of the horses. Most of her responsibilities relate to customers.

Tips from the Experts —
Shonda Nelson, Registrar, ApHC

- Take advantage of the opportunities that come your way.

- Become educated about all aspects of horses and the equine industry.

- Realize education by life experience is as important as a formal education.

- Believe in your product. The horse is the best product in the world — it doesn't pollute the air, and it teaches young people responsibility and adaptability.

- Whether dressage, rodeo, horse shows, or distance riding, equine sports teach people how to win well and, more importantly, how to lose well.

STANDARDBRED HORSE

The United States Trotting Association is one of the largest registries, with a staff of nearly 80 people. Positions include clerical, technical licensing, management, accounting, and human resources. Salaries range from $15,000 to $100,000, with a benefit package that includes health, dental, eye care, vacation, retirement, and educational reimbursement. Standardbred background is desirable, but not required.

AMERICAN PAINT HORSE

The American Paint Horse Association (APHA) was founded more than 30 years ago by horse people who loved the abilities of the Western stock horse, but who also appreciated unusual painted coat patterns. The organization grew from a registry of 3,800 horses to more than 360,000 horses worldwide. More than 50,000 foals were registered in 1997, making APHA the second largest equine registry in the United States, based on the number of foals registered annually.

APHA employs 133 staff members. According to Ed Roberts, executive secretary, APHA positions include administrative assistants, managers, secretaries, department heads, and clerical staff. There are positions in the registration department, accounting, data processing, performance, marketing, and member services. The association publishes a monthly magazine produced by editorial, advertising, and production staff. Salaries range from $10,000 to more than $60,000. Hours are 8:00 A.M. to 4:30 P.M. Benefits include a 401K pension plan, insurance, a bonus plan, personal days, and vacations. Horse experience is helpful but not mandatory for all jobs. Depending upon the position, applicants may be required to have a high school education, a college education, computer experience, clerical skills, managerial skills, or horse knowledge.

RESOURCES

American Hanoverian Society. Hugh Bellis-Jones, Executive Director. 4059 Iron Works Pike, Bldg. C, Lexington, Kentucky 40511. (606)255-8467. A registry with three full-time employees and one part-time employee. Salaries range from $20,000 to $40,000.

American Paint Horse Association. Ed Roberts. P.O. Box 961023, Fort Worth, Texas 76161-0023. (817)834-2742. Fax: (817)834-3152.

Appaloosa Horse Club. Heather Tiel, Keri Minden-LeForce, and Shonda Nelson. P.O. Box 8403, Moscow, Idaho 83843-5578. (208)882-5578. Fax: (208)882-8150.

DNA Diagnostics, Inc./Shelterwood Laboratories. Dr. Melba Ketchum. P.O. Box 215, Highway 79E, Carthage, Texas 75633. (903)693-6424. (800)693-6424.

Haflinger Registry of North America. Melissa Shanahan. 14640 State Route 83, Coshocton, Ohio, 43812-8911. (614)829-2790.

Harness Horse Youth Foundation. Ellen Taylor. 14950 Greyhound Court, #210, Carmel, Indiana 46032-1091. (317)848-5132.

Kurzeja, Richard E., Executive Secretary. International Buckskin Horse Association. P.O. Box 268, Shelby, Indiana 46337.

Horse Industry Directory. American Horse Council. 1700 K Street NW, Suite 300, Washington DC 20006. (202)296-4031. Lists 133 breed descriptions, registries, associations, contact data, publications, and annual meeting dates.

Palomino Horse Association. Raelene Rebuck. HC63, Box 24, Dornsife, Pennsylvania 17823. (717)758-3067.

Paso Fino Horse Association. C.J. Marcello, Executive Director. 101 North Collins Street, Plant City, Florida 33566-3311. (813)719-7777. Fax: (813)719-7872. *pasofino.cjmarcello@worldnet.att.net*.

Pony of the Americas Club. Jean Donley, Executive Secretary. 5240 Elmwood Avenue, Indianapolis, Indiana 46203-5990. (317)788-0107. Fax: (317)788-8974.

Tennessee Walking Horse Breeders' and Exhibitors' Association. Sharon Brandon, Secretary/Treasurer. P.O. Box 286, Lewisburg, Tennessee 37091-1286. (800)359-1574.

United States Trotting Horse Association. 750 Michigan Avenue, Columbus, Ohio 43215-1191. (614)224-2291. Fax: (614)224-4575.

Chapter Fourteen

The Publishing Industry

Writing is many things. It is communicating with words, painting a picture with language, sharing exciting events, expressing feelings, and describing facts and details. But being an author involves much more than writing. Writers must have information or stories to share and their messages have to be presented in an organized, concise, and interesting manner. Writers often need

persistence to stick with long and tedious tasks. Whether working at home, in an office, full time, part time, or as a hobby, writers must be self-motivated and disciplined, because they rarely have a boss who holds them accountable. Family, friends, and neighbors frequently view writing as more of a hobby than a career and often think nothing of distracting the writer with calls and activities.

GETTING STARTED AS A WRITER

Generally speaking, the writing process is the easiest, least time-consuming part of a project, compared to the editing and re-writing process, sending queries to and getting commitments from publishers, compiling resource lists and bibliographies, conducting interviews or research, gathering photos, and marketing. Writers keep abreast of the industry by reading current market guides and writer publications. Finding out about copyright laws, keeping accurate financial records, and staying informed about tax laws also take time. Many writers feel that less than 20 percent of their time is actually involved in the writing process.

If you are considering a writing career, try working your way through the Checklist for the Aspiring Writer on the next page.

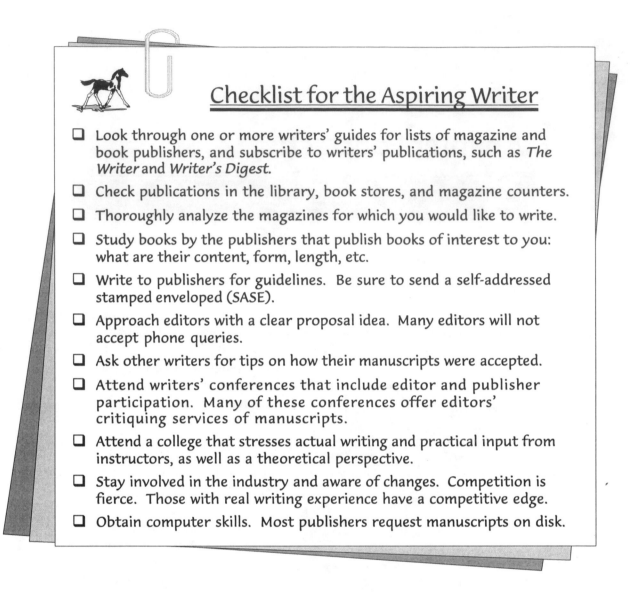

Checklist for the Aspiring Writer

❑ Look through one or more writers' guides for lists of magazine and book publishers, and subscribe to writers' publications, such as *The Writer* and *Writer's Digest*.

❑ Check publications in the library, book stores, and magazine counters.

❑ Thoroughly analyze the magazines for which you would like to write.

❑ Study books by the publishers that publish books of interest to you: what are their content, form, length, etc.

❑ Write to publishers for guidelines. Be sure to send a self-addressed stamped enveloped (SASE).

❑ Approach editors with a clear proposal idea. Many editors will not accept phone queries.

❑ Ask other writers for tips on how their manuscripts were accepted.

❑ Attend writers' conferences that include editor and publisher participation. Many of these conferences offer editors' critiquing services of manuscripts.

❑ Attend a college that stresses actual writing and practical input from instructors, as well as a theoretical perspective.

❑ Stay involved in the industry and aware of changes. Competition is fierce. Those with real writing experience have a competitive edge.

❑ Obtain computer skills. Most publishers request manuscripts on disk.

PUBLISHERS' PERSPECTIVES

The magazine publishing industry has faced major challenges in recent years as paper prices have risen and postage rates have increased. Even though television, the Internet, movies, sports, and recreational activities all vie for people's attention, magazines are still popular reading material. Not surprisingly, many publications related to nearly every aspect of the subject of horses are available to readers today. The *Horse Industry Directory* of the American Horse Council lists 250 magazines and publications about horses or the horse industry.

Publishers are always looking for a fresh new voice and approach. Of course, writers are not the only people employed by publishers. People manage the publication, select articles, edit, layout, publish, market, and keep financial records. Some publications rely entirely on volunteers. Others have employees who, along with other responsibilities, prepare the publications. Still others have staff columnists, but also accept and pay for freelance articles, and employ full-time editorial and publication personnel. The number of staff people depends on many factors: the size of the publication, the company or organization behind it, the part of the industry it represents, and its publication schedule (daily, weekly, monthly, or bimonthly).

A Newspaper

The *Daily Racing Form* publishes race track statistics, articles, and editorials. Printed each day in newspaper form with color highlights, this daily publication has a regular staff of 25 plus a couple hundred staff writers. These staff writers, according to News Editor Peter Berry, work at the tracks, compile data, make charts, and calculate handicaps. Every race in the country is represented in this newspaper.

A Weekly Magazine

Mark Simon has been editor of the *Thoroughbred Times* since 1985. This weekly publication has an impressive full-time staff. It also uses the resources of freelance writers around the country, most of whom correspond from race tracks. To write for the *Thoroughbred Times*, writers need to be genuinely interested in and knowledgeable about the horse industry, and their journalistic skills must include the ability to write in a coherent, understandable manner. Mark estimates full-time staff writers make $20,000 to $30,000. Editors make $35,000 to $75,000. Circulation of the magazine, publication frequency, education, and experience are all factors in determining salaries.

A Monthly Magazine

Fleet Street Publishing Corporation is the publisher of *Equus, HorsePlay, Dressage Today*, and *TT.E.A.M. News International*, a quarterly newsletter compiled by Linda Tellington-Jones. *Equus*, with a circulation now of about 146,000, was the first magazine the corporation published.

Mary Kay Kinnish is editorial director of the corporation. Eighteen years ago, Mary Kay accepted an internship with *Equus* while she was still in college. Upon graduation she accepted the position of assistant editor and worked her way up through the ranks. The corporate office, where Mary Kay now works, employs twelve people, including the president, executive president, vice president, editorial director, product marketing, marketing analysis, controller, accounting staff, office manager, product fulfillment coordinator, and office staff.

Mary Kay describes herself as a "word jockey." Her goal is to make others look better. According to Mary Kay, the key to success for writers and editors is the ability to think. Writers and editors must be able to express themselves in a logical and understandable language, which readers can identify with and understand in a practical, usable sense.

Laurie Prinz serves as the executive director for *Equus*. After acquiring her college degree in journalism, Laurie accepted a job in public relations for *Steeple Chase* magazine. Desiring to use more of her journalism training, she responded to an advertisement by *Equus*, and shortly thereafter she came on staff. As executive director, Laurie formulates each issue's lineup, works with freelance writers, reviews all material before and after editing, performs first-line editing, oversees much of the magazine production, and helps produce special products and books.

Laurie says her greatest frustration is freelance writers who submit inappropriate articles. It wastes her time and the writers' time. She suggests writers carefully examine several issues of a magazine for content, style, target market, article length, and topics. Submit written queries, not phone queries. By mail, request publishing guidelines from the magazine (many publishers expect you to enclose a self-addressed stamped envelope with your request).

Equus, along with *HorsePlay*, and *Dressage Today*, frequently assign articles to freelance writers. Interested writers should submit résumés and samples of previously published materials. For those desiring editorial positions, Laurie recommends a good college background and the development of excellent writing skills.

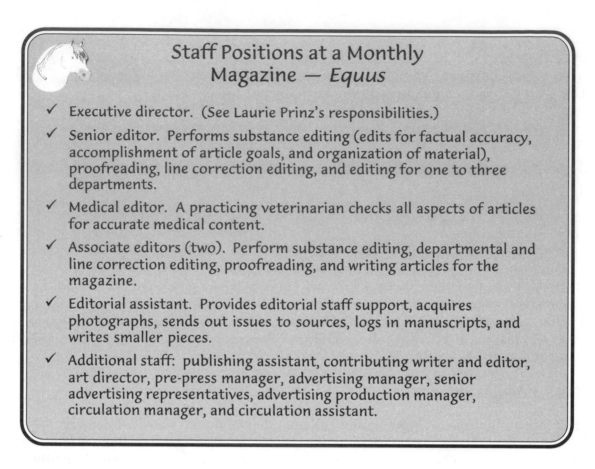

Staff Positions at a Monthly Magazine — *Equus*

- ✓ Executive director. (See Laurie Prinz's responsibilities.)

- ✓ Senior editor. Performs substance editing (edits for factual accuracy, accomplishment of article goals, and organization of material), proofreading, line correction editing, and editing for one to three departments.

- ✓ Medical editor. A practicing veterinarian checks all aspects of articles for accurate medical content.

- ✓ Associate editors (two). Perform substance editing, departmental and line correction editing, proofreading, and writing articles for the magazine.

- ✓ Editorial assistant. Provides editorial staff support, acquires photographs, sends out issues to sources, logs in manuscripts, and writes smaller pieces.

- ✓ Additional staff: publishing assistant, contributing writer and editor, art director, pre-press manager, advertising manager, senior advertising representatives, advertising production manager, circulation manager, and circulation assistant.

Association Magazines

Debbie Tuska is administrative assistant for *The Blood Horse* magazine, printed weekly, and for *The Horse: Your Guide to Equine Care*, printed monthly. Both are publications of the Thoroughbred Owners and Breeders Association. Debbie said that writers need not send queries if they have already written articles that are appropriate for the magazines. She does suggest that writers become familiar with each magazine to ensure that submissions are appropriate. Many writers for *The Blood Horse* magazine are correspondents who do their research at the race track and then submit their material.

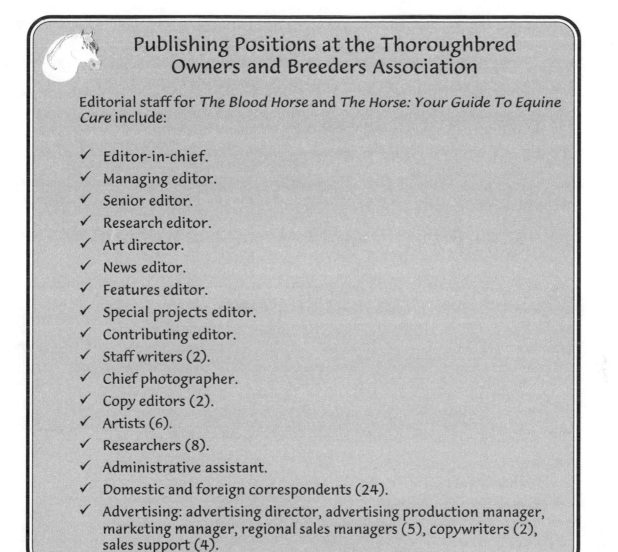

Publishing Positions at the Thoroughbred Owners and Breeders Association

Editorial staff for *The Blood Horse* and *The Horse: Your Guide To Equine Care* include:

- ✓ Editor-in-chief.
- ✓ Managing editor.
- ✓ Senior editor.
- ✓ Research editor.
- ✓ Art director.
- ✓ News editor.
- ✓ Features editor.
- ✓ Special projects editor.
- ✓ Contributing editor.
- ✓ Staff writers (2).
- ✓ Chief photographer.
- ✓ Copy editors (2).
- ✓ Artists (6).
- ✓ Researchers (8).
- ✓ Administrative assistant.
- ✓ Domestic and foreign correspondents (24).
- ✓ Advertising: advertising director, advertising production manager, marketing manager, regional sales managers (5), copywriters (2), sales support (4).

FREELANCE WRITING — AUTHORS' PERSPECTIVES

Betsy Lynch

Communicating is what Betsy Lynch does for a living, and all of her communications incorporate the written word. When she is a photographer, she writes an article to accompany the photos. When she is editing, she has an article of her own in the making. When she is marketing, she uses her writing skills to promote the product or program. When she runs her business, Third Generation Communications, she uses her skills in advertising, marketing, communications, and public relations. Betsy produces brochures, newsletters, and feature articles for horse publications. She contributed several chapters to *Legends*, published by Western Horseman, and co-authored, with Dr. Dwight Bennett, *Bits: Power Tools for Thinking Riders*. Two other books, one on Appaloosas and another on hackamores, are in the offing.

A horse lover from childhood, Betsy didn't pretend to ride a horse as a child, she pretended she was the horse. Owning a horse was not a privilege her family could afford, but Betsy found ways to ride. Showing and working with other people's horses became a way of life when she was a young girl. After earning a degree in agricultural journalism, she went to work for *California Horse Review* in the advertising department and copy editing department, became associate editor for *Appaloosa Journal,* and worked for *Horseman Magazine.* Each position change involved increased responsibility as well as salary.

In 1990 she started her own business, Third Generation Communications, and conducted public relations, advertising, marketing, and freelance writing. Although the company began as a diversified marketing communications company, the horse industry soon became her primary focus, with clients ranging from publishing companies to breed and professional organizations. Betsy is also a partner in a small publishing company that produces *Showtime Report.*

Betsy readily admits that while she loves journalism, the research and interviewing aspects are downright hard work. She is a regular contributor to such magazines as *Western Horsemen, Appaloosa Journal, Paint Horse Journal,* and *Performance Horse.* When she has an idea for an article, she contacts magazines to ascertain their interest level, pre-sells the article, and then writes it.

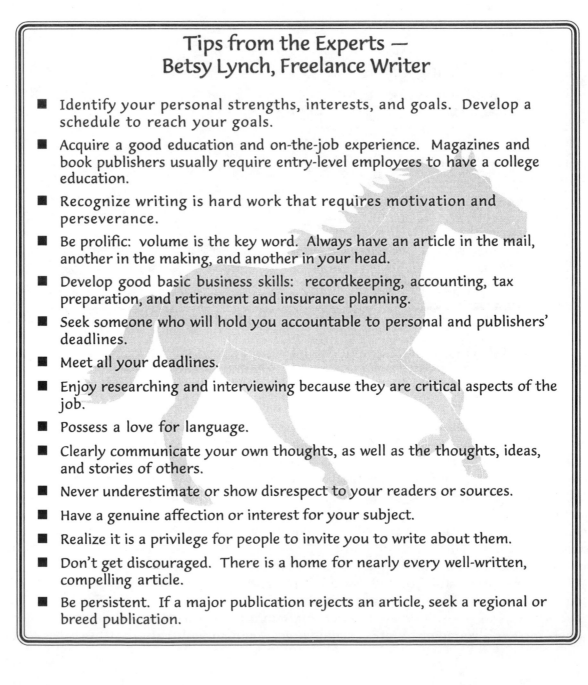

Tips from the Experts —
Betsy Lynch, Freelance Writer

- Identify your personal strengths, interests, and goals. Develop a schedule to reach your goals.

- Acquire a good education and on-the-job experience. Magazines and book publishers usually require entry-level employees to have a college education.

- Recognize writing is hard work that requires motivation and perseverance.

- Be prolific: volume is the key word. Always have an article in the mail, another in the making, and another in your head.

- Develop good basic business skills: recordkeeping, accounting, tax preparation, and retirement and insurance planning.

- Seek someone who will hold you accountable to personal and publishers' deadlines.

- Meet all your deadlines.

- Enjoy researching and interviewing because they are critical aspects of the job.

- Possess a love for language.

- Clearly communicate your own thoughts, as well as the thoughts, ideas, and stories of others.

- Never underestimate or show disrespect to your readers or sources.

- Have a genuine affection or interest for your subject.

- Realize it is a privilege for people to invite you to write about them.

- Don't get discouraged. There is a home for nearly every well-written, compelling article.

- Be persistent. If a major publication rejects an article, seek a regional or breed publication.

Cherry Hill

Cherry Hill is the author of many books, including *The Formative Years, From the Center of the Ring, Horsekeeping on a Small Acreage, Becoming an Effective Rider, Making Not Breaking, Maximum Hoof Power* (co-authored with Richard Klimesh), *Horse for Sale, Horse Owners Guide to Lameness* (co-authored with Dr. Ted Stashak), *Your Pony/Your Horse, 101 Arena Exercises, Horse Handling and Grooming,* and *Horse Health Care.* Currently she and her husband, Richard Klimesh, are working on several books and video series.

Cherry has combined her love of horses with initiative and hard work to formulate a career in the horse industry. Her interest in horses began in grade school where all her projects, term papers, collections, and hobbies related to horses. Encouraged by her parents to pursue a career with horses, she concentrated on taking science, math, and journalism classes in high school.

Cherry's career began as a trainer. In addition to learning by training horses, she earned a college degree in animal science, attended judging school, and sought apprenticeships with well-known judges. Once she was carded, she accepted show assignments for national shows. Because of her expertise and versatility, she was asked to teach equine courses at several universities in the United States and Canada.

After ten years of teaching many twelve-hour days, often seven-days a week, she reevaluated her priorities. She enjoyed writing, wanted to work at home, and perceived a need for instructional horse training books. The idea for the book, *The Formative Years* came while she was teaching a class on the subject. There was no textbook so the students took voluminous notes. It took Cherry a year to write this step-by-step book and take 170 photographs for the book. After writing the book, Cherry contacted 20 publishers. She browsed through horse books, and wrote publishers whose format she liked. Six responded positively. Just as she had narrowed it down to one, she saw another published book she admired. She contacted that publisher, and they offered her the best deal yet. With one successful book to her credit, Cherry was contacted by other publishers with ideas they wanted her to develop and requests to view future works. Cherry's career as an author was launched.

Writing takes discipline. Cherry's outgoing mail holder, a gift from her husband, says, "The art of writing is applying the seat of the pants to the seat of the chair." The phrase, "The art of writing is applying the seat of the pants to the *seat of the saddle*," could have been used when two of Cherry's books were being produced, because they were composed from the saddle. As she developed the exercises for *101 Arena Exercises* she dictated the procedures into a tape recorder as she took horses through the exercises. Most of *Becoming an Effective Rider* was also written on horseback using a tiny tape recorder.

Cherry has also written more than 700 articles for such magazines as *Horse and Rider, Michael Plumb's Horse Journal, Quarter Horse Journal,* and *Chronicle of the Horse.* She continues to keep sensitive to the industry by training, judging, and speaking. Her practical experience, combined with her writing skills and initiative, have shaped much of her success.

Part-Time Writers

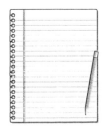

Writing can also be a part-time, supplemental profession. For instance, Anna Jane White-Mullin, a champion hunter and hunt seat equitation rider (see Chapter Six), used her expertise and background to write *Judging Hunters and Hunter Seat Equitation* and *Winning: A Training and Showing Guide for Hunter Seat Riders.*

Dave Millwater, founder of the Guild of Professional Farriers, uses his farrier expertise and desire to communicate through the written word in his supplemental career as a writer. His first article was written to correct misinformation published about the horseshoeing business. He also wrote articles for *Horseworld, Western Horsemen, Western Horse, Equus, Paint Horse Journal, HorsePlay,* and *Anvil.*

When the managing editor of *HorsePlay,* Lisa Kiser, needed a farrier advisor, she asked Dave, and he served in that capacity for some time. In 1994, Dave started a hoof care column entitled "Behind the Hoof" for *American Pioneer,* North Carolina's largest equine publication. He also writes "Farrier's Open Forum and Idea Exchange" for Southeastern Horseshoers on Education. Although the columns are not money-makers, they give Dave and his company, Millwater Horseshoeing, considerable exposure. He is the author of the *Pocket Dictionary of Farrier Terms and Technical Language,* a labor of interest and love.

FINDING A PUBLISHER FOR YOUR BOOK

Non-fiction books and magazines form an important part of today's vast information industry. People want to read material that shares information and instructions, interviews of people, tips for success, and opinions backed by research and experience, personal success stories, and facts. Horse people are especially eager to learn and grow in their knowledge and skills.

Even with such a receptive audience and 50,000 book publishing firms in the United States (only about 100 are considered big firms), finding a publisher takes a great deal of skill, effort, and time. A good place to start is a guide called the *Writer's Market.* This guide lists 4,000 markets for everything from books to greeting cards, and it is updated every year. *Writer's Market* also includes a wealth of information about manuscript format, taxes, copyrights, and writing contests and awards.

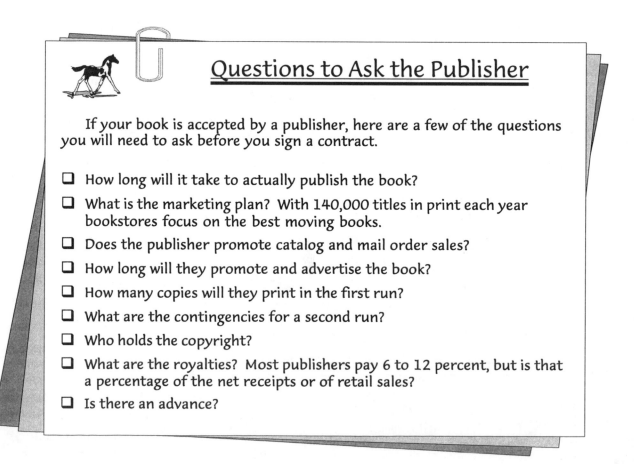

Questions to Ask the Publisher

If your book is accepted by a publisher, here are a few of the questions you will need to ask before you sign a contract.

❑ How long will it take to actually publish the book?

❑ What is the marketing plan? With 140,000 titles in print each year bookstores focus on the best moving books.

❑ Does the publisher promote catalog and mail order sales?

❑ How long will they promote and advertise the book?

❑ How many copies will they print in the first run?

❑ What are the contingencies for a second run?

❑ Who holds the copyright?

❑ What are the royalties? Most publishers pay 6 to 12 percent, but is that a percentage of the net receipts or of retail sales?

❑ Is there an advance?

After carefully selecting publishers to send queries to, remember you probably will have only one chance to convince them of the value of your book. Consequently, you must write an excellent query letter. Be sure to study the query procedure, using *Writer's Market* or another resource. Then make your query an impressive example of your writing that will entice a publisher to request the opportunity to preview your book.

Subscribing to writer's journals, reading relevant books, and attending conferences and writer's groups are helpful ways to learn the trade and make contacts with publishers. Acquiring an agent, a growing trend in the industry, is another way to approach publishers. Some publishers prefer working with agents, others do not. Writers' journals and market guides offer suggestions regarding acquisition, rates, services, and effectiveness of agents. The resources listed at the end of this chapter will help you secure this knowledge.

Subsidy Publishers

An alternate approach to getting your book published is to go through a subsidy publisher or vanity publisher. Grant money (from the government, a foundation, or a university) or money out of the author's own pocket is paid to a publisher to cover publication costs. Recently there has been an increase in author subsidy publishing, and much of the stigma of previous years is vanishing.

Every issue of all the writers' magazines includes numerous advertisements for subsidy publishers. However, it is important to carefully check all the details before selecting this avenue. Evaluate the contract carefully and be sure you understand that marketing, storage, and success of the book usually depend on you, the author.

Self-Publishing

A third alternative is self-publishing. This is a viable alternative for the author who has business skills. Dan Poynter, author and self-publisher, chose this avenue in 1973. His effort met with exceptional success, and he has since written a book on the subject entitled, *The Self-Publishing Manual*. Detailed instructions and a hot-line to Dan Poynter are included in the instruction to writers on how to by-pass the middleman, deal directly with a printer, and handle marketing and distribution.

Attorney Julie Fershtman used *The Self-Publishing Manual* as a major resource for establishing her own publishing company, selecting a printing company, and then successfully marketing her book. Julie specializes in equine law in Bingham Farms, Michigan. She realized early in her career that equine law courses and books were nearly non-existent. She spent many long days in the research library documenting pertinent equine law cases, precedents, and legislation. *Equine Law and Horse Sense,* published in 1996, was the result of her labor.

When Julie approached publishers, they either didn't agree with her stance about not publishing form contracts in the book, or the publishing date was set too far in the future. She realized most publishers only print runs of 5,000 books and her aspirations far exceeded that number. She decided to take matters into her own hands, and sales of the resulting book have exceeded those predicted by the publishing companies she originally queried. Julie markets the book as she speaks throughout the country.

Forming Your Own Publishing Business

Equistar Publications, Ltd., was formed in 1996 when a need was perceived for a comprehensive, detailed, scientifically accurate, well-illustrated book on horse anatomy and common disorders of the horse. Identifying the need was just the first step. Then came an expensive and time consuming process. After spending 20 years in practice with a major emphasis on horses, Ronald J. Riegel, D.V.M., was not only willing but was also capable of writing the book. Susan E. Hakola, owner of Hakola Studios, Inc., and a board certified medical illustrator, was more than qualified to do the illustrations. The next step was acquiring investors. Legal contracts were drawn up. Steve Ritchie and Jeffrey Hakola, with combined background in the scientific, business, and publishing worlds, rounded out the team. Steve says forming the company has been quite a challenge.

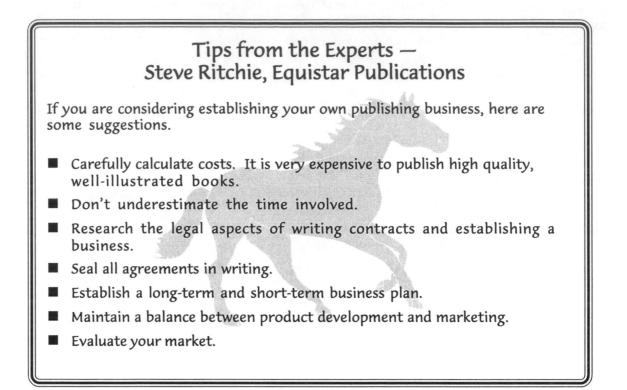

Tips from the Experts — Steve Ritchie, Equistar Publications

If you are considering establishing your own publishing business, here are some suggestions.

- Carefully calculate costs. It is very expensive to publish high quality, well-illustrated books.
- Don't underestimate the time involved.
- Research the legal aspects of writing contracts and establishing a business.
- Seal all agreements in writing.
- Establish a long-term and short-term business plan.
- Maintain a balance between product development and marketing.
- Evaluate your market.

Writing as a Livelihood

Earnings of freelance writers depend on production, persistence, acceptance, and the pay schedule of the targeted markets. Unless a writer is employed full time by a magazine or book publisher, most find it necessary to supplement their incomes. For those who are employed in the publishing industry, salaries depend on the company, how much you write, and the other duties you perform.

Although a college education is not a prerequisite to becoming a freelance writer, it is definitely an asset. Staff positions for magazine and book publishers usually require a minimum of a bachelor's degree in English, journalism, agricultural journalism, or a related field. Horse experience is essential in most cases.

A Career in Equine Photography

For the artistic horse lover, equine photography may be the ideal career option. Magazine and book publishers are always seeking quality pictures. Breed organizations, horse show committees, advertising agencies, race track operators, owners, breeders, and horse publications all engage horse photographers who can catch the essence of the animal.

A thorough knowledge of horse psychology and the ability to capture the essence of a horse are special talents. While no formal training is required, knowledge of equipment, lighting, horse anatomy, equine behavior, breed conformation, performance requirements, and ease in the presence of horses are among the basic requirements for an equine photographer. Photography classes are available through extension programs, college fine arts programs, and private studios. A volunteer internship with a successful photographer is a valuable way to gain experience and make contacts.

To test your ability, make contacts, and find a variety of horses, settings, lighting, and poses to capture with your camera, you can attend 4-H shows, local rodeos, roping competitions, and show circuits with Eastern and Western classes.

Income ranges from not even meeting expenses to $5,000 per assignment. Depending upon the location, and the photographer's willingness to travel, marketing skills, initiative, area of specialty and appeal, and the breaks received, it is possible to make from $30,000 to $50,000 a year. Fees vary from $10 to $150 for black and white photos and from $25 to $300 for color photos. Many established photographers charge a fee of $800 a day. Good used equipment usually runs in the vicinity of $2,000 and is an economical way for a new photographer to start in the business.

Specialties in Communication

In the communications industry, publishers, writers, editors, and photographers are only a few of the career options available. In the *Writer's Market* section entitled "How Much Should I Charge," employment categories for the freelancer are listed along with common fees. The categories range from advertising and audiovisuals to book jacket blurbs and church history. The abundance of job ideas and services is mind boggling. Picture editing, photo brochures, computer editing, screen writing, research — the list goes on and on. All these indicate that opportunities in the communications industry are abundant. Just keep searching for your niche.

RESOURCES

Blood Horse, The. Debbie Tuska. 1736 Alexandria Drive, Lexington, Kentucky 40504. (800)866-2361.

Books in Print. Available in the reference department of the library. Lists by author, subject, and title all books currently available.

Bowker, R.R. Catalog. 249 West 17th Street, New York, New York 10011. (212)645-0067. Contact for a catalog of publishing resources, and for sample copies and subscription rates for these: *Publishers Weekly, Library Journal,* and *School Library Journal.*

Copyright Office. Library of Congress, Washington, D.C. 20559. *Copyright Basics* (order Circular 1) and *Publications on Copyrights* (order Circular 2).

Daily Racing Form. Peter Berry. 2231 E. Camelback Road, Suite 100, Phoenix, Arizona 85016.

Directory of American Booksellers. American Book Sellers Association. 560 White Plains Road, Tarrytown, New York 10591. (914)631-7800. Fax: (914)631-8391. Lists 20,000 publishers. Available in most libraries.

Equistar Publications, Ltd. Steve Ritchie. P.O. Box 26895, Columbus, Ohio 43226.

Fershtman, Julie. *Equine Law and Horse Sense.* Horse and the Law Publishing Company. P.O. Box 25069, Franklin, Michigan 48025-0696 (1996). (800)662-2210.

Fleet Street Publishing Corporation. Mary Kinnish, Editorial Director. 656 Quince Orchard Road, Gaithersburg, Maryland 20878; (301)977-3900. Publications include: *Equus, HorsePlay, Dressage Today, TT.E.A.M. News International.*

Hill, Cherry. P.O. Box 140, Livermore, Colorado 80536.

Horse Industry Directory. American Horse Council. 1700 K Street NW, Suite 300, Washington DC 20006. (202)296-4031. Lists 250 horse publications.

Literary Market Place. Available in the reference department of the library. Lists agents, artists, reviewers, associations.

Poynter, Dan. *The Self-Publishing Manual: How to Write, Print, and Sell Your Own Book.* Para Publishing. P.O. Box 8206, Santa Barbara, California 93118-8206. Details every aspect of writing, publishing, and distribution. Lists many resources.

Publishers, Distributors, and Wholesalers of the United States. Available in the reference department of the library. Provides resources for self-publishing.

Publishers' Trade List Annual. Available in the reference department of the library. Includes a list of 1,500 publishers' catalogs.

Stuart, Sally. *Christian Writers' Market Guide.* Harold Shaw Publishers. Box 567, Wheaton, Illinois 60189. (708)665-6700. Targets writers who have a Christian perspective.

Third Generation Communications. Betsy Lynch. 5512 Rix Road, Fort Collins, Colorado 80524. (970)224-5332.

Thoroughbred Times. Mark Simon, Editor-in-Chief. P.O. Box 8237, Lexington, Kentucky 40533. (606)260-9800.

Writer, The. 120 Boylston Street, Boston, Massachusetts 02116-4615. (617)423-3157. Magazine offers practical articles on how to write for publication and tips on how and where to market manuscripts.

Writer's Digest. 1507 Dana Ave. Cincinnati, OH 45207. (800)333-0133. Considered one of the best magazines for freelance writers, it presents information on improving writing skills and locating publishers and markets.

Writer's Guide to Book Editors, Publishers, and Literary Agents: 1997-1998. Prima Publishing, Rocklin, California (1997). (916)632-4400. Profiles 500 publishing houses, includes many writer tips.

Writer's Handbook: The New 1997 Edition. The Writer Inc. Boston, Massachusetts (1997). Lists 3,000 markets for manuscripts of all types; writing instruction; publishers in 45 categories including animals (with horse publications listed); and sources for 168 cash prizes for unpublished works.

Writer's Market: Where and How to Sell What You Write. Writer's Digest Books, F&W Publications, 1507 Dana Avenue, Cincinnati, Ohio 45207. 1997. Comprehensive writer's resource includes information on queries and book proposals, agents, format, trends, contracts, taxes, fees, an overview of the Internet, book publishers, magazines listed by category (Animals and Sports categories list horse magazines). Updated every year with new markets, new editors, and information on publishers that no longer accept freelance unsolicited manuscripts.

Chapter Fifteen

Supporting the Equine Industry

Professionals in the legal, financial, insurance, and real estate fields support the equine industry in a variety of ways. Among these professionals are attorneys, consultants, expert witnesses, appraisers, accountants, insurance companies and agents, and real estate companies, brokers, and agents. Although these jobs don't provide extensive opportunities to work directly with horses, they do provide valuable support to the horse industry and allow people to be involved in a viable way with horses.

ATTORNEY AT LAW

Where there are people, there are differing opinions, and where there are differing opinions, there is a need for someone with legal knowledge and expertise to provide a fair and just solution. Professional legal counsel is frequently needed for the 7.1 million people involved in the horse industry as volunteers, horse owners, employers, employees, and business owners. Attorney Julie Fershtman describes *equine law* as the practice of law that involves horses and horse activities, businesses, organizations, and facilities. Clients range from individual owners, breeding farms, race tracks, insurance companies, syndication, partnerships, trainers, instructors, commercial haulers, associations, and veterinarians.

Law schools do not offer specializations in equine law, so anyone who is interested in knowing more about this field should refer to the books listed in the Resources section at the end of this chapter, speak with lawyers in the field, be willing to study and conduct research independently, and possess a solid knowledge of horses. The percentage of a practice dedicated to equine law varies according to the lawyer's desire, knowledge, reputation, and marketing focus. Location is also a factor. The larger the horse population, the broader the equine clientele base.

Specializing in Equine Law

George Johnson, Attorney at Law. George Johnson is an attorney with Johnson Law. This firm is located in Colorado, a state with one of the largest equine populations. Keeping this in mind, George feels it would be difficult for any lawyer to dedicate his practice entirely to equine law. Depending on the circumstances, his equine business ranges from 10 to 90 percent of his practice.

George's lifetime involvement with horses influenced his interest in equine law. His horse background, in addition to his expertise in tax law and property law, and his willingness to conduct research, are among his key qualifications. Nearly fifteen years into his practice, George was approached by a client friend who needed a legal contract drawn for leasing a horse. George created a horse lease and a new extension to his practice began. His equine practice includes horse injury cases, rodeo leases for non-sanctioned jackpot rodeos, drawing up releases for horse-related liability issues, contract agreements, risk management, and legal consultation for those acquiring, selling, or setting up a horse business.

George wrote the book, *In the Balance: A Horseman's Guide to Legal Issues*, which offers tips on how to form an equine business, keep good records, find an equine attorney, buy horse property, and handle liability and insurance issues.

Krystyna Carmel, Attorney at Law. Krystyna Carmel attended law school with the goal of entering international law and diplomacy. A horseback rider all her life, she subscribed to and thoroughly consumed, *Chronicles of the Horse.* An advertisement for a lawyer specializing in equine law peaked her interest. She called the lawyer and the following summer she found herself working for his firm. Her interest in equine law grew and upon graduation she joined the firm. One of her responsibilities included putting together a newsletter entitled, *Equine Law and Business Letter.* When the firm's focus changed, Krystyna purchased the newsletter and became a partner at another firm.

Krystyna's practice consists primarily of equine-related business law ranging from insurance and sale disputes, training agreements, retainers and fees for trainers, consignment and lease agreements, bills of sale, boarding contracts, and agency agreements. Her clients range from individual owners and buyers to large stables and boarding facilities. Hunter-jumper horses are popular in Virginia, and it is not unusual for buyers to pay $10,000 to $500,000 for a single horse. Some purchases involve overseas transport. Legal counsel can save investors a great deal of difficulty by settling simple issues before they become major complications.

Krystyna recommends the pursuit of equine law more out of a love for law than horses. Experience with horses is important, but equine lawyers deal with criminals, fraud, research, and disputes on a daily basis. Furthermore, a lawyer who wants to eventually have an equine law practice will probably have to put in some time as an associate for a large firm where cases are assigned to, not selected by, the associate. This allows little room for individual preference.

Julie I. Fershtman, Attorney at Law. Julie I. Fershtman became aware early in her career that many camps and programs were forced to discontinue horse operations or pay unbearably high insurance premiums. She knew there was a nationwide movement to limit the liability of horse and stable owners in an effort to revive the recreational equestrian industry. Julie aspired to make a difference in the horse world, and she knew that there was an abundance of equine law precedents buried in law libraries. She began researching. Motivated by the wealth of information, she listed her name as an equine lawyer in a newsletter. She was encouraged by her first call and began a marketing and educational campaign that now includes speaking at such conventions as Equitana USA, Equine Affair, National Conference on Equine Law, and the annual meeting of the American Horse Council.

Today, as a defense attorney, Julie also handles insurance, business, and employment disputes across the country. Litigation cases, where a stable or equine operation is being sued, comprise the biggest part of her practice. Julie is the author of *Equine Law and Horse Sense* and an article entitled, "Considering a Career in (Equine) Law," which she will share with any serious minded equine law candidate.

Tips from the Experts —
Julie I. Fershtman, Attorney at Law

- Be persistent but not pushy.
- Develop good people skills.
- Be a good listener.
- Be a good communicator. Consider enrolling in speech and journalism classes.
- Learn how to effectively interview clients.
- Learn how to give practical, not scholarly, advice.
- Keep current on legal issues by reading legal publications. Keep current on horse issues by reading a variety of horse publications.
- Understand the court system. Attend and read about court.
- Develop leadership skills.
- Participate actively in organizations by accepting and fulfilling leadership duties.
- Network with other professionals by joining groups, such as the bar association.
- Be visible. Advertise, publish articles, give speeches.
- Don't give your services away. Many equine industry people are capable, do-it-myself people. They may seek just enough free information to do their own legal work.
- Before promoting yourself as an equine lawyer, become proficient in the basic skills of practicing law.
- Consider working with a proficient lawyer or firm.
- Understand that developing a clientele takes time.
- Develop a good reputation by providing good, honest service.

Pursuing a Career in Equine Law

Law is a demanding occupation. A strong desire to attain a high level of academic achievement and professional responsibility is essential. Although law schools are diverse in their education and training missions, they have several things in common. Admission is competitive, a prerequisite bachelor's degree or three years of course work toward a bachelor's degree from an accredited institution is standard, the passing of the Law School Admission Test (LSAT), the submission of credible references (including a statement of background, career goals, and experience), a grade point average of 3.0 or better, and, after admission, three to four years of concentrated study. Before practicing law, a state board examination must be passed.

Experience in a law firm is advantageous. Some firms hire prospective law students as clerks, who run legal filings to court and perform basic office tasks. Little hands-on law experience is obtained, but the contacts and a feel for law office routine can be very valuable.

Once a student is admitted to law school, the person can benefit greatly from the hands-on experience of an internship.

The competition in the legal profession is intense, which makes it possible for clients to shop for lawyers. The experienced, reputable lawyer, who has done a good job of marketing, will have the advantage. Specialization can create a competitive edge if the specialty is appropriate for the locale.

Typically lawyers work as salaried employees with large firms, as self-employed business owners, or as partners in law firms. An associate's annual salary ranges from $25,000 to $40,000, and owners and partners make more than $100,000 per year, depending on the locale and demand.

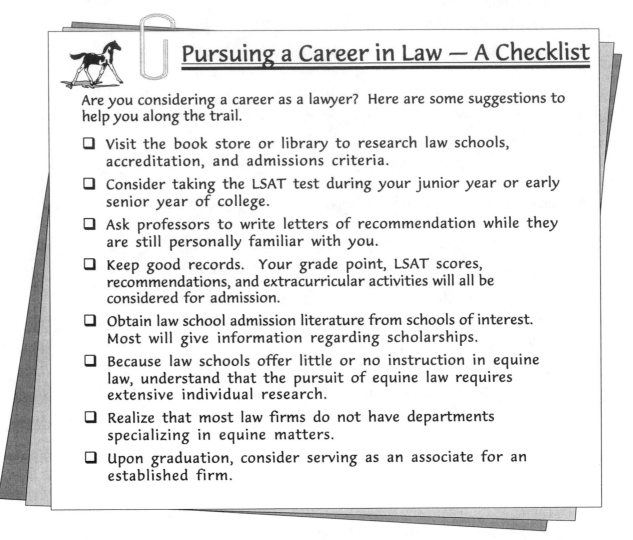

Pursuing a Career in Law — A Checklist

Are you considering a career as a lawyer? Here are some suggestions to help you along the trail.

❏ Visit the book store or library to research law schools, accreditation, and admissions criteria.

❏ Consider taking the LSAT test during your junior year or early senior year of college.

❏ Ask professors to write letters of recommendation while they are still personally familiar with you.

❏ Keep good records. Your grade point, LSAT scores, recommendations, and extracurricular activities will all be considered for admission.

❏ Obtain law school admission literature from schools of interest. Most will give information regarding scholarships.

❏ Because law schools offer little or no instruction in equine law, understand that the pursuit of equine law requires extensive individual research.

❏ Realize that most law firms do not have departments specializing in equine matters.

❏ Upon graduation, consider serving as an associate for an established firm.

EQUINE CONSULTANTS

The equine industry is spread around the world. It encompasses many recreational and career options and it involves people from different economical, cultural, and social backgrounds. There is no single governing agency. With such diversity in the industry, situations arise that require expert counsel that includes detailed research conducted by an expert in a specific equine area. When legal issues arise, the busy horse person seldom has the time or resources to obtain the needed documentation. Lawyers and government officials, trained in colleges that offer little equine law, often seek the services of people with specific horse expertise.

Expert Witness Services

Expert witness services exist across the country to provide lawyers with specialized expert witnesses. Some services are: Technical Assistant Bureau, National Consultant Referral, Expert Resource, Inc., Expert Knowledge Corporation, and Technical Advisory Service For Attorneys (TASA).

TASA contracts with 24,000 experts with expertise in about 7,000 disciplines. More than 40 are specialists in the equine industry and according to Suzanne Olita, vice president of TASA, there is plenty of room for more equine experts.

Laws, regulations, and technologies are constantly changing. Frequently complex legal matters arise, which call for the knowledge only experts can provide. Experts are consulted to help evaluate the merits of cases or to help with case preparation, research, and strategy. Approximately 90 percent of the cases are settled out of court.

As part of a screening device, potential TASA experts fill out a detailed application stating their expertise, education, training, and qualifications. Once registered with TASA, consultants set their own fees, which range from $150 to $300 an hour. TASA adds on a fee for their services. Attorneys contact TASA and TASA puts the attorneys in touch with experts in their geographic areas.

Expert Witnesses, Consultants, Appraisers — Four Professionals

Kathy Kusner. Kathy Kusner uses her years of experience and expertise in the equine world to assist others in making knowledgeable decisions. Kathy was the first licensed female jockey. She rode in the Olympics at Tokyo and Mexico City, and in Munich she earned a silver medal. She has won countless international competitions, and in 1990 she was inducted into the Show Jumping Hall of Fame. She gives clinics and lectures internationally and is an established teacher and trainer.

Currently, in addition to teaching, Kathy assists lawyers as a horse expert witness for cases involving horse litigation. Most of these cases require accident reconstruction to establish how and why an accident occurred and to establish if there was or was not any negligence involved. Kathy has worked long and hard to obtain her expertise, but she purposefully keeps her fees at a moderate level. She charges $100 an hour. A retainer of $1,000, half of which is non-refundable, is applied toward her hours of work. She is registered with five expert witness service companies.

Pat Rippee. A registered expert witness with TASA, Pat Rippee's fields of expertise include horsemanship, transporting horses, trail rides, and specializing in Arabians, show Thoroughbreds, and Morgan horses. Pat has trained with top notch trainers, served as an American Horse Show Association guest judge, and created equine courses at several community colleges.

In addition to working with TASA, Pat runs her own company, New Horizon Equine Consultant, for the purpose of acquiring, creating, and distributing equine educational materials. She serves as a consultant to buyers who seek an expert opinion about horses they are considering purchasing. She also provides judging, training, and consulting services for equestrian activities and legal cases. Pat's transition from trainer/teacher/judge to consultant is relatively recent. She says the change has required hard work, effective marketing, and perseverance.

Tips from the Experts — Pat Rippee, Expert Witness

Here are some of the qualifications required of an expert witness specializing in horses.

- Knowledge of breeds.
- Knowledge of training disciplines.
- Knowledge of dispositions, heat cycles, and temperaments.
- Capability to do research on the records of a horse's background, training, ownership, and abuse history.
- Knowledge of pedigrees and how to research pedigrees.
- Knowledge of state equine-related laws.
- Ability to make a professional decision regarding fault and possible prevention.

Richard A. Beck. Among the several careers of Richard A. Beck, owner of Penosa Blood Stock, are those of equine consultant and appraiser. Most of his consulting work is in the legal realm. He has provided consultation throughout the United States and he has also testified before the Internal Revenue Service. Richard states that years are often invested on a case before a financial reward is received. He worked on one Justice Department tax case that lasted five years. When the case came to court, he earned 50 percent of his total fees. The court session lasted four days.

Richard feels people can earn more than $30,000 a year as a consultant if they actively market their skills and really hustle. But credibility and expertise must come first. If you are going to represent yourself as a witness in the federal courts, he recommends you have enough experience and knowledge to hold your own. Lawyers may not know the equine industry, but they do know law.

Richard is a professional horsemen whose background includes a degree in equine science, certification as an American Horse Show judge, publication of books for six breeds, magazine articles, appraisal work, bloodstock agent, and a partner in an Egyptian Arabians breeding operation. He is registered with TASA, but most of his cases come from previous clients and by word of mouth. He is currently listing his services on the Internet.

Richard says that some attorneys use attorney-advisory services such as TASA, but also use experts from their own locale. If you are an expert, consider contacting attorneys who deal with horse-related issues, and present them with a résumé documenting your expertise. Also contact one of the advisory service organizations listed in the Resources section at the end of this chapter.

Dave Johnson. Dave Johnson, president and general manager of North American Equine Services™, confirms the fact that everyone who wants to be an expert witness or appraiser must have extensive background and involvement in the equine world. For the past 20 years, Dave and his company have specialized in evaluating horses and horse-related activities for the legal community. Eighty percent of the business involves equine litigation and commands fees of $150 an hour and $1,500 per day plus expenses.

Tips from the Experts - Dave Johnson, Appraiser

Here are some suggestions for anyone considering a career as an appraiser.

- Enjoy the law and research.
- Desire to learn new things.
- Love horses and people.
- Understand that law is history and the horse business is history in action.
- Be willing to gain experience and expertise.
- Stay involved with horses.
- Get a good college education. Many horse people are doctors, attorneys, and businesspeople, and you need to be able to effectively communicate with them.

Dave didn't just jump into this business. He has more than 25 years experience as a trainer, breeds hunter/jumpers, is a licensed judge with a *large R status* in Arabians, and a coach for such organizations as the United States Equestrian Team. When committee and volunteer positions came his way in the American Equine Appraisers, American Horse Show Association, American Quarter Horse Association, and International Arabian Horse Show Association, he willingly accepted them.

Aware that the horse world consists of many intelligent and educated people who enjoy dealing with experienced, informed experts, Dave attended law school for several years after receiving his master's degree in English and history. He loves everything about his work and horses, and believes in what he does because he believes in horses. They give so much for so little, says Dave.

Qualifications and Income Expectations

Qualifications for expert witnesses, consultants, and appraisers are similar. It is not unusual for people to provide all three services while continuing to work in a specific horse field.

Jay Proost is executive director of the American Society of Equine Appraisers, which recruits knowledgeable people who can judge equine value, certify appraisers, and provide performance criteria and limited training for others desiring certification. It serves the Internal Revenue Service, FDIC, insurance companies, bankruptcy courts, and large national lenders and businesses related to the equine industry. According to Jay, sincere, honest, and dependable people are needed today to render professional appraisal services to existing and new customers. Qualifications for certification by the American Society of Equine Appraisers are: a minimum of five years in an equine or equine-related business, and completion of an application for membership presented and approved by the board of directors.

The current fee charged by appraisers is $40 an hour. Appraisers, according to the American Society of Equine Appraisers, earn $4,000 to $35,000 a year on a part-time basis and can command full-time incomes up to $100,000. Membership, which includes a copy of the *Appraisers Handbook*, promotional and appraisal information, and a sample appraisal, costs $295, with semi annual dues of $55.

INSURANCE

There are 6.9 million horses in the United States. Many owners are emotionally attached to their horses to the extent of considering them valuable family members. Aside from emotions, billions of dollars are invested in horses. With individual investments ranging from $1,000 to $750,000, insurance is an important issue.

Insurance Agencies

Butch Human, president of Horse Insurance Specialists in Pilot Point, Texas, realized the importance of equine insurance. A horse enthusiast and active show horse rider, he spent his weekends at horse shows while owning a small insurance agency in North Carolina. When people learned he was in insurance they asked about horse coverage, and Butch realized the potential market. He researched the industry, found the best suppliers, and began a specialty insurance agency. Within three years his business grew to include clients throughout the United States, with the most in Texas. Consequently, in 1987 he moved the business to Texas. Today he employs fourteen people, eight are licensed agents, six are receptionists, accountants, and policy processors.

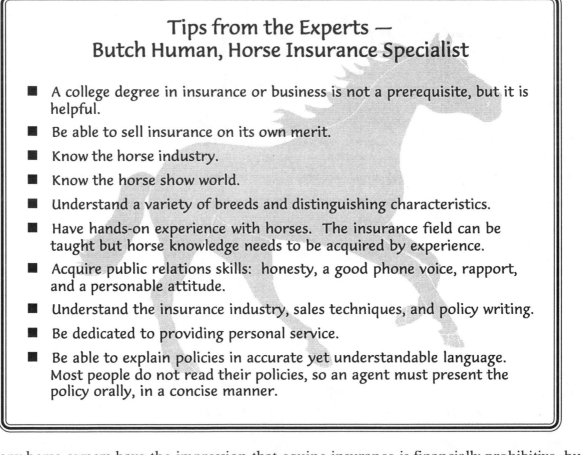

Tips from the Experts —
Butch Human, Horse Insurance Specialist

- A college degree in insurance or business is not a prerequisite, but it is helpful.

- Be able to sell insurance on its own merit.

- Know the horse industry.

- Know the horse show world.

- Understand a variety of breeds and distinguishing characteristics.

- Have hands-on experience with horses. The insurance field can be taught but horse knowledge needs to be acquired by experience.

- Acquire public relations skills: honesty, a good phone voice, rapport, and a personable attitude.

- Understand the insurance industry, sales techniques, and policy writing.

- Be dedicated to providing personal service.

- Be able to explain policies in accurate yet understandable language. Most people do not read their policies, so an agent must present the policy orally, in a concise manner.

Many horse owners have the impression that equine insurance is financially prohibitive, but Butch knows otherwise. Mortality insurance for a $10,000 horse runs around $350 a year. A breeding stallion can be insured for loss of fertility at one-half to one percent of the horse's value. Limited mortality coverage runs about one percent of the horse's value and covers the loss of a horse due to fifteen different types of risk, such as flood, earthquake, barn fire, wind, or lightning. Butch recommends insuring a horse if the loss will cause a big financial burden.

New agents who work for Horse Insurance Specialists earn about $20,000 a year plus a bonus if they exceed production goals. Within several years, earnings can reach $50,000. Commissions are paid on renewals whether the agent is actively involved in the renewal or not, so it is not unusual for an agent to earn $100,000. A college education is not required for agents, but a degree can open many doors. Courses in insurance and business are helpful. Butch recommends subscribing to major horse publications, viewing advertisements, calling companies of interest, introducing yourself, and asking about employment opportunities.

Major Insurance Companies

Horse Insurance Specialists, like other agencies throughout the United States, represent major insurance companies that have an agricultural division, which is responsible for equine liability, stable liability, and farm and ranch insurance policies. One such company is American Equine Insurance Group (AEIG). This company is unique as an independent underwriting manager specializing exclusively in equestrian insurance. AEIG serves as the intermediary between the actual insurance carrier and the insurance brokers who serve client needs.

John Hart, chief executive officer, started AEIG from scratch. He recognized a need for a company that stays in tune with the horse industry, keeps abreast of constant changes, and focuses specifically on horse and horse owner insurance. AEIG underwrites risks, issues policies, customizes coverage, sets rates, develops marketing strategies, renders statistical analyses, and basically handles everything for the carriers. AEIG works with several hundred brokers and their agents, ranging from small one-person agencies dealing exclusively with equine policies to large diverse agencies. There are fifteen employees, including underwriters, industry liaisons, and support staff. Most have horse background.

Amy Daum, public relations and marketing director of AEIG, received a degree in English and equine business management. She feels the insurance business offers her the best of both worlds. She has the opportunity to travel to special events, such as Equitana, work in the insurance industry, and ride horses after hours. She feels a college degree is a valuable asset that exposes people to many career opportunities.

Doug Panhorst, AEIG manager of underwriting, is assisted by Chris Phillips, a graduate of Johnson and Wales equestrian program, and Jim Griffith, charter property and causality underwriter (CPCU). These three are responsible for reviewing every application to determine if coverage will be granted. They ascertain if any exclusions are necessary and develop the contract. The recommended prerequisites for underwriters are good communication skills, a mind for analysis, insurance experience, and/or a four-year degree in business, communications, or an equine-related program. The advanced training certification, charter property and causality underwriter certification (CPCU), can be obtained at a private school or through independent study. This rigorous program includes twelve courses with accompanying tests. Underwriting assistants receive a starting salary in the $20,000 to $30,000 range.

Claims Adjusting

Claims adjusting for AEIG is done by National Equine Adjusting. Fred Whittet and his staff of seven monitor and assess claims to insure they are in compliance with the legal contract of the insurance policy. This only comprises half of their responsibility because most policies include major medical coverage. The policy holder is required to inform the company when a

183

horse is ill. Unlike human health plans, equine insurance has the adjuster work directly with the owner and veterinarian to make sure the horse receives proper care, medication, and surgery. If a horse dies, the adjuster researches the legal ownership and establishes the horse's worth. The adjuster also provides access to equine medical specialists who work with the local veterinarian to secure the best plan for a horse's recovery.

Equine claims adjusters should have a background in the equine industry and a college degree or previous insurance experience. Other large companies that write equine policies are the American Bankers Group Insurance, North American Live Stock Insurance, Redlands Insurance Company, and American Live Stock Insurance Company.

Liability Insurance

Coverage of horses and facilities is only one aspect of the equine insurance business. With the increasing trend toward lawsuits, there is a noticeable need for liability insurance coverage. Consumers who are unwilling to accept responsibility for a mishap are quick to sue and thereby direct blame away from themselves. Farriers, for instance, were seldom sued in the past, but the trend is changing. A full-time farrier shoes an average of 32 horses a week; this equals nearly 1,600 potential suits a year.

In response to the litigious climate and the high dollar value of horses today, Markel Insurance Company developed a general liability policy that protects farriers against claims of bodily injury or property damage due to shoeing activities; coverage for products sold, work performed, and equipment set up on someone's property that causes an injury; care custody and liability control for claims against a farrier who injures a horse; and equipment and supply floaters that cover loss, theft, or damage to horseshoes, tools, and supplies transported in a truck. Markel presented this coverage plan to the American Farriers Association and received their endorsement.

Agent and broker requirements vary from state to state. Some require a state mandated short course and licensing exam. Mathematical aptitude, a business degree, and equine background are helpful.

BOOKKEEPERS, ACCOUNTANTS, CPAS

Recordkeeping systems and tax returns range from relatively simple procedures to very complex. Owners keep their own books or hire a bookkeeper or accountant. Some business people file year-end returns themselves, and others turn their records over to a tax service, accounting firm, or certified public accountant (CPA). Large businesses often hire or contract with a CPA to do their books. Accounting and bookkeeping positions in the horse industry are available for people with the appropriate education and experience, combined with an analytical mind and horse background.

Accountants and bookkeepers assist businesses by setting up their books, keeping records, selecting a computer program, and paying taxes. Equine accounts usually comprise only one segment of the accountant's clientele. Most accountants, except during tax season, work 40 to 50 hours per week. Yearly salaries range from $30,000 to $100,000.

The horse industry is constantly in flux. A CPA can be a valuable asset to a business by helping with strategic planning, risk management, retirement and pension plans, merging a solid business plan with new technologies, locating and securing capital, reviewing software and hardware, and suggesting Internet strategies. In tax situations, only CPAs can represent a client before the IRS or state tax board.

Qualifications for Becoming an Accountant

Colleges and universities offer bachelor's degrees and master's degrees in accounting and financial planning that prepare individuals for accounting jobs with business and accounting firms. To obtain the next level of education — the certified public accountant (CPA) — a person must have a minimum of a bachelor's degree and pass a state test. Contact the state associations of certified public accountants or a local CPA for specific information pertaining to your state.

A college accounting degree is not required to provide tax preparation assistance. Shirley Mayfield, a partner of Better Income Tax Service in Colorado, has a degree in nursing. When the opportunity arose to enter the tax business she took a two-year course in accounting and tax preparation. To keep current, she attends a week-long course each year. She prepares a number of year-end accounts for horse industry people, and these comprise a small portion of her business. She feels anyone who tries to specialize in only horse industry accounts will have a difficult time.

American Institute of Certified Public Accountants (AICPA)

The national professional organization for all CPAs is the American Institute of Certified Public Accountants. Founded in 1887, this organization of 320,000 members established accountancy as a profession distinguished by rigorous educational requirements, high professional standards, a strict code of ethics, a licensing status, and a commitment to serving the public interest. AICPA provides products, publications, conferences, tax information phone service, and technical services, including an accounting and auditing hotline, library service, professional services, and financial planning hotline. AICPA offers an information packet on career alternatives, including public service, environmental accounting, forensic accounting (fraud investigation), information technology services (design and implementation of specialized advanced computer systems), management consulting, personal finance planning, tax advisory services, industry, government, and education.

To qualify for CPA certification, an individual must complete an accounting program (of 150 hours) at a college or university, pass a uniform CPA exam developed by the AICPA, and, in most states, have a certain amount of professional work experience in public accounting. Entry-level salaries range from $23,000 to $32,500 depending on the size of the firm. Large companies with more than $500 million in sales pay their CPAs up to $295,000. Accountants must acquire equine background through individual study and research.

Gary Bratton — An Equine CPA

Gary Bratton, of Bratton Financial Corporation, is a CPA who dedicates his practice to financial planning. Gary is a former racehorse owner and loves the horse world. He is especially drawn to the Thoroughbred horse industry, and has developed a rapport with about a half dozen trainers. Through these trainers, he has found an accounting niche in the Thoroughbred syndication industry. Working with five or six people, he develops syndication and partnership agreements that best represent all parties involved.

Previously, Gary prepared tax returns for people in the equine industry. Today he devotes his time to financial planning and refers any tax preparation accounts to an associate. Because it is common for people in the horse industry to only seek an accountant at the end of the year to prepare their tax returns, Gary feels that specializing in equine accounting is too limiting. Accountants with horse experience can successfully use their background to expand a practice, but can seldom build a practice entirely on horse accounts. He recommends reading syndication and partnership agreements, and a book by Arnold Kirkpatrick entitled, *Successful Thoroughbred Investments and a Changing Market.*

REAL ESTATE

Selling Horse Properties

Selling horse properties is the specialty of William Hummer. A long-time horse enthusiast, William and his wife own and raise Thoroughbred and Arabian horses. Seeking a profession in which he could work for himself and blend his selling skills, desire to be outdoors, and love for horses, he left the National Institute of Health and studied at the Real Estate Institute.

After William graduated and obtained his state license, he began selling horse properties. He soon found several obstacles in his path and set about creatively overcoming them. One obstacle was lenders. Nearly all lenders refused to finance vacant land. So William teamed up with Robert Moore of Cherry Creek Mortgage Company to provide buyers with quality customer service, knowledge, and commitment to drawing up equitable loan contracts.

The next obstacle was acquiring effective title searches. Horse properties frequently come on the market when large ranchers feel compelled to sell part of their land to pay taxes. The ranches may have been in the owners' hands for generations, and some date back to homestead rights. Dealing with the complex title issues, water rights, surveys, and zoning regulations requires a knowledgeable, experienced person. Keith Bohall of North American Title Company joined forces with William and Robert to provide that service.

Tips from the Experts —
William Hummer, Horse Property Sales

- Realtors are self-employed and must plan their budgets and lifestyles accordingly, and provide for insurance, retirement, recordkeeping.

- Earned income depends on initiative, industriousness, foresight, and effective use of time.

- A state license is required, which demands comprehensive knowledge. Take a two-week or three-week course, rather than self-study. Contact your local realty board for a list of recommended schools.

- Develop a vision suited to your personality, skills, and interests, then research and pursue it.

- Work with buyers to make sure deals are in the best interest of all parties.

- Stay involved in the industry.

Guest and Dude Ranch Properties

Carolyn Callaway and her family spent many vacations on dude ranches. When Carolyn lost her husband, and her children headed for college, she called the owners of a ranch she had visited and asked if they had an opening. The next thing she knew she was working in the office, filling in as cook, and serving in the diningroom. Sensing it was time for another change, she headed for Fort Collins, Colorado, began a career in real estate, and formed Callaway Country Real Estate, a division of Coldwell Banker, Everett, and Williams Real Estate.

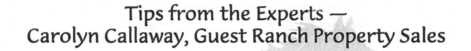

Tips from the Experts —
Carolyn Callaway, Guest Ranch Property Sales

- Be flexible. You have to fit into the schedule of buyers and sellers.

- Maintain contact with dude ranches, whether they are for sale or not. If the time to sell emerges, sellers need to feel comfortable and secure with their realtor.

- Become familiar with the dude ranch style of living.

- Know and love history. Many ranches date back to early ranch operations. Being able to describe their historical background increases interest and appeal.

- Love the business of real estate.

- Develop good communication skills.

- Give wise counsel. Know and understand the buyers' strengths and limits, then counsel them in finding the best match.

When a client expressed interest in guest ranches, Carolyn's business took a new direction. Today most of her sales are guest ranches, and it doesn't take many to make this a profitable career.

On the low end of the market, a dude ranch on leased land is listed at around $850,000. The average cost for a ranch is closer to $2,000,000, and ranches list as high as $7,750,000. Most ranches are turn key operations: the new owner can just step in and start business. Ranches come completely furnished with horses, tack, furnishings, equipment, and vehicles.

Horse Communities

Ted Yelek took another approach to real estate sales. After ranching for several years, he changed careers, teamed up with Dwight Eaton, a real estate broker, and began buying and selling for a profit. Recently Ted purchased 2,800 acres of land with a 10,300 square-foot indoor arena, 17 indoor stalls, and 5 acres of corrals. The property is located in the foothills of the Front Range of the Colorado Rocky Mountains, and Ted realized the area lent itself naturally to a subdivision. He divided it into 80 horse property lots and calls the development Sedona Hills. This private horse community has paved roads, underground utilities, and easy access to several cities. Perhaps the greatest attraction is the opportunity it affords horse enthusiasts to board, exercise, train, and ride right in their own backyards.

Internet

Gene Kilgore developed a marketing company that consists of a network of affiliate and associate brokers who specialize in recreational and working ranch properties. The Kilgore Ranch Network Real Estate can be accessed on the Internet. The network lists and describes a large selection of available ranches. The network consists of affiliate and associate brokers who specialize in recreational and working ranch properties. The properties include both small and large ranches, wilderness lodges, and cattle ranches, as well as unimproved land.

Career Opportunities

We live in a very mobile society. People move often and among those moving are horse people desiring their piece of the West. Whether people are looking for horse industry businesses, guest ranches, or just a place where they can keep their own horse and have access to riding trails, there will always be a market. Serving the horse community by finding properties to meet these different styles of living is one more career option.

While college education is not required to become a realtor, many colleges provide majors in real estate. In most states, people with four-year degrees in real estate do not have to take additional course work to obtain their licenses. However, they do need to pass the state exam. In the sunbelt states or states experiencing growth spurts, licensing procedures are more stringent.

Each state has its own set of criteria for real estate licensing, and laws are continually changing. Contact your state regulatory board (state division of real estate or state commission of real estate) for specifications. Fortunately for those already in the field, most laws are not retroactive, and only apply to new entrants. For instance, in January 1997 a new bill passed by the Colorado legislature was enacted that redefined real estate agent and broker titles: an *associate broker* is a broker employed and supervised by another broker; an *independent broker* is a self-employed broker with no employed licensees; and an *employing broker* is a broker who employs and supervises other licensees. With these redefinitions came requirements for additional course work. For more information, as well as a list of approved schools, contact the state of Colorado Real Estate Commission.

RESOURCES

Attorney Resources

Annual Equine Law Seminars. University of Kentucky. College of Law. Office of Continuing Legal Education, Suite 260 Law Building, Lexington, Kentucky 40506. (606)257-2921. Seminar materials presented by top equine lawyers.

Blood Horse: The Source, The. 1736 Alexander Drive, Lexington, Kentucky. (606)276-4450. Lists attorneys involved with equine law.

Carmel, Krystyna, Attorney at Law. *Horse Law News.* P.O. Box 579, Redwood City, California 94064-0579. *http://www. piebaldpress.com.*

Carmel, Krystyna, Editor. *Equine Law and Business Letter.* P.O. Box 4285, Charlottesville, Virginia 22905. E-mail: *kcarmel@aol.com.*

Fershtman, Julie, Attorney at Law. *Equine Law & Horse Sense.* Horses and the Law Publishing Company. P.O. Box 25069, Franklin, Michigan 48025-0696. (800)662-2210. Office: 30700 Telegraph Road, Suite 3475, Bingham Farms, Michigan 48025-8645. (248) 644-8645.

Internet. For law schools and descriptions, use a search engine to call up Law Schools. In some cases it is possible to submit an application via e-mail.

Johnson, George, Attorney at Law. Johnson Law Firm. 1775 Sherman Street, Suite 1825, Denver, Colorado 80203.

Johnson, George, Attorney at Law. *In the Balance: The Horseman's Guide to Legal Issues.* Pica Press. Golden, Colorado 80403. (800)279-2001, extension 209.

Law School Admission Test (LSAT). Box 2000, Newton, Pennsylvania, 28940-0998. (215)968-1001.

Martindale Hubbell Law Directory. 121 Chanlon Road, New Providence, New Jersey 07974. (908)464-6800.

Expert Witness/Appraiser Resources

American Society of Equine Appraisers. Jay Proost. Blue Lakes Office Park, Suite 1130, 834 Falls Avenue, Twin Falls, Idaho 83303. (208)733-1122.

Expert Knowledge Corporation. 2899 Agoura Road Suite 805, West Lake Village, California 91361. (800)401-4016.

Expert Resource. 4700 N. Prospect Road, Suite B, Peoria Heights, Illinois 61614. (800) 383-4857.

Kusner, Kathy. 1053½ N. Stanley Avenue, West Hollywood, California 90046. (213)654-7266.

National Consultant Referrals. 4918 North Harbor Drive, Suite 103, San Diego, California 92106. (800)221-3104. *http://www.referrals.com.*

New Horizon Equine Consultant. Pat Rippee. 3015 E. Hardie Road, Gibsonia, Pennsylvania 15044. (412)449-9909.

North American Equine Services™. Dave D. Johnson. 35644 North 11th Avenue, Phoenix, Arizona 85027. (602)582-8635. E-mail: *davidj@goodnet.com.*

Penosa Blood Stock. Richard Beck. 38220 Weld County Road 13, Windsor, Colorado 80550. (970)686-2865.

Technical Assistant Bureau. (800)336-0190. *http://www.intr.net/tab.*

Technical Advisory Service for Attorneys (TASA). Suzanne Olita. 1166 DeKalb Pike, Blue Bell, Pennsylvania, 19422-1853. (800)523-2319).

Insurance Resources

American Bankers Group Insurance. 11222 Quail Roost Drive, Miami, Florida, 33157.

American Equine Insurance Group. John Hart, Amy Daum, and Doug Panhorst. 5005 Newport Drive, Suite 600, Rolling Meadows, Illinois 60008. (847)398-7787.

American Livestock Insurance Company. 200 S. 4th Street, P.O. Box 520 Geneva, Illinois 60134-0520. (630)232-2100. E-mail: *als@inil.com.*

Blood Horse: The Source, The. 1736 Alexander Drive, Lexington, Kentucky. (606)276-4450. Lists insurance agents involved with the equine industry.

Horse Insurance Specialists. Butch Human. 1013 South Highway 377, Pilot Point Texas 76258. (800)346-3271.

Markel Insurance Company. 167 E. Main Street, Suite 305, Lexington, Kentucky 40507. (606)254-5782.

National Equine Adjusting. Fred Whittet, President. P.O. Box 571, Frankfort, Kentucky 40602. (800)783-9418.

North American Livestock Insurance. P.O. Box 930, Ocalla, Florida 34478-0930. (352)351-4799.

Redlands Insurance Company. Omni Center Office Park, 300 West Broadway, Suite 1600, Council Bluffs, Iowa 51503. (800)999-7475.

Accounting Resources

American Institute of Certified Public Accountants (AICPA). Kim Walsh. 1211 Avenue of the Americas, New York, New York 10036-8775. (212)596-6213. *http://www.aicpa.org.*

Better Income Tax Service. Shirley Mayfield, 321 W. Olive, Fort Collins, Colorado 80521.

Bratton Financial Corporation. Gary G. Bratton, CPA. 6555 Quince Road, Suite 104, Memphis, Tennessee, 38119. (901)756-6099.

Horse Industry Directory. American Horse Council. 1700 K. Street, NW, Suite 300, Washington DC 20006. (202) 296-4031.

Kirkpatrick, Arnold. *Successful Thoroughbred Investments and a Changing Market.* Thoroughbred Publications, Lexington, Kentucky.

National Association of Thoroughbred Owners. P.O. Box 878, Unionville, Pennsylvania 19375-0878. (800)545-7777.

Real Estate

Better Homes and Gardens. William Hummer, Robert Moore, Keith Bohall. 7061 South University Avenue, Littleton, Colorado 80122. (303)706-0269. E-mail: *wkh_hummer@msn.com.*

Callaway Country Real Estate. Carolyn Callaway. 2900 South College Avenue, Fort Collins, Colorado 80525. (970)223-6500.

Hudson, Karen. Jones Real Estate Colleges. 2150 South Cherry Street, Denver, Colorado 80222. (800)276-7031. Fax: (303)758-5332. Subsidiary of Dearborn Financial Institute. Classes prepare brokers for licensing under new Colorado legislation.

Kilgore Ranch Network. *http://www.ranchweb.com/restate-about/kilg//.htm.*

Real Estate Commission. Department of Regulatory Agencies, State of Colorado. 900 Grant Street, Suite 600, Denver, Colorado 80203.

Sedona Hills, Eaton, and Company Real Estate. Ted Yelek. 2517 County Road 29, Loveland, Colorado 80537. (907)667-8200.

Chapter Sixteen

Manufacturing, Distribution, and Sales

The $112.1 billion impact of the horse industry on the U.S. economy affects many facets of the employment market. Employment opportunities are extensive in the companies that produce the equine goods and services that are valued at $25.3 billion annually. Several of these companies are profiled in this chapter.

HORSE PRODUCTS: MANUFACTURING AND DISTRIBUTION

Farnam Industries

Farnam Companies, Inc., is one of many companies that serve the horse industry by manufacturing, distributing, and selling horse products. Founded in 1946, the company produces 250 horse products under three different brand names: Farnam, Equicare, and Horse Health Products. These products target both professional and pleasure horse owners, and are supplied to 12,000 retail outlets, including tack stores, feed stores, saddle shops, co-ops, and chain stores.

Positions with manufacturing and distribution companies provide little hands-on horse opportunities, but employees do work in a horse-oriented industry. Mark Steele, Farnam's director of human resources, maintains that in the sales and marketing division, equine experience is

perhaps even more important than an academic degree. Farnam looks for fresh perspectives, and therefore is receptive to horse event participants. However, a bachelor's degree with business and management courses is an important criterion.

The salaries of Farnam's employees are confidential, but are said to be competitive. They vary according to position, location, and qualifications. Employee benefits include 401K plans, gain sharing plans, and health, dental and life insurance. Mark Steele explained that career opportunities exist for qualified and motivated individuals. Personnel in sales, manufacturing, and distribution often enter at the ground level. As they show initiative and prove to be capable, opportunities for advancement and benefits increase.

Farnam's annual sales exceed $100 million, a figure that is growing by 10 percent yearly. They have 250,000 square feet of manufacturing and warehouse space located in Omaha, Nebraska, and Council Bluffs, Iowa. Besides sales and marketing, Farnam has several other divisions.

Veterinary Products Laboratory. This Farnam division conducts research and develops products that are shipped to 120 veterinary distribution centers, which in turn supply 17,000 veterinary practices. The division's focus is on horse health products. Twenty-five employees have educational backgrounds ranging from bachelor's degrees to a Ph.D. in nutrition, entomology, and veterinary medicine.

Charles Duff Advertising. This agency of Farnam designs labels, brochures, catalogs, advertisements, television commercials, info-mercials, multi-media sales presentations, and Internet advertising. About fifteen people are employed and qualifications include graphic arts, computer input, or journalism experience.

Spinworks. The goal of this public relations division is to reach dealers, distributors, and customers through trade publications, consumer magazines, journals, newspapers, radio, and special media events. The staff of two public relations professionals is predicted to grow.

Other Distributors and Manufacturers

Farnam is one of many distributors and manufacturers of equine products, health care products, feeds, and supplements. Equine products are also produced by such companies as Pfizer, Bayer Corporation, Franklin Fort Dodge Animal Health, Hoechst, Syntax, Buckeye, Farmland, Stamina Plus, and Purina Mills. These major distributors supply thousands of stores — stores that hire thousands of employees. To locate distributors and retail stores, consult *The Blood Horse: The Source;* the November special supplies and services issue of the *American Farriers Journal;* want ads and advertisements in equine magazines; and company representatives at horse expositions and clinics.

HORSE FEED: RESEARCH AND MANUFACTURING

Purina Mills

Purina Mills, Inc., founded in 1894, has its headquarters in St. Louis, Missouri; a research laboratory and an 1,188-acre experimental farm in Gray Summit, Missouri; 56 manufacturing plants located in 26 states; and 4,000 Purina dealers. As leaders in the animal nutrition industry, they employ 260 people in the central headquarters and 2,500 people nationally. About one-eighth of their business is dedicated to the equine industry.

Dave Nelson, a graduate of Louisiana Tech University in equine science and agricultural business, holds the position of operations manager. His responsibilities include the development of short-term and long-term growth plans, marketing strategies, advertisement placement, bag design, and educational programs, and the management of a traveling exhibit.

Purina Mills — Production and Manufacturing Personnel

✓ Executive officers. President and chief operating officer (CEO).

✓ Control, planning, and auditing personnel.

✓ Human resources staff.

✓ Marketing, public relations and communications staff.

✓ Operations managers and staff.

✓ Purchasing and transportation personnel.

✓ Researchers.

Purina's Experimental Farm conducts research pertaining to equine and other livestock nutrition. Dr. Kent Thompson, an equine nutritionist, was attracted to Purina in 1994 by the opportunities, the excellent research facility, and the qualified staff. His responsibilities include designing experiments, conducting experiments, data analysis, product development, and technical service.

Additional animal researchers and animal technicians conduct research and experiments for breeding and foaling of horses, including all ages and activity levels of performance and pleasure horses. Other researchers collect, record, and input data in the computer. Purina also engages field equine specialists who are stationed throughout United States. These people communicate with and ascertain the needs of equine owners, ranchers, and business people.

Purina Mills — Other Personnel

✓ Animal researchers and animal technicians.

✓ Business group directors. Oversee animal retail sales and marketing functions.

✓ Equine nutritionist.

✓ Farm staff. The 3 full-time employees and 1 part-time employee in the equine section of Purina's farm, which has 60 head of Quarter Horses, include: farm manager (oversees the running of the farm), veterinarians, and equine specialists.

✓ Field equine specialists.

✓ Marketing managers.

✓ Regional vice-presidents. Work with sales managers in their assigned regions.

✓ Sales managers and sales representatives. 450 professionals support 4,000 dealers.

✓ Veterinary services. Four veterinarians, including one equine specialist.

Purina is dedicated to communities and education. In an effort to involve local experts and inform the equine industry of the latest research and techniques, the company offers the Purina Education Series. More than 900 classes in the series are taught by local volunteer experts, such as nutritionists, veterinarians, and farriers. These workshops give experts visibility in their own communities and provide Purina with advertising exposure.

Purina also contributes to United Way, National 4-H, National Future Farmers of America (FFA), graduate research, university teaching programs, and scholarships for students seeking degrees in education and animal agriculture. Another outreach effort is America's Horse Country, an interactive equine educational exhibit, that travels to major equine events, state fairs, and community training events. The exhibit travels about 75,000 miles each year and reaches approximately 50,000 people. It contains a nutrition area presented by Purina Mills and a health care area sponsored by the American Association of Equine Practitioners.

The field for research and development of products is a growing field. Thirty percent of all the products sold by Purina have been developed in the last five years.

WHOLESALE AND RETAIL BUSINESS

Lextron, Inc.

Lextron is a wholesale/retail corporation that serves the agricultural sector throughout the United States. Lextron sells retail to the public, with 45 retail locations accommodating walk-in business, and the corporation sells wholesale to veterinarians and farm stores. Lextron also has an exclusive private label line of biological products.

The whole agricultural market is targeted, but geographic locations determine which products and specialty items will be emphasized. For instance, the divisions of Lextron in California and Florida are more involved with equine product sales than those located in other areas. The Colorado division targets feed lots and dairies, with a side market being feed lot cowboys and their horses. Lextron employs nearly 400 people.

Alycia Carmin, formerly the marketing coordinator at Lextron, accepted her position immediately after graduating from college. She found that her experience as a horse owner since early childhood, her work-study experience at a Colorado feed lot, and her dual major in animal science and agricultural economics were assets in acquiring the job.

Alycia found that her horse, feed lot, and educational qualifications helped her communicate with and win the confidence of farmers, veterinarians, cowboys, and sales managers. However, she says that someone who is just starting to work in the animal health industry shouldn't be too focused on one aspect of the industry because this will limit initial opportunities for employment. Companies need to offer a broad line of products to be profitable. Consequently, a potential employee needs to have a broad base of skills and interests.

Wholesale and Retail Positions

The following Lextron positions are found in most of the industry.

- ✓ Chief executive officer (CEO). Presides over the corporation, concentrating on the company's growth and future.

- ✓ Chief operating officer. Oversees the operation of the company.

- ✓ President. Works with division managers and vice presidents to assure smooth operations on the state and local levels.

- ✓ Chief financial officer. Responsible for all financial aspects of the company.

- ✓ Human resource personnel. In charge of benefits, payroll, background checks of potential new employees, and advertising for positions.

- ✓ Marketing coordinator. Sets up store displays, marketing strategies, and training.

- ✓ Division managers. Responsible for stores and sales representatives in the 15 divisions.

- ✓ Sales representatives. About 12 people for each of the 15 divisions sell products to farm and ranch stores, veterinarians, feedlots, and ranchers.

- ✓ Sales, counter, warehouse and telemarketing personnel. Work in Lextron's 45 retail stores.

RESOURCES

American Farriers Journal. Magazine of the American Farriers Association. P.O. Box 624, Brookfield, Wisconsin 53008-0624. (414)0782-4480. *Lesspub@aol.com.* A special edition of farrier supplies and services, published each November, lists 100 companies in the Products: Feed and Supplements section. Special edition price: $25.

Blood Horse: The Source, The. P.O. Box 4710, Lexington, Kentucky 40544-4710. (800)582-5604. Lists 100 feed businesses, with contact and merchandise information.

Carmin, Alycia. 31544 Hwy. 34, Kersey, Colorado 80644.

Charles Duff Advertising Agency. P.O. Box 34820, 301 West Osborn, Phoenix, Arizona 85013. http://*www.farnam.com.*

Farnam Industries. Mark Steele, Director of Human Resources. P.O. Box 34820, 301 West Osborn, Phoenix, Arizona 85013.

Horse expositions and shows. Have booths sponsored by major manufacturers and distributors wishing to promote their companies.

Lextron. 630 O Street, Greeley, Colorado 80631.

Purina Mills. Dave Nelson, Marketing Manager, and Dr. Kent Thompson, Research. 1401 South Hanley, St. Louis, Missouri, 63144.

Want ads and advertisements in equine magazines. Promote many suppliers and distributors.

Chapter Seventeen

Government and Law Enforcement Opportunities

Equine-related employment opportunities exist at the federal, state, and local levels of government and law enforcement. The U.S. Department of Agriculture has more than 1,000 equine-related positions. There are fewer positions available with the U.S. Forest Service, U.S. Department of the Interior, Fish and Wildlife Service, and Bureau of Land Management. Horse-related jobs with local government agencies are available in some metropolitan areas and counties. In addition to paid work opportunities, government equine programs also provide a variety of volunteer options.

U.S. DEPARTMENT OF AGRICULTURE (USDA)

Animal and Plant Health Inspection Service (APHIS)

Dr. John Zisk was head of the USDA Animal and Plant Health Inspection Service (APHIS) Horse Protection Act (HPA) program from 1992 to 1997. Before joining APHIS he was in private practice and served as a state veterinarian for the Wagering Division of the Florida State Regulation Commission.

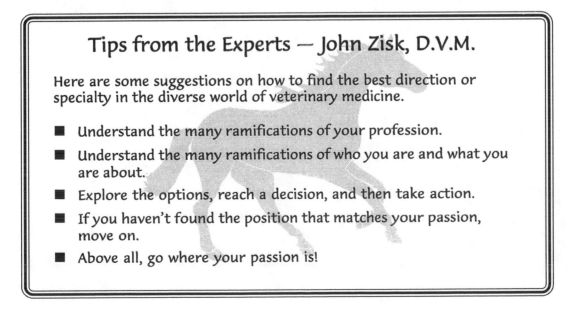

Tips from the Experts — John Zisk, D.V.M.

Here are some suggestions on how to find the best direction or specialty in the diverse world of veterinary medicine.

- Understand the many ramifications of your profession.
- Understand the many ramifications of who you are and what you are about.
- Explore the options, reach a decision, and then take action.
- If you haven't found the position that matches your passion, move on.
- Above all, go where your passion is!

According to Dr. Zisk, APHIS is the largest employer of veterinarians in the United States. There are about 1,000 veterinary professionals who hold various positions in Washington, D.C. and throughout the United States. Their goals are to insure humane care and treatment of show horses protected under the HPA; enforce the Animal Welfare Act, which covers certain animals used for research, exhibition, or sale through wholesale channels; work to prevent the introduction of and eradication of destructive exotic pests and diseases; and facilitate the international trade of horses and other animals. Currently the agency is developing humane treatment guidelines for horses that are transported to slaughter. APHIS veterinarians are involved in animal husbandry, behavior, reproduction, nutrition, and infectious disease research.

APHIS also employs animal care investigators who work in various field locations and need a minimum of a two-year degree in an equine-related field, combined with equine experience.

Most positions in APHIS do not involve hands on work with horses. However, many employees do work in and around the animals by conducting inspections of their surroundings, equipment, care, and overall health.

Other agencies of the federal government hire veterinarians for various research jobs and inspection positions. Brief job descriptions can be seen on the Internet at *www.usajobs.opm.gov* or information can be obtained by telephone at (912) 757-3000. As with most career opportunities it pays to be persistent. If no positions are available on your first contact, check back regularly.

Standard annual salaries for APHIS veterinarians range from $55,000 to $75,000, and take into consideration educational background, experience, and years of employment with the federal government. Animal care investigators' salaries range from $35,000 to $50,000. Benefits include medical and dental care and life insurance, as well as retirement, sick leave, and annual leave packages.

Advantages to Working as a Veterinarian for the USDA

✓ Know and be known by many people.

✓ Work as a veterinarian without having to intern for a long period of time.

✓ Receive a good benefit package, predictable income level, and advancement scale.

✓ Work a regular 40-hour week.

✓ Be free of the pressure of running your own business.

✓ Avoid the stress of working with a demanding public.

✓ Have exposure to and opportunity to work around horses.

✓ Apply for a variance that allows a veterinarian to also run a private practice.

U.S. FOREST SERVICE (USFS)

Jim Miller from the Washington, D.C. office of the U.S. Forest Service (USFS) says there are limited horseback riding job opportunities in the U.S. Forest Service. Most of those are in the Western states of Montana, Wyoming, New Mexico, Arizona, and Idaho.

The U.S. Forest Service is part of the U.S. Department of Agriculture, which consists of ten regions. Each region has 2 to 34 national forests with ranger districts responsible for recreation, trails, wilderness, and range management. The Forest Service maintains 133,000 miles of all-use trails, so employees in the trail and recreational maintenance program may have occasion to work on horseback. The range management districts, on the other hand, offer opportunities for full-time stock use. They hire packers to take supplies to remote forest ranger stations and to remote areas where bridge and other construction projects are under way. The pack trains, consisting of five to nine mules, usually include one permanent full-time rider and two permanent part-time riders. Most part-time employees work other jobs during the winter. The packers' responsibilities focus entirely on the stock.

If you are interested in U.S. Forest Service positions, you should contact the national forests in the Western states. Bob Hoverson, forester and regional packer for the Ninemile Ranger District of the U.S. Forest Service in Huson, Montana, entered his profession by doing just that. During his college years he applied for a position at a local ranger station and was turned down. At his wife's insistence, he reapplied. Someone had resigned and he was hired on the spot. He became close friends with another forester who became his sponsor. Seven years after Bob received a bachelor's of science degree in forestry, he took a full-time position with the Ninemile Ranger District. He has been with the Forest Service for 27 years.

Tips from the Experts —
Bob Hoverson, Forester and Packer, USFS

If you are interested in working for the Forest Service, here are some suggestions.

- Contact a specific forest or ranger office. There is a limited application period — usually a two-week period in April.
- Be persistent.
- Don't be particular about where you enter the system. The key is to get your foot in the door. Once you are a part of the system, opportunities to select specific areas are apt to open up.
- Make friends and contacts. Advancement opportunities are enhanced by good recommendations from respected people in the department.

Bob runs the Northern Region Pack Train during the summer. He and his crew pack into the back country with supplies and equipment to support back-country projects. It is not unusual for him to travel 800 to 1,000 miles a season on horseback. He also oversees the Primitive Skills Training Center during the winter months, runs the Leave No Trace Stock Use Education Program, and makes educational appearances in parades, fairs, and special events.

Limited stock-related opportunities with the Forest Service exist in trail, recreation, wilderness, and range management. Some trails are only accessible by horseback; thus, seasonal jobs maintaining trails by horseback may exist. Permanent full-time jobs and part-time jobs are scarce, but do exist for the person who is persistent and willing to start on the bottom rung of the ladder. Hiring is dependent on annual budgets, so the number of jobs fluctuates yearly.

Salaries are determined by a standardized scale. The lowest level is around $7 an hour. Increases depend on experience, education, and years with the Forest Service. A GS pay schedule can be obtained from the U.S. Department of Agricultural Forest Service District.

U.S. Department of the Interior

Fish and Wildlife Service

When people think of the Fish and Wildlife Service, they might imagine many opportunities to work on horseback. This is not always the case, according to the Fish and Wildlife Service's Division of Law Enforcement. There are special agent positions that require agents to ride, but horse experience is not a prerequisite. Agents stationed in such states such Montana, Idaho, and Nevada are required to perform some duties on horseback, but horses are considered one of many tools.

The philosophy of the Division of Law Enforcement of the Fish and Wildlife Service is to broaden employees' background by assigning new staff from rural backgrounds to metropolitan areas. Once experience is gained and seniority is established, there may be opportunities to return to a rural environment.

The Fish and Wildlife Service's Division of Law Enforcement suggests that individuals who have experience with horses and the desire to utilize that experience in a job with the Fish and Wildlife Service contact their local federal office of personnel management.

Duties of Fish and Wildlife Agents

✓ Enforce U.S. Code Title 16 Conservation Statutes.

✓ Enforce criminal law under U.S. Code Title 18.

✓ Investigate criminal violation of wildlife laws.

✓ Assist state wildlife agencies when interstate transportation is involved.

✓ Assist national wildlife refuges when needed.

✓ Work in import and export when conservation laws are involved.

✓ Work cases when an illegal animal is transported from state to state.

✓ Oversee implementation of endangered species laws.

Bureau of Land Management

The Bureau of Land Management operates the wild horse and burro program. According to Bob Abbey and Susan Mielke from the Colorado Division of the Bureau of Land Management, helicopters, four-wheel drive vehicles, and all-terrain vehicles have basically replaced the use of horses to gather and otherwise manage the wild horses and burros in the program. When it is necessary to get back into country where only horses can tread, the bureau usually contracts with local outfitters.

In many states, an organization called the Back Country Horsemen assists the Bureau of Land Management. This nonprofit organization maintains and manages resources in an effort to keep public lands open to recreational stock use. Clubs in California, Wyoming, Nevada, Oregon, Washington, New Mexico, Idaho, Colorado, and Utah have about 6,000 total active members. Although no paid positions are available, the experience volunteers gain can produce excellent references because many trainers, breeders, and horse industry professionals belong to the organization. Contact your state Bureau of Land Management for information about a Back Country Horsemen organization in your state.

LOCAL LAW ENFORCEMENT

Mounted Police Patrols

The police departments of some large metropolitan areas have mounted police patrols. Joyce Sheppard described her experiences with the Baltimore Police department in the March 1997 issue of *Equus* magazine. Joyce, already a police officer, was given the opportunity to work on the mounted police unit of the Baltimore Police Department. She immediately pursued riding instruction. Once she acquired the necessary skills, she was teamed with an experienced officer for apprenticeship training. Today she patrols streets, controls crowds, and arrests armed robbers and drug dealers — all from the back of her horse.

Lexington Mounted Police Headquarters at the Kentucky Horse Park.

Salaries for mounted police officers vary depending on seniority and location, but they generally run in the vicinity of $25,000 to $50,000, according to freelance writer Kay Frydenborg. Some departments require a four-year degree in addition to 500 to 700 hours of police academy training. Good physical condition, experience with horses, enjoyment of riding (in all kinds of weather and conditions), courage, sound judgment, and quick responses are additional characteristics of the mounted police officer.

The Denver mounted patrol conducts daily patrols in the downtown Denver area. During patrol, mounted officers may chase down robbery suspects, assist in directing traffic at accident scenes, handle fights, deal with disturbances, cover radio calls, and arrest drug traffickers. They use their horses for crowd control on special occasions and at Bronco games. In the past, the mounted patrol has helped protect visiting dignitaries, such as the Pope and the President. They also assist in mob control when demonstrations become violent.

Not all large cities have mounted police divisions. Check with the police departments in the cities you are interested in if you want to combine a law enforcement career with horseback riding.

Volunteer Law Enforcement

Excellent volunteer opportunities for the horse person exist with local sheriff posses. David Wilson, an engineer with the City of Loveland, Colorado, has been a Larimer County Sheriff Posse member for ten years and has served as the captain of the posse. This posse has 35 regular members and 25 reserve members. Members provide personnel, vehicles, and horses. They assist the Larimer County Sheriff's Department by participating in search and rescue efforts and by patrolling the Larimer County Fair, where they undertake full responsibility for the junior and senior rodeos. Posse members also assist with road blocks, and help secure the sites of such incidents as accidents, shootings, homicides, and suicides.

Dave Wilson assisted with crowd control when the Pope visited Denver.

Tips from the Experts —
David Wilson, Larimer County Sheriff Posse

- Contact a local sheriff posse member to discuss qualifications in detail.
- For more information and an application, call your local Sheriff's Department.
- Ascertain if you have enough time to effectively serve on the posse.
- Be willing to devote six months to classroom instruction.
- Be flexible. Hours vary. Summer and fall are the busiest seasons because of fair activities and searches for hikers and hunters.
- Make sure you have good horse skills.
- Understand that you need a good quality handgun (a semi-automatic or revolver).

To qualify as a member, individuals must own a horse, demonstrate good horse skills, and successfully complete an oral test demonstrating an understanding of posse members' responsibilities in relation to full deputy sheriff responsibilities. Applicants and their horses are tested on a variety of levels. Horses and riders must complete a trail course and are tested for their trailer loading and unloading skills. Applicants are evaluated on their use of tack and saddling ability. Applicants' horses must be able to remain calm when exposed to distractions. (Members and their horses train extensively on crowd control techniques, including exposure to loud, sudden noises.) Applicants must also submit to a background and integrity check by the Sheriff's Department. Members are expected to attend nine out of twelve meetings per year, successfully complete classroom instruction about vicarious liability and basic legal procedures, and pass a firearms course and a first aid/CPR course.

Sheriff posses contribute valuable services to their communities, and they also provide opportunities to meet other horse people from varied backgrounds. Every year on Labor Day weekend, members of all the posses in Colorado meet for competitions and fellowship.

RESOURCES

Bureau of Land Management, Colorado Division. Bob Abbey and Susan Mielke. 2850 Youngfield Street, Lakewood, Colorado 80215. (303)239-3937.

Frydenborg, Kay. "Labors of Love." *Equus*. 656 Quince Orchard Road, Gaithersburg, Maryland 20878. (301)977-3900. March 1995. Pages 26-35.

Ninemile Ranger District. Bob Hoverson. 20325 Remount, Huson, Montana 59846.

U.S. Department of the Interior, Fish and Wildlife Service. Jim Neal. P.O. Box 3247, Arlington, Virginia 22203.

U.S. Forest Service. Jim Miller. 201 14th Street SW, Washington, D.C. 20090-6090.

Wilson, David, former Captain. Larimer County Sheriff Posse. For information: Larimer County Sheriff's Department, 200 West Oak, Fort Collins, Colorado 80521. (970)482-6442.

Zisk, Dr. John. U.S. Department of Agriculture, Animal and Plant Health Inspection Service. P.O. Box 827, Jessup, Maryland 20794. (301)734-7833.

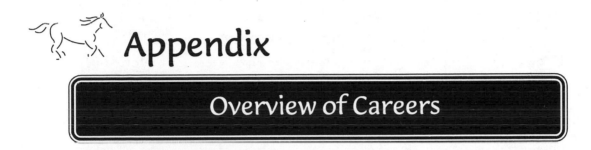

Appendix

Overview of Careers

AUCTIONEERING & HORSE SALES
Bid caller
Clerk/cashier
Instructor
Owner of auction, sale barn, or school
Ring assistant or spotter
Sales manager

BOARDING
Exercise rider
Groom
Instructor or trainer
Owner/manager

BREEDING
Farm manager
Ground & stable maintenance
Office personnel
Owner/manager of facility
Public relations & promotion
Sales
Veterinarian
Veterinary technician
Researchers
   college or university personnel

BREED REGISTRY/ASSOCIATION
Accounting personnel
Administrative personnel
Clerical staff
Data processors
Human resources staff
Judges
Marketing personnel
Member services staff
Operations personnel
Registrations registrar
Show department personnel
Stewards
Technical & licensing staff
Youth program staff

BUSINESSES, MISC.
Accessories with equine theme:
   commemorative memorabilia
   crafts
   leather products
   personal & household items
   toys
Child care at horse events
Clothing
Computer software
Consulting services
Educational & instructional items:
   books
   courses, programs, seminars
   videos
Engraving & embroidery services
Horse sitting services
Internet services
Music
Photography & art:
   calendars
   portraits
Printing services

Saddles, tack, gear:
   design & production
   sales
Transportation
Travel services

FARRIERY
Clinician/consultant
Contest shoer
Farrier school personnel:
   owner, administrator, staff
   teacher
   guest lecturer
Instructor
Product developer & manufacturer:
   sales
   tester or certification expert
   video production
Writer

GUEST & DUDE RANCHES, YOUTH CAMPS
Cook
Counselor
Entertainer
Farrier
General maintenance staff
Groundskeeper
Housekeeper
Office staff
Owner/manager
Recreation director
Riding instructor
Server
Trail guide
Veterinarian, on-call
Wrangler/stable hand

HEALTH CARE
(See also Veterinary Medicine)
Acupressure/acupuncture practitioner
Chiropractor
Dental technician
Electrical stimulation
Homeopathic practitioner
Magnetic field therapy
Massage
Nutritionist
Physical therapy

HORSE RACING
Announcer (track, television)
Appraising & consulting
Bloodstock agent
Broker or agent for:
   claiming, sales, syndication, training
Clerk of course
Clerk of scales
Clocker
Dental technician, equine
Driver
Exercise rider
Farrier
Government licensing clerk
Groom
Handicapper

Horse owner (see also Breeding):
Identifier
Information systems management
Investigative agent
Jockey
Jockey agent
Jockey valet
Journalist (see Publishing)
Lab technician, equine
Lobbyist
Off-track betting site personnel
Pari-mutuel betting personnel
Photo finish operator
Race horse adoption programs
Race timer
Race track management:
   accountant/controller
   computer operator
   judge: patrol, paddock, placing
   paymaster of purses
   program director
   public relations/publicity/marketing
   racing secretary
Racing commission
Security control
Simulcasting personnel
Stable superintendent
Starter
State or racing veterinarian
Steward/steward secretary
Totalisator
Track maintenance crew
Trainer & assistant trainer
Training center management
Transportation
Wagering personnel

HORSE TRAINING
Trainer of horses of a:
   specific breed
   specific discipline
   specific sport
Assistant trainer
Clinic/workshop presenter

JUDGING

LAW ENFORCEMENT
City police departments:
   mounted police patrols
County sheriff's departments:
   volunteer sheriff posses

MANUFACTURING & SALES
Accountant & bookkeeper
Administrators/operating officers
Data entry staff
Graphic artist/computer designer
Human resource staff
Management
Marketing specialist
Public relations staff
Researcher
Salespeople, retail & wholesale
Support staff
Wholesale distributor

OUTFITTER
Cook
Guide
Owner/operator
Packer
Wrangler

POLO
Club owner & personnel
Event volunteer or employee working as:
    goal judge
    referee
    scorekeeper
    timekeeper
    umpire
U.S. Polo Association personnel:
    administrative staff
    clerk
    collegiate field representative
    professional umpire
    scholastic program representative

PUBLISHING
(Books, brochures, magazines, newspapers, advertising materials)
Administrative personnel
Advertising personnel
Art director/artist
Circulation personnel
Copy editor
Copy writer
Correspondent
Editor-in-chief
Features editor
Managing editor
Marketing staff
News editor
Photographer (staff & freelance)
Press personnel
Regional sales staff
Research editor
Researcher
Special projects editor
Support staff
Writer (staff & freelance)

RIDING INSTRUCTION
Instructor of people who:
    are a specific age or ability level
    ride a specific breed
    ride a specific discipline
    ride a specific sport
Camp or guest ranch instructor
Instructor of disabled riders
Assistant instructor
Clinic/workshop presenter

RODEO
ProRodeo Cowboy Association personnel:
    animal welfare representative
    computer/data entry staff
    media relations staff
    points & membership personnel
    professional judges
    sponsor information staff

Rodeo participants:
    announcer
    bareback bronc rider
    barrelman/clown/bullfighter
    barrel racer
    bull rider
    calf roper
    chute laborer
    pickup man
    saddle bronc rider
    specialty (contract) act
    steer wrestler
    stock contractor
Rodeo personnel:
    administrator/office staff
    logo producer
    maintenance staff
    photographer
    rodeo secretary
    ticket office
    timer
Support personnel:
    cleanup crew
    concessions
    doctor
    program seller
    veterinarian

STABLES
Owner/manager
Riding instructor
Trail ride guide
Wrangler/stable hand

SUPPORT PROFESSIONS
Accountant/CPA working in:
    environment
    forensics (fraud investigation)
    personal finance planning
    tax advisory services
Appraiser
Attorney at law
Bookkeeper
Consultant
Expert witness
Insurance:
    agent/salesperson
    claims adjuster
    company owner/CEO
    public relations/marketing staff
    underwriting personnel
Realtor specializing in:
    guest/dude ranches
    horse properties
    horse communities

U.S. DEPARTMENT OF AGRICULTURE
Animal care investigator
Veterinarians working in:
    animal husbandry research
    animal welfare
    behavior research
    infectious & contagious disease control
    nutrition research
    reproduction research

U. S. FOREST SERVICE
Forester
Packer
Recreation services
Trail maintenance

U. S. DEPARTMENT OF INTERIOR
Bureau of Land Management:
    contractor for Wild Horse & Burro Program
Fish & Wildlife Services:
    special agent

VETERINARY MEDICINE
Veterinarian (D.V.M.) working in:
    blood typing labs
    breed associations
    breeding facilities
    disease control & management programs
    DNA/pedigree test labs
    drug & pharmaceutical companies
    environmental toxicology research
    equine behavior research
    equine geriatrics
    genetic disorders/ engineering
    immune functions
    international quarantine agencies
    manufacturing & feed companies
    nutrition research
    pain management research
    private practice (equine or mixed)
    research (university or commercial)
    surgery
    teaching
Veterinary technician working in:
    anesthesiology
    animal health product sales
    breeding facility
    breed registry/association
    equine dentistry
    equine sports medicine
    farm management
    feed company sales
    laboratory
    pedigree evaluation, analysis
    radiology
    research
    utrasound
    veterinary clinic/hospital

WAGON TRAINS & TRAIL RIDES
Entertainer/presenter
Owner/operator
Packer
Trail Boss
Wagon Master
Wrangler

Index

ORDER FORM

New Horizons Equine Education Center, Inc.

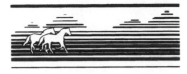

The Complete Guide to Horse Careers

- Fax Orders: (970) 224-9239
- Phone Orders: (970) 484-9207
- E-Mail Orders: nheec@frii.com
- Postal Orders: New Horizons Equine Education Center, Inc.
                      425 Red Mountain Road
                      Livermore, CO 80536
- Internet: http://www.frii.com/~nheec

Other resources available from New Horizons Equine Education Center, Inc.:

EQU	**101-110**	Step-by-step, study at home lessons. Course covers essential elements of horse ownership, care, and managment.
AQU	**101-110**	Parallels EQU 101-110. Approved by the American Quarter Horse Association, and tailored to the American Quarter Horse.
PNT	**101-110**	Parallels EQU 101-110. Approved by the American Paint Horse Association, and tailored to the American Paint Horse Association.
APL	**101-110**	Approved by the Appaloosa Horse Club. This series offers the same comprehensive program as EQU 101-110 and targets Appaloosa enthusiasts.
ARA	**101-110**	Approved by the Arabian Horse Association. This series offers the same comprehensive program as EQU 101-110 and targets Arabian enthusiasts.

Additional courses cover trailering, stable management, genetics, breeding and reproduction, horse psychology, and first aid.

Please send me _____ copies of New Horizons **The Complete Guide to Horse Careers for $29.95 plus $5.00 shipping. Colorado residents add 3.65% sales tax.**

☐   **I would like more information on New Horizons' courses. Please send me a free catalog.**

Name:_____
                    (Last Name)   (First Name)   (M..I.)
Address:_____ City_____
State: _____ Zip:_____ Home Phone: (____)_____ Work Phone: (____)_____

My payment is being made in the following way:

☐Check   ☐Money Order   ☐VISA   ☐Master Card

Name of Cardholder: _____

Card Number: _____ Expiration Date:_____

Signature of Cardholder: _____